Charles L. Dodso

Graduate Education Today

EDITED BY Everett Walters

Graduate

Education

Today

AMERICAN COUNCIL ON EDUCATION

Washington, D. C.

PRINTED IN THE UNITED STATES OF AMERICA BY
GEORGE BANTA COMPANY, MENASHA, WISCONSIN
3-67/2M

Editor's Introduction

EVERETT WALTERS

GRADUATE education has now received clear-cut recognition of its importance as a national resource. The Higher Education Facilities Act of 1963, the present largest graduate enrollment in educational history, and President Johnson's recent message to Congress on education represent the most dramatic proof of this development. And there is a host of less-publicized indications of the nation's concern for the role of graduate education.

Few people would deny the need for an expansion of graduate education facilities. The call for persons with the doctorate and the master's degree is heard everywhere. Educational leaders, congressmen, businessmen, industrial leaders, newspaper editors, and dozens of others publicly express alarm about the present shortage of college teachers and ask what can be done to avert the serious crisis predicted for the 1970's. Even with the greatly increased graduate student enrollments, many colleges and universities will be forced to employ teachers who lack adequate preparation. Other employers of doctors and masters, usually able to pay higher salaries than can educational institutions, also voice concern over the limited production of higher degrees by the nation's graduate schools. At Federal agencies such as the National Aeronautics and Space Administration, over 3 percent of the professional personnel have the doctorate; at the International Business Machines Corporation, over 10 percent of the research and engineering employees have the Ph.D.; at the Systems Development Corporation of Santa Monica, California, over 75 percent of its 2,000 professional staff are college graduates and 200 have the doctorate; and hundreds of other government agencies, businesses, research institutes, industries, and banks employ large numbers of staff holding doctor's and master's degrees. And all of these employers expect to hire proportionately larger numbers in the coming years.

v

The Higher Education Facilities Act supplements in many ways other financial assistance given to graduate education during the last fifteen years. This assistance has come primarily from the Federal and local governments and to a lesser, but nevertheless important, degree from industry and the philanthropic foundations. The Federal Government has poured out vast sums for research, graduate fellowships, training grants, and special facilities. State and local governments have provided large amounts for aid to graduate students and to research at publicly supported universities. Industry has aided through research funds, fellowships, teaching grants, facilities, money, and lectureships. And such foundations as Ford, Carnegie, Lilly, and Kellogg have made generous grants for fellowship programs, training programs, independent study, and similar purposes.

Any institution heavy with tradition and custom cannot be changed without considerable turmoil and consternation, and graduate education is no exception. Since World War II, the criticism of graduate education, especially of the doctoral programs, has become increasingly severe. Although much of it repeats what had been said soon after the establishment of graduate study in the United States—and continued to be said sporadically thereafter—the postwar objections have been sharper and more widespread. Also, as pointed out above, there is now a great demand for doctors, a new phenomenon. Only a few decades ago many educators and educational associations were decrying the number of young men and women who were working toward doctoral degrees, for it seemed they had no future, either in the colleges and universities or in industry or government.

Recent censure of graduate education began when, in 1948, the President's Commission on Higher Education pointed out what it believed to be the major defects in the nation's graduate schools: the outmoded requirements for advanced degrees, the type of instruction offered, the absence of programs for teacher preparation, and the lack of student guidance.[1] In general, the Commission complained that the traditional graduate program was designed to produce research scholars whereas, in fact, most doctors became college teachers who did little or no research. It also objected to the increasing specialization of faculty members which made it difficult for students to obtain a broad general education. To meet the great shortage of teachers which it anticipated, the Commission recommended several devices, including fellowship and teaching internship programs. In the late 1940's there was a spate of conferences on college teaching, usually sponsored by one or more educational associations. These conferences, uniformly critical of graduate education, resulted in pamphlets which were widely distributed throughout the educational world. The most important of these were Theodore C. Blegen and Russell M. Cooper (eds.), *The Preparation of College Teachers* (Washington: American Council on Education, 1950), and Fred J. Kelly (ed.), *Improving College Instruction* (Washington: American Council on Education, 1951). Similar criticisms of graduate study were published in the report of the Committee of Fifteen, *The Graduate School Today and Tomorrow,* sponsored by the Fund for the Advancement of Education; Clarence Lindquist (ed.), *Staffing the Nation's Colleges and Universities: Report of a Conference,* U.S. Office of Education, (Washington: 1951); and also the Office's bulletin *Toward Better College Teaching;* and in 1956 the American Council's report of still another conference, Charles G. Dobbins (ed.), *Expanding Resources for College Teaching.*

. The most severe criticism was expressed by four graduate deans in a 1957 Association of Graduate Schools committee report.[2] This report, which attracted national attention when it was published in the *New York Times* and later *Time* only several weeks after the launching of Sputnik, acknowledged that "current pressure forces us to examine our myth-enveloped Ph.D. with candor." The deans' examination provoked them "ruefully [to] conclude that the Ph.D. is tortuously slow and riddled with needless uncertainties. . . . The basic flaw is: we have never clearly defined this protean degree." Their criticisms and recommendations were discussed widely and debated in speeches and articles. Almost every graduate dean and educator commented on them in approbation or in disapproval.

A few years later, former U.S. Commissioner of Education Earl J. McGrath, now executive officer of the Institute of Higher Education, Teachers College, Columbia University, wrote a slashing attack on the failure of the graduate schools to give proper training to future college teachers.[3] He charged that the graduate schools have stressed narrow specialization and vocationalism and thus have tempted the liberal arts colleges to place too much emphasis on research and on heavy majors for undergraduates. The graduate schools, McGrath asserted, have led liberal arts colleges to abandon their chief purpose, which is to instruct the young people "in the Western European intellectual and spiritual traditions." Other persons, inside and outside graduate education, have strongly backed McGrath's view; some, without necessarily agreeing that the liberal arts college has declined, called for new programs which would ensure that prospective college teachers be given more specific training and experience in teaching. Others would add the provision that they should have broadly conceived courses in Western cultural traditions and in the role of science in today's world. There have been some advocates of new degrees—doctor's, D.Arts, D.Phil.; and master's, M.Phil.—for teachers so prepared.[4]

Still another criticism concerns the nature of graduate work and the function of the graduate school. At certain universities, the graduate school awards the Ph.D. only in the arts and sciences; at others, doctor's degrees in applied and professional fields are granted by the respective colleges and schools, such as the Doctor of Education in colleges of education and the Doctor of Business Administration in schools of business. Yet, in perhaps half of the nation's graduate schools, the Ph.D. is the only doctorate offered, and it is given in all subjects—accounting, animal science, home economics, education, German, nursing, nuclear engineering, physical education, veterinary pathology, zoology. Advocates of the traditional Ph.D. protest against stretching the requirements for this well-established degree to accommodate candidates in the applied fields who, they believe, should have professional doctorates as defined by professional needs. Proponents of a single doctoral degree, however, believe that the Ph.D. has a well-established position in the academic community and that it can be made sufficiently flexible to encompass advanced study in both the older disciplines and the applied and professional fields.

In 1960 Bernard Berelson published the most comprehensive study of graduate education yet undertaken.[5] This work, based primarily on extensive questionnaires, explored the attitudes of graduate deans, graduate faculties, recent recipients of the doctorate, college and university presidents, and representatives of industrial firms that employ doctors. Berelson's study (required reading for anyone interested in graduate study) also reviews in detail the usual criticisms, commenting on them with observations gleaned from his questionnaires. In general, Berelson concludes: "By and large, the graduate school is doing a reasonably good job or better, as judged by both the students and the employers," and he adds that graduate deans and faculty members agree that the total graduate educational process is better than it was in the past. Berelson himself supports these conclusions, although he advances a number of eminently sound recommendations, recommendations which, in his words, are "realistic" in relation to the past and present of graduate education.

It is in this context of growth and criticism that these essays have been written. The present writer, formerly the dean of a large graduate school, has come to believe that graduate deans have not properly responded to the criticisms of their own area of academic responsibility and that they would do well to express themselves to the nation at large. All the contributors to this volume have had years of experience in graduate education and have written extensively about it. All of them are or have been deans of graduate schools that are members of the Association of Graduate Schools and of one or more other organizations of graduate schools. They have had important roles in the creation of the recently established Council of Graduate Schools of the United States. Each of them is a scholar in his own discipline, and here sets forth his own views without regard for the official position of any association of graduate schools.

The essays are designed for those persons concerned with the problems of higher education, especially those not intimately involved in graduate study. It is the hope of the authors that their efforts will be useful for congressmen, businessmen, government officials, newspaper people, and many others who seek to understand the complicated process known as "graduate education."

This collection of essays has the strengths of similar collections but few of the weaknesses. Each author is an authority on his subject: he knows what he is writing about; he has reviewed the literature in preparing his essay; and he has written specifically for this volume. His work is the "latest word" on the subject, and in some instances it is the only article available. The weaknesses of this collection are minor: conflicting points of view among the authors (in reality a strength), some unavoidable repetition of historical and factual material, lack of smooth transition from one essay to the next, and sharp differences in style. It is the hope of the editor that readers will find, as he has, that the essays present a fresh, up-to-date, authoritative picture of graduate education in the United States.

Finally, to the authors themselves, I wish to express my appreciation for their willingness to take time to write these essays. All university administrators are busy these days, and graduate deans are no exception. Indeed, they are busy with the problems about which they write in this volume.

Both Dr. Gustave O. Arlt's essay, "New Trends in Graduate Study in the Humanities," and Dean W. Gordon Whaley's "New Trends in Graduate Study in the Biological Sciences," appeared in slightly different versions in *The Graduate Journal* (Fall 1962). Permission has been given to reprint these essays in this volume.

I wish to thank Miss Olive Mills, production editor of the American Council on Education—she does have a way with words—and Mrs. Helen Lindstrom and Miss Fay Moore, my secretaries at Boston University, for their most generous and skillful assistance in editing, typing, and preparing these essays for publication.

NOTES

[1] *Higher Education for American Democracy,* Vol. IV: *Staffing Higher Education,* (New York: Harper & Bros., 1948).

[2] *Journal of Proceedings and Addresses of the Fifty-eighth Annual Conference of the Association of American Universities and the Ninth Annual Conference of the Association of Graduate Schools* (Columbus, Mo.: 1957), p. 35.

[3] McGrath, *The Graduate School and the Decline of Liberal Education* (New York: Bureau of Publications, Teachers College, Columbia University, 1959).

[4] Cf. Oliver C. Carmichael, *Graduate Education: A Critique and a Program* (New York: Harper & Bros., 1961), chaps. 11–12 and p. 201.

[5] Bernard Berelson, *Graduate Education in the United States* (New York: McGraw-Hill Book Co., 1960).

Contents

List of Tables

The Rise of Graduate Education

EVERETT WALTERS

O F THE several American colleges, not yet universities, that offered graduate work during the first half of the nineteenth century, Yale was the first to establish work leading to the doctorate and also the first to award the degree Doctor of Philosophy. In August 1846 the Yale Corporation authorized a faculty committee (led by the scientist Benjamin Silliman and Theodore D. Woolsey, the latter soon to become president) to look into the possibility of offering studies beyond the bachelor's degree for graduates of Yale and other institutions.[1] One year later, in August 1847, the Corporation approved the formation of a Department of Philosophy and the Arts to "offer advanced work in the arts and sciences not already being taught and their application to the arts."[2] The new department would complement the departments of theology, law, and medicine. Created at the same time as a division of the department was the School of Applied Chemistry, which became (in combination with the School of Engineering), first, the Yale Scientific School and, later, the Sheffield Scientific School.

EVERETT WALTERS, vice-president for academic affairs at Boston University, was graduate dean at Ohio State from 1956 to 1963. On leave from Ohio State 1962–63, he served as director of the NDEA Title IV Fellowship Program, U.S. Office of Education. He edited the *Journal of Proceedings* of the Association of Graduate Schools for four years and also acted as secretary-treasurer of that organization. In 1961–62 he was chairman of the Midwest Conference on Graduate Study and Research. Dr. Walters is a contributing editor on graduate education to the *Journal of Higher Education*. A native of Pennsylvania, he attended Swarthmore College, the University of Cincinnati (A.B., 1936), and Columbia (Ph.D., 1947). He was a member of the history department of Ohio State from 1946 to 1963. His published works include two books and a dozen articles on late nineteenth-century American politicians and political movements and numerous articles on higher education.

1

Eleven students enrolled in the new department during the academic year 1847–48. Instruction was quite unsystematic and individual: there were no entrance requirements, no examinations, and no degree. By 1852, however, the graduate work in philosophy, history, languages, and pure science became formalized: the Bachelor of Philosophy was to be offered after two years of study and satisfactory completion of a final examination. That year fifty-five students were registered, among them, Daniel Coit Gilman, who, later, was to become the foremost leader in graduate education.

In 1860, following a memorial from the Scientific School professors, the Yale Corporation authorized the department to offer the degree Doctor of Philosophy so as "to retain in this country many young men, and especially students of Science who now resort to German Universities for advantages of study no greater than we are able to afford."[3,]* Young Gilman, in 1856, then on the staff of the Scientific School, had prompted the memorial through his original pamphlet concerning a doctoral program, "Proposed Plan for the Complete Organization of the School of Science Connected with Yale College." This pamphlet was, in effect, the blueprint for graduate programs in the United States.[4] In 1861 Ph.D.'s were awarded to three students who had already been studying in the department.[5] Requirements for this first American Ph.D. called for two years of postbaccalaureate study, a final examination, a thesis "giving evidence of high attainment in the studies to which [the student] has attended, and an acquaintance with Latin and Greek if bachelor's degree did not show such knowledge."

THE BEGINNINGS OF GRADUATE EDUCATION, 1789–1861

Graduate work at Yale and the other early universities did not, however, spring full-blown like Athena from the head of Zeus. Rather,

---

* The mounting interest in graduate education at Yale had been reflected in 1856 by James D. Dana, Silliman Professor of Natural History, when, in addressing alumni, he asked, "why not have here, THE AMERICAN UNIVERSITY!" And he went on to advocate higher studies in a wide variety of fields, "literary as well as scientific," for "the number of resident graduates would greatly increase, and a new era dawn upon American learning." Not until this had been accomplished, he warned, "can we hope to prevent our youth from seeking in the atmosphere of Germany the knowledge for which they yearn." (James D. Dana, "Science and Scientific Schools," *American Journal of Education*, II [1856], 374.)

it evolved slowly, growing out of national developments that began to take shape soon after the adoption of the Constitution, and maturing as the nation matured. Conditions were simply not favorable for advanced learning beyond the college years in a new country, with a predominantly rural society and few cities, with a lack of broadly established traditions for scholarly learning, with colleges founded on the English pattern that was devised to give cultural education to a relatively few young men, and with a widespread feeling of distrust of intellectual pursuits. And, paralyzing the entire collegiate system was a rigid curriculum based on instruction in the classics and offering little or nothing of other subjects, and, at many institutions, the understanding that a college education prepared young men for the ministry or for schoolteaching.

In the years following the founding of the nation, some concern for advanced education had been both expressed and implied. Several leaders—among them, Benjamin Rush and George Washington—called for a national university, with quite obvious implications for graduate and professional education. Others had called for local universities. In retirement, Thomas Jefferson wrote exhaustively about educational systems, from elementary grades to professional and graduate levels. His original plan called for the University of Virginia to be a graduate institution. George Ticknor, who had studied at the University of Göttingen, attempted in the 1820's to bring about educational reforms at Harvard, but without success.[6] Most of his recommendations stressed the need for persons with advanced, or graduate, education. The other three members of the famous quartet who in the early 1820's received degrees from Göttingen—Edward Everett, George Bancroft, and Joseph Green Cogswell—also contributed to the growing interest in graduate education at Harvard. By 1850 almost two hundred American students had followed in the footsteps of this quartet and had registered at German universities, chiefly Göttingen, Berlin, Leipzig, Halle, Heidelberg, and Freiburg.[7] They too returned to American shores imbued with the German spirit of freedom of thought, scholarly thoroughness, and hard work. Whenever possible, they sought to stimulate similar qualities of dedication to learning in American higher education.

The influence of these European-trained minds was considerable from 1820 to 1850, for there were numerous expressions by prominent leaders for the expansion of existing institutions into universities similar to the traditional European universities or for the founding of new universities. Among these were Theodore D. Woolsey, president of Yale, 1846–71, Francis Wayland, president of Brown University from 1827 to 1855, and Henry P. Tappan, president of the University of Michigan, 1852–63. All advocated drastic reforms in higher education, especially in liberalizing the classics-based curriculum and instituting graduate work. Tappan, who sought to "Prussianize" the entire educational system in the state of Michigan, carried through his part of the general plan, and in 1858 his young university offered graduate courses leading to master's degrees. Similarly, attempts were made to introduce German teaching devices, especially the seminar—or "seminary," as it was called in the early nineteenth century. In 1831 at Harvard, for example, Charles Beck, a German-born classicist with a Tübingen doctorate, projected a seminary but it was never put into operation.[8]

In the early nineteenth century other developments also contributed to the founding of graduate education. Probably the most powerful of these was the rapid rise of interest in scientific discovery, almost all of which took place outside the colleges and universities. Both here and abroad few higher institutions offered instruction in the sciences even though large numbers of scientists were closely studying physical and biological phenomena and writing about them. The influence of European scientific activity on American scientists was great, for some had themselves emigrated from Europe and others had studied abroad, chiefly in German universities.

Throughout roughly the first half of the century, another factor, closely related to the emerging role of science, brought pressure for the teaching of practical, applied sciences in the colleges and universities. Frontier conditions had formed the American people into a primarily practical-minded people, and instruction in industrial, mechanical, and agricultural arts began to be demanded.*

* These demands also contributed to the passage of the Morrill Act of 1862 which established the land-grant institutions, "the most original and characteristic American contributions to higher education." (Earle D. Ross, "Contributions of Land-Grant Colleges and Universities to Higher Education," William W. Brickman and Stanley Lehrer (eds.), *A Century of Higher Education* [New York: Society for the Advancement of Education, 1962], p. 94.)

In combination, these significant forces led, as we have seen, to the beginning of graduate work at Yale. And, significantly, the 1860 appeal for the Ph.D. came from the Scientific School faculty.

Unquestionably the desire to found a "real" university (in the European sense) stimulated the desire to offer graduate work and graduate degrees. The educational leaders sought to have the traditional four faculties: law, medicine, theology, and philosophy—the latter to embrace the arts and the sciences on an advanced level. The new institutions would not merely duplicate the German universities in every regard but, rather, would make concessions to the American tradition. As eager for reforms as Ticknor, for example, was, he agreed that "we must accommodate ourselves more to the spirit and wants of the times and country in which we live."[9] Furthermore, these early educators usually maintained that the American students should remain in the United States for their advanced education. The cultural nationalism expressed by Emerson in "The American Scholar" in 1837 had grown with the years. Important too was the growing availability of young college graduates who wished to study beyond the baccalaureate degree and who encouraged the faculties to provide advanced education. Harvard had had "resident graduates" as early as 1826 (including Ralph Waldo Emerson, A.B.), Princeton in 1829, and Michigan in 1852.

Other institutions in mid-century struggled to establish formal graduate work but without success. Despite broad educational and diplomatic experience, Edward Everett, president of Harvard from 1846 to 1849, was unable to launch recognized graduate programs at his college. His preference for gradual change, the sharp differences in his faculty, and the Corporation's serious indecision over the reform of undergraduate instruction, all combined to stall advancement. Confusing the whole issue was a $50,000 gift from Abbott Lawrence in 1847 to support a scientific school. Similarly, the extensive plans for graduate education in New York came to naught, at New York University, at Columbia, at Union, and at Albany, where there were great plans for a new university. Efforts at the University of Pennsylvania failed completely. Tappan's imaginative plan for Michigan in the late 1850's did attract a few graduate and special students for several years but soon collapsed when the fiery and controversial educational leader was forced to leave Ann Arbor.

George T. Strong, New York merchant and reform mayor, who

dreamed of a real university for Columbia, summed up the basic cause for failure: "The full grown plant we are sticking into the ungenial soil of New York will take no root. The utmost I hope is that when it withers and perishes it may leave some nucleus or germ surviving whence there may be natural development and expansion hereafter."[10]

It should be noted that in these early years many college graduates received a Master of Arts degree, usually in recognition of their good behavior for three years and a five-dollar fee. Ironically, these master's degrees were conferred "in course."

INFLUENCE OF GERMAN UNIVERSITIES, 1861–1900

In the post-Civil War years graduate education began to develop rapidly. The two earlier forces—the migration of American students to German universities and the demand for graduate work—grew dramatically. By the end of the century graduate education had become an established part of higher education.

The early nineteenth-century stream of Americans going to the German universities widened into a veritable flood. Despite four years of Civil War and the disturbed years that followed, during the 1860's more than 1,000 American students matriculated at the German universities, historic and modern, eminent and obscure. In the 1880's, the number rose to a peak of 2,000, then declined during the 1890's and the years before World War I. It has been estimated that about 10,000 Americans made academic pilgrimages during the nineteenth century and that more than half of them studied in the departments of philosophy at German universities, which included those subjects not pertaining to theology, law, or medicine.[11] Thus approximately 5,000 Americans matriculated in what may be called "graduate work." Just how many received doctorates is not known; certainly a majority merely attended lectures for part of a regular term or for a summer session. In a volume prepared for the 1893 Chicago World's Fair, at a time when there was considerable interest in higher education, it was estimated that in 1891–92 there had been 445 Americans studying at German universities—253 in philosophy, 133 in medicine, 46 in theology, and 13 in law—and that in 1892–93 the total had dropped to 383.[12]

By far the most popular German institution with American students was the University of Berlin, where approximately one-half of the great nineteenth-century American intellectual migration matriculated. Unquestionably, the rapid rise of Berlin in population, culture, sophistication, and position as capital of the newly created German Empire were factors that contributed to the popularity of its university. Leipzig, Heidelberg, Halle, Bonn, Munich, Göttingen, Würzburg, Marburg, Tübingen, Freiburg, and Breslau attracted few in numbers but not necessarily because of inferior faculties. Outside Germany, sizable numbers of American students enrolled in the University of Vienna and in several of the Swiss universities, institutions that were under the influence of the German tradition.

A more slender yet only somewhat less influential migratory stream of German educational influence was embodied in the hundreds of Germans who came to American colleges and universities during the nineteenth century. Many of them were distinguished scientists; others were scholars in literature, language, history, political science, and philosophy. Trained at the German universities, they brought with them the philosophies, method, and, above all, the spirit of the German university tradition. Perhaps the most distinguished of this group were Francis Lieber, the famous political scientist and historian, first at the University of South Carolina and later at Columbia; Hermann von Holst, the great historian of the American Constitution and political life, professor at German universities and at the University of Chicago where in 1892 he became the first head of the Department of History; and Albert A. Michelson, the outstanding physicist, winner of the Nobel and other prizes, at Case School of Applied Science, Clark, and Chicago.

The German university idea in all its aspects meant an exciting adventure for the young American either in a German lecture hall listening to a great scholar or in an American classroom learning from a scholar trained in the German tradition. Most dramatic, of course, was the emphasis on freedom of teaching and learning. Here was a principle that was captivating: it meant that teacher and student were seekers after the truth without regard for the consequences, whatever they might be. They were in the service of truth. Thus, a subject would be pursued without concern for current public opinion, religious strictures, political restrictions, historical traditions, or established concepts. How compelling for young Americans were the words of the German philosopher Fichte:

> I am a priest of the truth; I am in her service; I have bound myself to do and to dare and to suffer everything for her. Should I be persecuted and hated for her sake, should I even die in her service, what should I be doing that is remarkable, what should I be doing further than what I simply had to do?[13]

Beyond this exciting freedom was the respect for the logical arrangement of thought and intellectual orderliness. Included in this intellectual discipline were the gathering of information or data, the classification and ordering of things, the reporting of discoveries. And these procedures were followed by "rigorous and pitiless methods of investigation and deduction. Their [the German scholars] analysis was their strong point."[14] All of this involved the worth of the intellect—the widest possible use of the human mind. Here was "Man Thinking."

Also compelling were German teaching methods and scholarly paraphernalia. The most famous of these was the lecture. Far different from the American classroom recitation or the English tutorial system, the lecture was devised to bring to the hearer:

> an introduction . . . of the whole field, through a living personality, in a series of connected lectures. It should enlighten him concerning the fundamental problems and essential conceptions of this science, concerning the stock of knowledge acquired and the method of its acquisition, and finally concerning its relation to the whole of human knowledge and the primary aims of human life, and should in this way arouse his active interest in the science and lead him to an independent comprehension of the same.[15]

Friedrich Paulsen, the historian of the German university idea, saw many advantages in the lecture system: the personality of the lecturer; the flexibility and freedom of the lecture over the textbook; the perception (visibility) of lecture material; the benefits to the lecturer himself; and, finally, the usefulness of the lecture in communicating between teacher and students.[16] An American student recalled with vividness a lecture by von Holst:

> Suddenly an electric shock seemed to pass through the man. The dull eyes blazed, the hollow cheeks became brilliantly red, the voice rose to

a commanding pitch, the words rushed out in a steady stream, the weak form started from the chair. The man was lost in his subject; the veritable soul of history was crying out.[17]

The other renowned method was the seminar, or "seminary," as it was known. It was a training method for independent investigation of a significant problem. Seminars were, Paulsen commented,

the nurseries of research; their particular service is to familiarize the student with practical scientific methods. The method of solving problems varies with various fields of research such as history, philology, natural science, or mathematics. In general, however, an expert in research gives a problem to his students, or encourages them to find such problems for themselves, and the work of solving it is then done under his guidance; expert criticism and advice are at the service of the halting endeavors of the inexperienced. Thus they learn to know and handle with skill the tools and methods of work. The aim is to make the pupil himself a master, hence, first of all to enable him to do independent scientific work; the dissertation is intended to be the proof that he has acquired the necessary ability.[18]

An American professor, trained in Germany, echoed Paulsen's description of the seminar method when he observed:

No man is truly a student of any branch until he is an original student. He is never fully interested in study till he begins to pursue it for himself by original methods. Hence it is the duty of all institutions which will fit their students for the highest intellectual service in the world, to train them in this method.[19]

Every American student quickly came to know the other scholarly elements of the German university scene: the university library, the museum, and the laboratory. Here were great storehouses and generators of information, the wherewithal of research. No contemporary American university, it should be noted, had a decent library; customarily, the few volumes on the library shelves were not readily accessible to students.

The American, in his lectures and seminars, came to appreciate the values of independent thinking, of pursuing a course not laid out for him, and of patient, unremitting thoroughness in scholarship, of care in every detail. So, too, he became interested in studies such as psychology and economics or in new aspects of established fields such as physics, chemistry, and biology. German philosophy opened up a new world. And in the German university community he discovered the enviable social position of "Herr Professor"—quite different from that of the unsophisticated American professor.

Not all persons in higher education relished the flow of students to Germany. As noted earlier, the founders of the Ph.D. program at Yale believed that students should remain in this country for graduate work and advanced this as one reason for establishing the Ph.D. Similar expressions of disapproval were voiced in the following years. A Harvard professor in 1894 urged college professors to encourage their students to attend American rather than German universities. Several years later another professor, in an article for the *Educational Review,* protested what he called "the migration of a race." He urged Americans to stay at home.[20]

DEVELOPMENT OF THE DOCTORATE, 1861–1900

Meanwhile, important changes were taking place in scores of American universities. Harvard, having solved its internal difficulties and having seen the success of Yale, announced in 1872 that its faculty was prepared to offer formal graduate work for which the degrees Master of Arts, Doctor of Philosophy, and Doctor of Science would be offered. The M.A. "in course" would no longer be given. As at Yale, the Ph.D. was to be awarded after two years of postbaccalaureate study, the passing of an examination on this study, and the submission of a satisfactory dissertation. The S.D., apparently the first to be offered in the United States, was to be given to college graduates after three years of advanced study (two years only for Harvard graduates) in at least two subjects, the completion of a thorough examination, and "some contribution to science" or "attainments in some special scientific investigation." That year the Harvard catalogue listed three candidates for the M.A., seven for the Ph.D. (three in physics, two in philology, and one each in history and mathematics), and five for the S.D. (three in natural history and one each in physics and mathematics-physics).[21] Harvard's first Ph.D. and S.D. were awarded in 1873.

Cornell University from its very founding in 1868 announced that graduate work would be one of its major educational concerns.

Suiting action to the word, in 1871–72 its catalogues provided for an earned master's degree and for the Ph.D. The requirements for the latter degree, in addition to a knowledge of Latin (Greek was added in 1872) and the passing of an examination, embraced a "meritorious thesis based on an original investigation in one of the departments in which [the students] have studied," and two years of study taken in resident graduate courses, "not strictly professional in character." There must already have been several "resident graduates" at the fledgling university on the shores of Lake Cayuga because in the following year an earned master's and a Ph.D. were awarded.[22] By its fifth year of existence, Cornell had sixteen graduate students, including one each from Harvard, Oxford, Western Reserve, and Swarthmore. In its twelfth year it announced the availability of the Doctor of Science degree.

A fortuitous combination of enlightened trustees, substantial financial resources, and outstanding leadership led to the establishment of Johns Hopkins, from its very beginning in 1876, the leader in American graduate education. Under the dynamic presidency of Daniel Coit Gilman, the university declared graduate and advanced education as its most important mission. Gilman and his splendid faculty in short order set up in Baltimore a university combining the worthiest elements of the German university and the American college-university which had evolved in the two hundred and forty years since the founding of Harvard. The influence of the German university tradition was strong, for Gilman and almost all of his faculty had studied at German universities; thirteen of them had the German doctorate. Johns Hopkins' avowed purpose, Gilman stated in his inaugural address, was "the most liberal promotion of all useful knowledge; . . . the encouragement of research; the promotion of young men; and the advancement of individual scholars, who by their excellence will advance the sciences they pursue, and the society where they dwell."[23] For college graduates, there was study leading to the Doctor of Philosophy degree. Freedom of teaching and learning was cultivated as was freedom from traditional American instructional methods. Professors were chosen for their ability to do original investigation and were not burdened with extensive teaching duties; for them the advancement of science and learning was paramount. The pervading spirit was that of scholarship:

"questioning, doubting, verifying, sifting, testing, proving that which has been handed down; observing, weighing, measuring, comparing the phenomena of nature, open and recondite."[24] Provisions were made for study in a wide variety of applied areas and for professional education. Gilman believed from the beginning that the university would be a training place for professors and teachers for the highest academic posts, and that the university must house great libraries, laboratories, and museums. He also believed that, to transmit the fruits of research, the university must sponsor scholarly and scientific journals and operate a university press.

Within a few years Johns Hopkins had come to set the standards for graduate education. Sidney Lanier's words sang of the quick maturity: "So quick she bloomed, she seemed to bloom at birth." The level of scholarship and of research, the emphasis on freedom of teaching and research, and the excellence of the doctoral programs were soon copied at other universities, both those which had been long established and those which were just emerging. Harvard, Yale, and Cornell, already offering doctoral work, profited enormously. Charles W. Eliot, president of Harvard, in 1902, summed up the great contributions of Johns Hopkins:

> I want to testify that the graduate school of Harvard University, started feebly in 1870 and 1871, did not thrive until the example of Johns Hopkins forced our faculty to put their strength into the development of our instruction for graduates. And what was true of Harvard was true of every other university in the land which aspired to create an advanced school of arts and sciences.[25]

Other Eastern universities such as Columbia, Pennsylvania, and Princeton followed, as did the state universities of the Midwest and the West—Wisconsin, Minnesota, Ohio State, Illinois, and California. Closely following Johns Hopkins' lead were two new universities, Clark and the University of Chicago. At the former, G. Stanley Hall, a former psychologist at Johns Hopkins, organized in 1889 a strictly graduate environment—a school for candidates for the Ph.D. and for established research scholars with the doctorate or its equivalent; at the latter, William Rainey Harper in 1892 set up a university primarily designed for graduate work. Although Hall and Harper both acknowledged the pioneer efforts of Gilman, they also criticized the latter for yielding to the offering of undergraduate work. Ironically, Clark and Chicago soon enough followed suit.

By the mid-1890's college graduates in numbers flocked to Johns Hopkins, Clark, Chicago, Yale, Harvard, Columbia, Michigan, Pennsylvania, New York, Princeton, California, Cornell, Stanford, Minnesota, and Wisconsin to work for the doctorate. Smaller numbers took doctoral work at the many universities that had established graduate study in a limited number of fields. Among these were Iowa, Virginia, Vanderbilt, Indiana, Missouri, Illinois, Cincinnati, Boston, George Washington, and Western Reserve. Boston awarded the first Ph.D. to a woman, Helen McGill, in 1877.

By 1892, Seth Low, president of Columbia University, was able to comment that twenty years earlier there had been almost no graduate work carried on in the country but that "Today it is a marked feature of higher education everywhere." Chiefly responsible for this development, as he saw it, was the influence of the university system of Germany—its emphasis on scholarly work by the individual for "It places at the service of the individual student great collections of books, unexampled opportunities for scientific investigation and research, and brings him into personal contact with the acknowledged masters of thought over a great range of learning." He gave high praise to the "most fruitful development" at Johns Hopkins.[26] His appreciation of these influences was firsthand, for his own institution was forging ahead rapidly in graduate work under John W. Burgess in the School of Political Science.

GRADUATE EDUCATION AT THE CLOSE OF THE NINETEENTH CENTURY

By 1900 the American university offering graduate work leading to the doctorate had become well formulated. It was basically the traditional four-year undergraduate college of arts and sciences and/or engineering and agriculture with a varying number of professional schools (medicine, law, and theology); graduate work was offered by departments of instruction of the colleges and schools. With an exception or two, there was no separate graduate school with its own faculty, buildings, and budget. Rather graduate work was added to undergraduate instruction, with common faculty and facilities. The graduate school, as such, did not exist. The problems of administration were handled by an organization known as the "graduate school" or an administrative committee (or board), with a dean to deal with problems of degree requirements, fellowships, and similar matters. At Harvard, for example, the Graduate Department, established in 1872, became the Graduate School in 1890, and the Graduate School of Arts and Sciences in 1905, and this became a fairly well established pattern. Faculty appointments, course offerings, and facilities were the responsibility of the undergraduate dean and the department chairmen. Von Holst's declaration in 1893 that "There is in the United States, as yet, not a single university in the sense attached to this word by the Europeans" remained true. American institutions in 1900 were, as he said:

> either compounds of college or university—the university as an afterthought, figuring still to some extent as a kind of annex or excrescence of the college—or hybrids of college and university, or finally, a torso of a university. An institution, wholly detached from school work done by colleges, and containing all the four faculties organically connected to a *Universitas literarum,* does not exist.[27]

A university in the European sense could not come into being in the United States. Rather the American university had evolved, as had so many things American, from a combination of European and native forces.

The Ph.D. pattern had become quite widely standardized in most universities; the S.D., it should be noted, was either dropped at most institutions or fell into bad repute. The Ph.D. requirements were surprisingly like those of the 1861 Yale degree: admission for students with bachelor's degrees; three years study (still two at some institutions); knowledge of French and German (Latin at several); general examinations, written or oral or both; and a dissertation (often called a thesis) which embodied original research, a defense of this dissertation before faculty members, and publication of the dissertation. In general, the master's degree requirements were one or two years of study in residence, an examination, and a thesis or essay. Fortunately, the honorary Ph.D. and the master's degree in course were almost abolished. The lecture and the seminar and independent study, all German imports, were widely accepted.

The evolution of graduate study, American style, had contributed two important new dimensions to higher education by the turn of the century. College teaching came to be recognized as a career for which one specifically prepared; and the college curriculum became more sharply divided into disciplines, or subjects, similar to those in which the teachers had done their graduate work. Thus, college faculty members came from the graduate schools rather than from the ministry or public service, and they were regarded as being chemists, economists, botanists, or historians. Here was born the idea of specialization, and here began the controversy over teaching and research. Closely related to this latter aspect of graduate education was the surging interest in science and the scientific method, the founding of professional societies such as the American Chemical Society (1876), the Modern Language Association (1883), and the American Mathematical Society (1888), and the establishing of such learned journals as the *Political Science Quarterly* (1886), the *American Historical Review* (1895), and the *American Journal of Physiology* (1898).

An unofficial statement of graduate enrollments in 1898–99 showed that at Brown there were 69 graduate students; Bryn Mawr, 61; California, 191; Chicago, 857; Clark, 48; Columbia, 342; George Washington, 68; Cornell, 68; Harvard, 329; Johns Hopkins, 210; Stanford, 97; Michigan, 66; Minnesota, 156; Missouri, 25; New York University, 159; Pennsylvania, 158; Princeton, 128; Radcliffe, 58; Vanderbilt, 37; Western Reserve, 28; Wisconsin, 128; and Yale, 283.[28] At perhaps two dozen more universities there was a handful of graduate students. In 1900 about 382 doctorates were awarded, perhaps twice the number conferred in 1890.

FORMATION OF THE ASSOCIATION OF AMERICAN UNIVERSITIES, 1900

Recognition of the new position of graduate study was marked in 1900 by the formation of the Association of American Universities. The presidents of Harvard, Columbia, Johns Hopkins, Chicago, and California issued an invitation to their counterparts at Catholic University, Clark, Cornell, Michigan, Pennsylvania, Princeton, Stanford, Wisconsin, and Yale to an organizational meeting, designed to represent "to foreign universities the importance of revising their regulations governing the admission of American students to the examinations for the higher degrees," to discuss the possibility of greater uniformity of conditions for degree candidates in American universities, "thereby solving the question of migration . . . ," to improve the opinion held of the American doctorate in Europe, and "to raise the standard of our own weaker institutions." These fourteen institutions, which awarded 88 percent of the doctorates at that time, became the charter members of the association, the prestige organization of the various higher educational associations. From time to time in the succeeding years, the association, founded "for the purpose of considering matters of common interest relating to graduate study and research," admitted new members, totaling forty-one by 1965, including the Canadian universities, McGill and Toronto.

The formation of the A.A.U., as it has been known over the years, represented a typical American response to the need for self-discipline and standardization. There had been a number of calls for protection of doctoral degrees during the 1890's. In 1893 the Congress on Higher Education at the World's Fair adopted a resolution that a committee be formed to cooperate with various educational and scientific bodies in finding ways "to protect the significance of the Doctor of Philosophy and Doctor of Science"; the abuses of degrees, it held, were owed to "the rage after titles and the Ph.D. is the highest." An organization to accredit graduate schools was suggested.[29] In 1894 the Ohio College Association defined requirements for a master's degree and recommended standards for the Ph.D.[30] At its several meetings the Federation of Graduate Clubs, representing present and former graduate students at the leading graduate schools, called for the regularization and standardization of master's and doctoral degrees, and vigorously opposed conferring the Ph.D. *honoris causa*.[31] Many educational leaders spoke and wrote in the same vein.

Perhaps the greatest work of the A.A.U. lay in its attempts to raise the standards of graduate study. From its very inception, each member institution, usually represented by both president and graduate dean, discussed such basic concerns as the nature of the dissertation, the meaning of research, the conditions of fellowship awards, admission requirements, preparation for college teaching, the role of the master's degree, and the foreign language requirements. These matters soon became the hardy perennials of the A.A.U. meetings, and the discussions about them became the required reading for graduate deans in and out of the A.A.U. To aspire to the recognized levels in graduate education meant to follow the standards of the A.A.U. members. To its credit, the A.A.U. never attempted to accredit graduate schools, although for many years it did maintain an approved list of undergraduate institutions. Other organizations did, however, attempt accreditation at various times during the twentieth century—the National Association of State Universities, the American Association of University Professors, and several regional associations. To this day accreditation, quite fortunately, remains a natural resolution: the quality of the graduate and the general prestige of the graduate school determine acceptability or nonacceptability.

EARLY CRITICISMS OF THE DOCTORATE

"The rage" after degrees, especially the Ph.D., was not welcomed on all sides. Professor James M. Taylor of Vassar College in 1894 typically expressed fear of domination by the Ph.D., specifying that too much emphasis on specialization might well bring about neglect of broad scholarship. He would redefine the master's degree and have it the degree for scholarship and learning.[32] President A. Lawrence Lowell of Harvard decried the conferring of advanced degrees, holding that results speak louder than degrees for original thinkers; he believed that graduate degrees were attracting a dangerous "mediocrity" which would later seriously affect school and college teaching.[33] Dean Andrew West of Princeton in 1912 questioned, "Why is the degree made the be-all and the end-all? It is beginning to be known like a 'union card' for labor."[34] Many condemned the failure of the Ph.D. as preparation for college teaching, a criticism that has been voiced with recurring regularity since 1900.

William James in 1903 took the new degree to task most savagely and urbanely in his famous essay, "The Ph.D. Octopus." Worried lest the degree damage the true spirit of learning, he joked at titles and degrees on pages of college catalogues which created an impression of "A terribly distinguished crowd,—their titles shine like stars in the firmament: Ph.D.'s, S.D.'s, Litt.D.'s, bespangle the page as if they were sprinkled over it from a pepper caster." America, he feared, was drifting into a situation "in which no man of science or letters will be accounted respectable unless some kind of badge or diploma is stamped upon him, and in which mere personality will be a mark of outcast estate." A degree such as the Ph.D., he charged, stifles freedom of interest, does not guarantee success as a teacher, promotes academic snobbery, and above all is a sham.[35]

Edwin E. Slosson echoed James's criticism of the booming popularity of the Ph.D. In 1909–10 for *The Independent* he wrote a series of articles on American universities; in his conclusion he declared that the Ph.D. was being imperiled by its popularity, that its financial value was becoming too great, and that too many people now came to measure an institution's stature by the Ph.D.'s on its faculty roster. He also questioned the meaning of the "original contribution" as applied to the dissertation. Two remedies he suggested to strengthen the degree were the requirement of publication of the dissertation to ensure its high standards, and an examination of Ph.D. candidates to determine their general breadth of learning.[36]

EXPANSION OF GRADUATE EDUCATION, 1900–1940

From 1900 to 1940 graduate education, like higher education in general, grew in phenomenal proportions. The growth rate in higher education from 1900 to 1920 outdistanced the growth in the total population; from 1920 to 1940 the rise was even more pronounced. Graduate student enrollments soared, as did the numbers of master's and doctor's degrees conferred. Graduate school enrollments doubled approximately in each decade: 5,831 in 1900, 9,370 in 1910, 15,612 in 1920, 47,255 in 1930, and 106,119 in 1940. Earned doctorates increased from 382 in 1900 to 615 in 1920, and to 3,290 in 1940; master's went from 1,583 in 1900 to 4,279 in 1920, and to 26,731 in 1940. During these decades the number of institutions conferring the doctorate also increased, but at a modest rate.

The reasons for the growth of graduate education lay in the ever-increasing demand for persons with advanced degrees; primarily, the demand stemmed from the belief that college teachers should have advanced degrees, preferably the doctorate. Fewer and fewer institutions were willing to accept teachers holding only bachelor's degrees and former ministers with or without a degree. Increasingly, regional educational associations and national educational groups, as well as the public at large, came to use the number of doctors on faculty rosters as an important measure of collegiate standards. The doctorate became the union card of the college teacher and the mark of academic respectability. Similarly, schoolteachers and administrators began to recognize the importance of graduate education, primarily that leading to the master's degree. In many school systems the possession of this degree meant an automatic, although not necessarily substantial, salary increase. A few persons with master's and doctorates found their way into government agencies, publishing, industry, and research.* In a way, the growth of graduate study reflected the maturing of the nation: the rise in its cultural level, the desire for education for democracy, and belief in the American dream. These were stimulated by the prosperity of the pre-World War I years and the 1920's. The Great Depression of the 1930's did not in any way diminish the general growth since many young people, unable to find jobs after graduation from college, enrolled in graduate schools.

This general growth, beginning roughly in the 1890's, was accompanied by the creation, within the traditional colleges of arts and sciences, of new fields of academic interest and of new departments of specialization in these fields.

One vigorous newcomer was education, whose purpose was the preparation of schoolteachers and of teachers to teach in the normal schools. Although most schoolteachers attended normal schools (many became state teachers colleges and, more recently, state universities), a considerable number of prospective schoolteachers attended universities that had developed departments of pedagogy, or departments of education, or schools or colleges of education. At the University of Chicago in the 1890's, the philosopher John Dewey, working from within the Department of Philosophy, developed a new Department of Pedagogy and an elementary school. In many institutions, especially the large state universities of the Mid-

* A typical exception was in chemistry. At Wisconsin from 1899 to 1919 only eight doctors in chemistry entered industry; from 1919 to 1928, of the 109 doctors in chemistry, 56 went into industry. (American Association of University Professors *Bulletin*, XIV, 621.)

west and the West, the schools of education admitted students as freshmen and offered four years of undergraduate work leading to a bachelor's degree and a teaching certificate. During the early years of this development, the teachers were drawn from the traditional fields of the arts and sciences. Soon after the turn of the century graduate work was offered in education itself, which had attained the status of a "professional" field. At most institutions graduate study was simply added onto the undergraduate program, and the same faculty members taught both groups; then and now two exceptions were Columbia's Teachers College and Harvard's Graduate School of Education, which offer only graduate work and have separate faculties. The school at Harvard led the way with a new degree, the Doctor of Education (Ed.D.) in 1922, and—with varying success—the degree has been widely adopted. From the beginning the Ed.D. was sharply criticized, especially by professors in the traditional colleges of arts and sciences, who ridiculed it as a second-class degree. Yet its defenders—and there were many—retorted that the degree was a realistic recognition of the profession of Education (it was generally capitalized) and that calling a doctorate a Doctor of Philosophy did not necessarily make it a good degree. At some institutions the degree was administered by the school of education; at others, by the graduate school.

Between 1900 and 1940 somewhat similar developments took place in agriculture, business education, engineering, and other fields. Undergraduate work in these fields was expanded into graduate study, usually at a high level of application. In agriculture, for example, the Ph.D. was offered in agronomy, animal husbandry, and horticulture. In business, the emphasis was on "administration," marketing, or finance, and the Ph.D. and, more recently, the Doctor of Business Administration (D.B.A.) were awarded. The prestigious Harvard Graduate School of Business Administration, founded in 1908, flirted briefly with the Doctor of Commercial Science in the 1930's and 1940's but then cast its lot with the D.B.A. In engineering, the Ph.D. and the Doctor of Science degrees were awarded at a few institutions. And in other fields doctoral work was offered as in social work, pharmacy, library science, home economics, and public health. Occasionally "named" doctorates were devised, the most unusual of which are the Doctor of Physical Education and the Doctor of Nursing. Not to be outdone, the professional schools, medicine, veterinary medicine, theology, and law, joined the new trend and offered the doctorate, although in the case of law only a few schools offered work leading to advanced degrees.

Paralleling the developments in doctoral work was the expansion of master's study. In addition to the traditional M.A. and M.S. were the Master of Education (a great favorite with schoolteachers across the country) and a host of so-called professional master's, of which the following are most widely recognized: Master of Social Work (M.S.W.), Master of Business Administration (M.B.A.), Master of Public Health (M.P.H.), and Master of City Planning (M.C.P.).

Criticism of both the scope and quality of graduate work was persistently voiced during the 1920's and 1930's.[37] Like all other levels of education, it was continually censured from within and without. At meetings of the A.A.U. the question of the preparation of college teachers disturbed both university presidents and graduate deans. Was the Ph.D. a degree for college teachers or for researchers, or could it serve for both, were questions discussed at virtually every meeting. The Association of American Colleges in the mid-1920's also examined the products of the graduate schools, since its members were the chief employers. In general, the findings of the association's committees were tepid. A study, prepared for the A.A.C. by President Raymond Hughes of Miami University in 1934, was based on estimates made by specialists in the various fields. In graduate departments of the arts and sciences about 20 percent were rated "distinguished," about 35 percent as "adequate," and about 45 percent as "inadequate."[38] The large number of students seeking graduate degrees continued to bother educational leaders as well as educational associations. A committee of the North Central Association in 1926 issued a typical word of warning:

> the crowding of the graduate schools has been so great as to raise some question as to the quality of work done and the value of the degree. Certainly in some way the young, ambitious teacher should be protected as far as possible from spending his time and money in acquiring a graduate degree which will not be regarded favorably by his colleagues.[39]

Undoubtedly the warning was directed primarily to students in education, but it could have been applied in other fields as well. A survey of the speeches of educational leaders and of association committees published during the 1920's reveals an uneasy concern with the quality of graduate study, closely linked with the belief that many of the M.A.'s and Ph.D.'s wou'.: be unable to secure employment.

THE NEW ROLE OF SCIENCE, 1940–65

World War II brought significant changes to higher education, as it did to almost every other facet of American life. Perhaps most important were the exalted role of research, especially in the sciences, and the effects of a soaring growth of population. During the war, research in every field of science (and in some social sciences) developed phenomenally: great contributions were made to basic science, and applications of basic concepts were extensively explored. Universities carried on much of this research, particularly in atomic energy, communications, control systems, and propulsion. Although the amount of Federal funds spent on university research during this period has not been estimated, the total probably reached well over $500 million.

After the war the research-oriented universities continued to obtain Federal funds for research: they had become intimately bound up in the country's realization that science is a major national resource and that research is a vital element in national security. The haunting fear of a third world war was subtly dominant. The universities were regarded as essential contributors to the national security because (1) they engaged in basic research for the discovery of new knowledge and also pursued extensive programs of applied research, and (2) they educated and trained young persons who would become the scientists of the future.

Federally sponsored research at the universities was chiefly under the aegis of the Department of Defense, the Atomic Energy Commission, the Department of Health, Education, and Welfare, the National Science Foundation, the Federal Aviation Administration, and the National Aeronautics and Space Administration. Through these agencies, money was provided for research to be performed primarily by university personnel—teachers and graduate students alike—in university buildings. In a few instances universities set up separate research centers, for example, the Los Alamos Scientific Laboratory in New Mexico, managed by the University of California.

The National Science Foundation, founded in 1950 to "promote the progress of science," in the main supported basic scientific research at the universities and also encouraged other Federal agencies to do the same. After the war, Federal support at universities was aimed primarily at strengthening the military establishment, although this emphasis declined in the late fifties. By 1960 an increasing proportion of Federal funds was stemming from the National Science Foundation, the Department of Health, Education, and Welfare, and the National Aeronautics and Space Administration.

In the fall of 1957, the research efforts of the nation were sharply jolted when the U.S.S.R. launched Sputnik I into celestial orbit. The American people were astounded to learn that Russia had achieved a major scientific feat and that the United States could no longer claim superiority in science. Within the space of a few years Russia's ability to produce nuclear weapons and to launch man-made satellites, some of them carrying human beings, seemed to prove that she had overtaken the United States and had, indeed, surpassed our scientific achievements. By the opening of the 1960's Russian scientific prowess had enabled her to threaten world security and to create an international tension that was made the worse by fear of atomic bombing and the horrors of fallout.

Immediately in the United States, the federally supported research programs at the universities and colleges were re-examined and new efforts undertaken. Congress voted huge sums of money to strengthen lagging Federal programs, and the role of scientific research was even further enhanced.

Concurrent with the increase in research for national security was the growth of research in industry. The applications of scientific knowledge, especially in the chemical and electronics industries, became one of the dramatic developments on the postwar economic scene.

The effects on graduate education were spectacular. First of all, there was a vast demand for research itself, from government and from private industry. Graduate faculty and students were caught up in this demand, for primarily they were responsible for research at the universities. Faculty members, especially, bore heavy responsibilities as both principal researchers on contracts and grants and teachers of the new generation of scientists. If this were not enough, they were expected to battle such problems as indirect costs, classified versus nonclassified research, the suitability of sponsored research (government and industrial) for master's theses and doctoral dissertations, the development of proposals and negotiation of contracts for research, and housekeeping related to purchasing and facilities. Second, the demand for master's and for doctor's, especially the latter, increased apace. The need for teachers (discussed below) was growing critically at the same time that highly trained employees were being recruited by Federal agencies and laboratories, independent research establishments (many with lucrative government research contracts), private companies bent on expanding their range of products, and local governmental agencies. Most of the new employers sought Ph.D.'s or holders of other doctorates in the sciences, mathematics, and engineering, and increasingly they looked for doctors in the applied fields of psychology, sociology, agriculture, economics, and business. Thus, it has been reported that one of the giant computer companies would willingly employ the entire crop of Ph.D.'s in mathematics; that the Federal Government has employed almost as many Ph.D.'s as the ten leading universities; and that doctoral candidates in psychology, especially those clinically oriented, were spoken for long before they received their degrees. And the nation's deep commitments to international peace and aid to developing countries have produced a sharp demand for political scientists, sociologists, historians, economists, and agriculturalists.

New demand for college teachers, 1955–65

The nation's population explosion and the increasing proportion of teen-agers seeking college educations, similarly created a major problem for graduate education. The tidal wave of college students predicted for the late 1950's, the 1960's, and the 1970's foretold serious shortages inasmuch as the graduate schools would be expected to prepare the teachers for these students. The annual production of Ph.D.'s could not possibly satisfy this need and the needs of government and industry as well. The situation in the physical sciences, mathematics, and engineering appeared to be particularly critical; that in the humanities, social sciences, and other fields was only somewhat less serious. The impending shortage of college teachers, first predicted by the President's Commission on Higher Education in 1948, became increasingly acute in the late 1950's and early 1960's.

In an effort to help the graduate schools face their heavy responsibilities, financial support was given by the Federal Government, by industry, and by the great foundations. The contribution of the Federal Government has been the heaviest. The National Science Foundation has financed, in addition to its research grants, several large graduate fellowship programs, a retooling program for college science teachers, and a system for granting assistance for graduate faculty members and graduate students. Three titles of the National Defense Education Act of 1958 (whose enactment was inspired by Sputnik) have materially assisted graduate students: title II established a repayable loan program; title IV created a substantial three-year fellowship program designed to help college graduates become college teachers and to expand doctoral programs; and title VI set up a program to assist in the teaching of modern foreign languages. In the health sciences, the National Institutes of Health have established extensive fellowship and training grants programs. To stimulate the training of research scientists for the nation's space effort, the National Aeronautics and Space Administration has granted large sums of money to the nation's leading universities for graduate fellowships and research assistance. Increasingly, other Federal agencies have developed programs for assisting graduate education. Indeed, the magnitude of this assistance, when added to the funds for sponsored research and facilities construction, has caused many observers to question the dependence of higher education on Federal support.

Industry, which profited so handsomely from university research, has contributed through such means as fellowship programs, unrestricted research grants, and lecture funds. The benefits from these have been impressive. Outstanding assistance has been given by the Ford Foundation grant to the Woodrow Wilson National Fellowship program, which annually finances about one thousand prospective college teachers through their first year of graduate study; important too has been the foundation's assistance in foreign studies programs and in business administration. The Carnegie, Lilly, and Danforth Foundations, among others, have given impressive support through study grants and fellowships.

Thus after the turn of mid-century, the strenuous demands placed upon the established graduate pattern of education renewed the questioning about graduate study and the traditional degree requirements. This round of criticism, however, was voiced more widely than in earlier years. Now graduate education was of national interest; the American people were worried about the impending shortage of college teachers and of scientists. Research seemed to have become the hope of the future: research, they believed, would bring about a better world, certainly a safer one, and one with better health benefits and even greater material prosperity.

The public press reported fully the annual meetings of the associations for higher education, which usually had one or more sessions related to graduate education. It also recorded the increasingly frequent comments of congressmen and local political leaders who sensed the future role of higher education in American life. The *New York Times,* always alert to the temper of the times, saw the newsworthiness of the Association of Graduate Schools committee report which criticized existing doctoral programs and reprinted it only a few weeks after the launching of Sputnik I. Less spectacular were the many other national and regional conferences on the preparation of college teachers and the educational associations' reports on the training of college teachers. All implied the failure of the nation's graduate schools adequately to train future college teachers.*

Not only were the graduate schools criticized for their failure to prepare college teachers, but also for continuing such "outdated" requirements as the foreign language requirement (at most institutions, French and German, although some graduate schools had relaxed this traditional requirement to permit the substitution of statistics or another tool subject), the year's residence requirement, and the dissertation as a contribution to knowledge. The most significant of these criticisms have been described above.

Despite these criticisms, the prestige of the Ph.D. has been stead-

* See Introduction, p. v.

ily enhanced—for those who possess it and for those who strive to acquire it. In the prestige-conscious society of the 1960's, the Ph.D. is highly desirable. It has become fashionable to introduce a Ph.D.-holder as "Doctor," not the "Mr." or "Professor" common in earlier times.

GRADUATE SCHOOL ORGANIZATION

One result of the growing stature of graduate education—and the criticisms—was the organization of graduate schools into associations and conferences. This typical American reaction to problems of a complex nature ("let's see what the other fellow is doing") brought about the formation of regional organizations of graduate schools, most of which were not members of the Association of Graduate Schools* or the Division of Graduate Work of the (then) Association of Land-Grant Colleges and Universities. Among these postwar regional groups were the New England Conference on Graduate Education, the Midwest Conference on Graduate Study and Research, the Conference of Deans of Southern Graduate Schools, the Western Association of Graduate Schools, and the Graduate Deans of the Slope Institutions of the Pacific. In some regions there were other informal groups. These conferences and associations held annual meetings; those with formal meetings published proceedings or minutes, following the custom of the A.A.U.-A.G.S. *Journal of Proceedings,* which has been published since 1900. A natural result of the duplication of effort by these organizations—some graduate deans attend at least four meetings annually—was the creation of a national organization to represent all graduate education. In 1960, the A.G.S., stimulated by its own limitations, especially its inability to speak as a national representative of graduate education before congressional committees, fathered a new organization, the Council of Graduate Schools of the United States. The growing fear that regional educational associations would begin to accredit was another important factor in founding the council.

In many ways the formation of the C.O.G.S. marked the coming of

---

* In 1948 the graduate deans established the Association of Graduate Schools in the American Association of Universities. In effect, then, the Association of American Universities became the organization of university presidents and the Association of Graduate Schools became an organization of graduate deans.

age of graduate education in the United States. One hundred years after the awarding of the first Ph.D.'s, the leaders in graduate education had come to feel sufficient unity and security to form a national organization, with an office in Washington and a full-time president. Such a development would not have been possible at an earlier time. As this essay has shown, the growth of graduate education has been slow, marked with uncertainty of direction and purpose, always with financial dependence and administrative subordination. University presidents and educational leaders all too often neglected it, indeed frequently denounced its growth in public. But post-World War II developments, especially the meteoric rise of science, drastically changed the scene and brought about recognition of graduate education and its role in higher education and in the nation's economic, cultural, and scientific growth. Significantly, the council was made possible by the representatives of the prestige graduate schools, who saw the new status of graduate study and its need for full national recognition. By 1964 the council, representing more than two hundred institutions, had become the spokesman for graduate education before Congress, the foundations, and the American people. Although only a few years old, it does represent a century of graduate education.

NOTES

1. Russell H. Chittenden, *History of the Sheffield Scientific School of Yale University, 1846–1922* (New Haven, Conn.: Yale University Press, 1928), I, 40–41.
2. Richard J. Storr, *The Beginnings of Graduate Education in America* (Chicago: University of Chicago Press, 1953), p. 55.
3. George Wilson Pierson, *Yale College: An Educational History, 1871–1921* (New Haven, Conn.: Yale University Press, 1952), p. 704.
4. Francesco Cordasco, *Daniel Coit Gilman and the Protean Ph.D.: The Shaping of American Graduate Education* (Leiden, The Netherlands: 1960), pp. 25–29.
5. Ralph P. Rosenberg, "The First American Doctor of Philosophy Degree," *Journal of Higher Education,* October 1960, p. 388.
6. Storr, *Beginnings of Graduate Education,* pp. 15 ff.
7. Charles Franklin Thwing, *The American and the German University: One Hundred Years of History* (New York: Macmillan Co., 1928), p. 42.
8. Storr, *Beginnings of Graduate Education,* p. 25.
9. Quoted in Storr, *Beginnings of Graduate Education,* p. 19.
10. Quoted in Storr, *Beginnings of Graduate Education,* p. 111.
11. Thwing, *The American and the German University,* pp. 42–43.
    Jurgen Herbst estimates that fewer than nine thousand Americans studied

in German Universities, 1820–1920 (*The German Historical School in American Scholarship: A Study in the Transfer of Culture* [Ithaca, N.Y.: Cornell University Press, 1965], p. 1).

12. W. Lexis, *Die Deutschen Universitäten* (Berlin: 1893), I, 128–30.

13. Quoted in Friedrich Paulsen, *The German Universities and University Study* (New York: Charles Scribner's Sons, 1906), p. 274.

14. Harris E. Starr, *William Graham Sumner* (New York: Henry Holt & Co., 1925), p. 64.

15. Paulsen, *German Universities*, p. 192.

16. *Ibid.*, pp. 193–98.

17. Lucie Hammond, "Hermann von Holst, the Historian," *American Monthly Review of Reviews*, XXIX (1895), 322.

18. Paulsen, *German Universities*, p. 312.

19. Quoted in Thwing, *The American and the German University*, p. 121.

20. Charles Gross, "College and University in the United States," *Educational Review*, January 1894, p. 31; Samuel H. Bishop, "University Study at Berlin and at Oxford," *Educational Review*, April 1898, p. 351.

21. *A Catalogue of the Officers and Students at Harvard College, 1872–73* (Cambridge, Mass.: Harvard University 1872–73).

22. *Catalogue of Cornell University 1871–72* (Ithaca, N.Y.: The University, 1872).

23. Quoted in W. Carson Ryan, *Studies in Early Graduate Education: The Johns Hopkins, Clark University, The University of Chicago* (New York: 1939), p. 28.

24. Daniel Coit Gilman, *The Launching of a University, and Other Papers* (New York: Dodd, Mead & Co., 1906), p. 147.

25. Quoted in Ryan, *Studies in Early Graduate Education*, p. 4.

26. Seth Low, "Higher Education in the United States," *Educational Review*, January 1893, p.'9.

27. Hermann von Holst, "The Need of Universities in the United States," *Educational Review*, February 1893, p. 113.

28. Edward Delavan Perry, "The American University" in Nicholas Murray Butler (ed.), *Monographs on Education in the United States* (Albany, N.Y.: 1900), p. 315.

29. William O. Sproull, "The Degree of Doctor of Philosophy," *Educational Review*, October 1893, p. 289.

30. Nicholas Murray Butler, "Notes," *Educational Review*, October 1894, p. 310.

31. Perry, "The American University," p. 312.

32. James M. Taylor, "Graduate Work in the College," *Educational Review*, June 1894, p. 72.

33. A. Lawrence Lowell, *At War With Academic Tradition in America* (Cambridge, Mass.: Harvard University Press, 1934), pp. 337–43.

34. Quoted in Bernard Berelson, *Graduate Education in the United States* (New York: McGraw-Hill Book Co., 1960), p. 19.

35. William James, *Memories and Studies* (New York: Longmans, Green & Co., 1911), pp. 332–34.

36. Edwin E. Slosson, *Great American Universities* (New York: Macmillan Co., 1910), pp. 490–96.

37. Berelson, *Graduate Education*, pp. 27–32.

38. Raymond Hughes, *A Study of American Graduate Schools Conferring the Doctorate, 1937–38 to 1941–42* (Ames, Iowa: 1946).

39. Committee on Graduate Degrees, North Central Association, *North Central Quarterly*, I (1927), 216.

The Doctor of Philosophy Degree

MOODY E. PRIOR

THE Ph.D. degree has become—to misapply a noble line of
Alexander Pope—the glory, jest, and riddle of the world
of higher learning in America. The standard joke about it is that it
is now the union card of the college professor, though like many
tedious official jests this one conveys indirectly an acknowledgment
of the importance of the thing being joked about. There is also the
one about the Ph.D. being a specialist who knows more and more
about less and less. The current jibes about the Ph.D. have, however, acquired an earnestness because of the serious questioning, severe criticism, and even intemperate attack which the degree has
inspired in recent years, and which have served to diminish the lus-
ter of our most distinguished academic emblem. Nevertheless, the
glory, though a bit tarnished, is still there. The Ph.D. is sought by
an ever-increasing number of able students. To those who can qualify for it, encouragement is offered in the form of a variety of support programs, some of them extensive and national in scope, and

MOODY E. PRIOR, formerly dean of the Graduate School, Northwestern
University, returned in 1964 to full-time teaching and research as Shafer
Professor of Humanities and English. Born in Fatsa, Turkey, in 1901, he
came to the United States in 1906 and became a naturalized citizen in
1914. He attended Northwestern University, receiving the B.S. and M.A.
degrees in 1923 and 1924. In 1930 he was awarded the Ph.D. from the
University of Chicago. Since 1930 he has taught in the Department of
English at Northwestern. His writings include many articles on the literature and history of ideas of the seventeenth and eighteenth centuries, the
drama, and Shakespeare. He is the author of two books, *The Language of
Tragedy* (1947) and *Science and the Humanities* (1962). In 1951 he
was appointed graduate dean. His vigorous and colorful defense of the
standards of graduate education coupled with his willingness to consider
innovations won him the presidency of the Association of Graduate
Schools in 1961–62.

those who have earned it are in demand not only in colleges and universities, but also in industry and government. Moreover, efforts to alter the basic character of the degree or to establish substitutes to better meet the needs of certain occupations for which the Ph.D. is now desired have regularly failed to secure the approval of those who employ the products of our graduate schools as well as of those who train them.

The present prestige and importance of the Ph.D. degree are closely bound up with the extraordinary rise of American universities in modern times as centers of learning, a development which is associated with the introduction and development of graduate study and which is responsible for the present identification of research and doctoral study as the distinguishing marks of a university. What needs to be emphasized here is the rapid rate of development, once its importance was generally understood, of the revolution in education which these events signalized. When the Association of American Universities was founded in 1900 with the avowed aim of promoting the improvement of our own resources for advanced study, American universities were still not capable of providing adequate training for scholars in many areas of learning. Migration of American students to European universities was at the time felt to be justified. Within half a century, however, a sizable number of American universities had acquired the capacity to train scholars at the highest level in every branch of modern knowledge, and their faculties were making contributions to learning which granted them world prominence. It is difficult to find a parallel to a development at once so rapid and impressive in the history of institutions of higher learning.

Inseparable from this growth to maturity and scholarly greatness was the growth of graduate study. The American graduate school has come in time to sponsor a great variety of educational activities, especially through the versatile character of the master's degree, but it is the Ph.D. which has called upon the total resources of our universities, and which has been the graduate school's chief educational product as well as its principal justification. Since World War II, we have witnessed a tremendous stepping-up in the research activities of the universities and, simultaneously, an increase in the number of doctoral students and of Ph.D. degrees. How vital these twin developments have become is demonstrated by the huge national efforts to stimulate and support both. As a final mark of its success, the American doctorate is at last gaining the respect of European scholars and is being sought by students from many countries.

The day of its apparent triumph, however, has not been signalized by paeans and congratulations. The paradox—the riddle, if you will—is that the Ph.D. is at the moment the most severely criticized, and even vilified, product of our system of higher education.[1] In its dual aspect of power and weakness, its dual role as hero and villain, the Ph.D. presents a series of contradictions not easy to resolve. To understand the place of the Ph.D. and its possible future in our education system it is necessary to appreciate some of the implications of this long and continuing controversy over its nature.

A suspicion has long been entertained by its critics that the graduate school and its doctorate were forcibly and unnaturally imposed as an import from Germany upon the traditional pattern of American education which had developed gradually from institutions originally modeled on those in Great Britain. In a report to the Association of American Universities in 1912—a report notable for its thorough review of the issues which had arisen around the Ph.D.— Dean Woodbridge alluded to this view: "It stands more for an ideal imposed upon our culture than for an ideal growing out of our culture."[2] Time has not eliminated lingering doubts about the wisdom of this transplantation from abroad. In 1959 Earl McGrath pointed to the influence of the German university as lying "at the root of most of our problems in higher education today," and affirmed that "this transplanted institution did not adapt well to the established system of higher education, based on the British tradition in which the college was central."[3]

Pragmatic considerations—notably the early appeal, the rapid development, and the present prestige of the Ph.D.—seem to argue against this view, and in fact it rests on a partial and not wholly accurate notion of the history of higher education in America. Immediately after independence was won from England, demands began to appear for a change in the direction of education from the established pattern. Thus, Benjamin Rush, in a proposal for a Federal university, envisioned that in contrast to traditional European education, "the youth of America will be employed in acquiring those branches of knowledge which increase the conveniences of life, lessen human misery, improve our country, exalt the human understanding, and establish domestic, social, and political happiness." It was in a similar spirit that Jefferson proposed in 1800 a university for Virginia "on a plan so broad & liberal & *modern*, as to be worth patronizing with the public support"—the italics are his. The Yale report of 1828, recommending the elimination of dead languages from the course of study, noted the widespread sentiments for change: "From different quarters, we have heard the suggestion, that our colleges must be *new modelled;* that they are not adapted to the spirit and wants of the age." This has been a persistent voice in the United States.

The reiterated demand to keep higher education in tune with the times and responsive to the needs of the country has been as much a part of our educational traditions as anything else. To this spirit in American educational thinking, there have been various responses, some of them far-reaching. One instance is the establishment of the land-grant universities. The research-oriented graduate school was the response of the late nineteenth century to new demands, and if the German universities served as a model, it was because what they were doing offered something so necessary in the United States that American students went to Germany to get it. Wilbur Cross, in a talk before the A.A.U. in 1925, recalled the young men who went to Germany and, upon returning, became aware of "how low college instruction had sunk in the United States." And just as the earlier English model underwent modifications through the influence of American conditions, so did the later German model. The rapid establishment and widespread acceptance of the Ph.D. belie the image of it as an unnatural hybrid. It has flourished and has shown an amazing capacity to reproduce its kind.

THE AIMS OF THE PH.D. DEGREE: ITS RESEARCH CHARACTER

This capacity of doctoral programs to grow and to proliferate has in itself been a cause for concern. Unlike the degrees for established professions such as medicine and law, the Ph.D. was not confined by any restriction of field of study or aim. Did it have any discernible character? Surveying the variety of fields in which it could be earned, Woodbridge asked in 1912, "for what does it essentially stand?" A committee of deans in a report to the Association of Graduate Schools in 1957 complained, "we have never clearly *defined* this protean degree." Yet in a very important sense the degree has been defined, both by various pronouncements on the part of those involved in developing and administering it as well as by the kinds of academic requirements which were imposed upon the early candidates and which have become traditional. The Ph.D. has been protean with respect to the diversity of fields of study; it has been reasonably consistent in its approach to these. This distinction was pointed out as early as 1902 in a talk during the third annual conference of the A.A.U.: "The justification for making study in such comparatively unrelated fields lead up to one degree, Doctor of Philosophy, must be sought in the methods of study common to them all." The chief common element has been the emphasis on independent investigation as a preparation for continued scholarly activity. Woodbridge, in the report referred to above, noted that "the degree aims at being the badge of the proved investigator"; and in a report to the A.A.U. in 1926, the association was urged to reaffirm "its previously pronounced policy that the Ph.D. degree shall be open as a research degree in all fields of learning, pure and applied." As long as a subject lent itself to this approach, the area of study has made little difference, provided the university in which the degree was being earned had on its faculty persons whose own studies had carried them far enough to act as mentors for the student and judges of his efforts. There are educational values which might well be an indirect by-product of doctoral study, but with which the graduate school has not directly concerned itself, or only half-heartedly. It has regarded it as the responsibility of other divisions of the university to concern themselves directly with the education of cultivated men and good citizens and with the cultivation of breadth and of those traits of intellect and sensibility which are the marks of the well-educated man.

The program for the Ph.D. has centered its attention on producing the learned scholar, with emphasis on depth of knowledge and on the cultivation of those tools and habits of mind which enable a man to go beyond what he has learned and to exercise independence in the understanding of his chosen branch of knowledge and in advancing it. This aim has been responsible for the academic requirements which have grown up around the degree—the specialized curriculum, the language requirement, the qualifying examination in the field, the dissertation. In specific details there have been changes over the years: the requirement that the dissertation be published has been abandoned; the language requirement has become less inflexible; formal course work has, perhaps unfortunately, been increased; and the qualifying examination, usually written, has become almost universal and has replaced in importance and in rigor the old oral "defense of the thesis." In the main, however, the basic aims and expectations have remained unaltered in essence.

Thus defined, the Ph.D. degree program possesses a clear logic and propriety. If the fact is not self-evident, it is because the degree possesses also an inherent versatility and flexibility that makes it adaptable to a wide variety of areas of study and a wide variety of aims, and because it does not lend itself readily to a fixed and clearly predetermined curriculum. The classic issues of the debates over the Ph.D. are a consequence in large part of these circumstances. The practice of listing the wide variety of subjects within which it is possible to earn a Ph.D. today, from archaeology to animal husbandry, and then asking scornfully, what kind of degree is this and what does it stand for, is really futile, since it approaches criticism of the degree from the wrong direction. The model has been there all the time, and it is easy to provide numerous excellent examples which demonstrate the reasonableness and the continued vitality of the aim and methods of the American doctorate; yet, at the same time, the whole phenomenon is complicated enough to provide grounds for the uncertainty, lack of confidence, disapproval, and disenchantment which find frequent and vigorous expression by writers on graduate education.

The years since World War II have been productive of circumstances that have provided fertile soil for the charges of confusion and even irresponsibility which have been brought against the graduate schools of the country. The increase in the number of graduate students is certainly an important complicating factor. More significant is the expansion both in knowledge and in university activity. Unprecedented demands are being made on the universities to increase research and to contribute to society and to meet new goals in providing highly educated persons for a great variety of services. Knowledge is growing at an increasing rate, and old established disciplines are being subdivided, new ones are being formed, and combinations of disciplines centering in pressing problems of general scope are being encouraged by the formation of programs, centers, and institutes, administrative entities that add to the forces which are modifying the structure and character of our universities. In addition, the Ph.D. is now sought in areas once thought to lie quite outside the established disciplines and not compatible with the character and aims of the degree.

THE PH.D. AS A PROFESSIONAL DEGREE

These circumstances have given a new interest to the question of the aims and purposes of the degree, one aspect of which is the current preoccupation with the "professionalization" of the Ph.D. Fears have been expressed that the program for the Ph.D. is being increasingly directed toward training for specific professional services and thus drifting away from the original and proper aim of the degree as education for scholarship. This statement of the issue bypasses an older and more basic question—whether, in fact, the Ph.D. is not itself a professional degree. One of the graduate deans who contributed an article, "Professionalization of the Ph.D. Degree," to a symposium in the March 1959 issue of *The Journal of Higher Education,* concludes that "the M.A. and the Ph.D. are professional degrees." On the other hand, an Association of Graduate Schools committee report in 1957 insists that "the Ph.D. is not a professional degree." Something more than a quibble is involved in this contradiction, but something less than a real difference of opinion.

We can agree at the start that the Ph.D. has for many years been regarded as almost indispensable to a secure position on a university faculty, and since teaching is certainly a profession, the Ph.D. is in that sense a professional degree. Moreover, the Ph.D. is regarded as a desirable preparation for many other sorts of endeavor. Almost no one today acquires a Ph.D. simply as a preparation for a private indulgence in the joys of learning. If one wishes to contend that any high-level program of study that enables a man to engage in an activity requiring advanced academic work is a professional program, then one can insist that the Ph.D. is a professional degree. This attitude is sometimes accompanied by the suggestion that those who disagree are the victims of a myth about the scholarly purity of the Ph.D. and not in touch with reality. The only thing wrong with this position is that it effectively obscures an important characteristic of the Ph.D. which differentiates it from such established professional degrees as those in law and medicine. One difference is that the Ph.D. is not, as is the case with the degrees in law and medicine, an absolute prerequisite for practice or even continued success in any of the activities for which it may be in demand, not even in teaching.

An even more important distinction is that there is a wide variety of activities for which a Ph.D. affords accepted preparation and to which it offers an entree with prestige and status. Mastery of a field of learning and training for independent inquiry in it are acquisitions which today are very valuable to our society in many ways. To insist that the Ph.D. in chemistry is a professional degree because one who possesses it is employed by an industrial organization is to disregard the fact that what industry wants from him is his knowledge of chemistry and his ability in research—the very attributes which doctoral training fosters for whatever final use and which also make one desirable on a university faculty. There is nothing in the training of a Ph.D. in economics which determines whether he will ultimately use his education to be an analyst in a department of government, a researcher for an international bank, or a university professor. Bacon said of books that they teach not their own use, and one might apply this principle to the Ph.D. From this point of view it is possible to insist that the Ph.D. is not a professional degree.

To the outsider, this argument may seem merely verbal, but it is important to establish these distinctions because they have a bearing on a development which does raise the question of professionalization in a special form. The fact that the Ph.D. provides for no explicit professional commitment has made it available to activities requiring advanced training but lacking a traditional degree of their own. This characteristic was noted at the meeting of the A.A.U. as early as 1902:

> The whole field of study not already pre-empted by these earlier degrees (of theology, law, medicine) has been appropriated by the degree of Doctor of Philosophy; and with the rapid expansion of the domain of knowledge in every direction, that has taken place since "philosophy" took over the unappropriated field, that term has lost the distinctiveness of its earlier meaning, and has come to be an "omnium gatherum."

As long as the degree stayed within the disciplines represented in the standard college curriculum, it was possible to view the proliferation of fields as a function of the advancing tide of learning. The situation became slightly different, however, as the newer professional schools which had become a part of the American university—business, journalism, speech, engineering, education—began to undertake graduate programs of study without an existing higher degree of their own having established traditions and prestige, as in medicine and law. These newer professional schools tended to adopt the one degree with prestige and character which lacked a clear professional label and was therefore available to any field that could establish a plan of study with language reading requirements, qualifying examinations, and a dissertation. What made this approach particularly appealing was that these schools wanted to provide for their teachers the same status as teachers had in other divisions of the university, and therefore turned to the Ph.D., which had become the identifying mark of a university professor. Certain professional schools sponsor both a professional degree (for example, the Doctor of Business Administration, Doctor of Engineering Science, Doctor of Education, Doctor of Music) and the Ph.D. on the analogy of medicine, but with only moderate success in some instances and with less general acceptance of the practice than in the case of schools of medicine, with their ancient and highly respected M.D. as a symbol of professional competence and the Ph.D. as a symbol of preparation for research and possibly an academic career.*

---

* The problem of the professional doctorate and the Ph.D. in professional schools is discussed below in the chapter "Other Doctorates," by John Ashton.

THE PH.D. AS A DEGREE FOR TEACHERS

The Ph.D. has accommodated itself in recent years to a variety of professional activities, but with the one profession which it was originally introduced to serve it has not yet made its peace. And as the need for college and university teachers—not to mention teachers for junior colleges—becomes critical, the failure of the Ph.D. to produce good teachers in large enough numbers has intensified the charge that the graduate schools have failed in their responsibility to teaching and have contributed to a decline of liberal education in America. It has become almost conventional to express astonishment and incredulity at the state of affairs which allows college teaching to remain the one profession which one may enter without any direct instruction in the performance of one's duties. It is a widespread opinion that, although the Ph.D. is required for college teachers, it does not actually prepare for teaching; and the low level to which undergraduate teaching has allegedly fallen, a lack of interest in teaching on the part of university professors, and indifference to good teaching as a basis for promotion on the part of university administrators, are laid at the door of the graduate school because of its sponsorship of a doctorate directed toward research.

To this criticism there is a partial and still valid reply. It is expected that college and university teachers will know a great deal about the subjects they profess, and it was the shortcomings of American universities in the best modern learning that sent American academic men to Europe during the latter nineteenth century. At the most elementary level of instruction, a limited amount of learning will serve, and scholarly activity is far less useful than an understanding of children, of how they learn, and of how much they are capable. As the student advances, the importance of learning on the part of the instructor increases. A college teacher who brings to his students a high level of comprehension of his subject has the great advantage of being able to speak with conviction and to convey an appreciation of the contemporary relevance of his studies. At the most advanced level, thorough knowledge of the field, a philosophical understanding of the theory and of the fundamental concepts underlying it, a critical attitude toward evidence and opinion, and a firsthand familiarity with the significant current investigations in the subject become essential. The graduate schools have fostered the training which is aimed at producing men with such qualifications, and to this extent they can be said to have contributed significantly to the training of college and university teachers. No responsible educator has ever claimed that the Ph.D. carries with it any implication, let alone guarantee, that one who has earned it will be a good teacher. The only claim which can be seriously made for it, and it is not a negligible one, is that without the kinds of qualifications for which the degree stands, one is not well equipped to teach at the college and university level, whatever other virtues and gifts he might possess.

The question remains, however, whether a degree program required of teachers can claim to have met its obligations if it fails to provide any training in the art for which it purports to prepare its students. Most Ph.D.'s still go into teaching, and teaching is not less difficult or demanding than any other profession. Proposals have been made, accordingly, for certain kinds of instruction to be included in the doctoral program with a view to providing a foundation for the teaching activities of the future Ph.D.'s. One suggestion is that instruction be provided in modern learning theory. There is a fascinating literature by psychologists on this subject, rewarding for its own sake; but it is not likely that those who set their hopes on it as a means to the improvement of college teaching are very familiar with its contents, since even authorities in learning theory have not claimed that, considered by itself, it has anything very useful in its present state to offer to those who will teach at an advanced level. Another recent suggestion is that all prospective college teachers be required to take a course in the history of American higher education and in the present curricula and administrative structure of our colleges and universities. This is an attractive idea, since it will presumably make the prospective teacher better informed about the general institutional environment which he plans to enter, if not the particular one in which he ultimately finds himself. The outcry, however, is for better teachers, and it is unlikely that such a course would make the doctoral student a better man in the classroom or laboratory or seminar. In an already full and demanding program, it is necessary to be selective, and for every possible addition it has to be determined whether it is essential or whether it can be left to later study and experience. It is in fact because they seem to promise too much that suggestions like these have failed to catch on.

What makes the anger against the graduate school for its failures less persuasive than it should be is that the proposals for reform in the training for teaching sedulously avoid consideration of an aspect of teaching which distinguishes it from the other learned professions. It is impossible to practice medicine without training in medicine and the care of patients, and it is dangerous to practice it with insufficient training. It is possible to practice teaching, and with success, without any formal preparation. Every year there are graduate students who leave with their degrees and face their first class, and demonstrate before the year is over that they can hold the attention of their class, provide interesting and useful materials for study, gain the respect of their students, and presumably have some salutary effect on them. This fact does not prove that direct instruction in the art of teaching is not possible, but until this common phenomenon is acknowledged and thoroughly understood, the bitter complaints about the failure of the graduate schools to provide proper training for teaching will sound like crusading without a program, the comparisons with medicine will remain improper analogies, and the complaints about the dearth of good teachers will be sympathetically noted as understandable outcries against nature.

Whether teaching can be taught is still an open and complicated question, at least for college teachers, but the proposals for providing such instruction within the doctoral program have not to date been very impressive. There is one practical approach, however, which has not been sufficiently developed. More imaginative and systematic use could be made of the teaching assistantship to prepare graduate students for assuming full responsibility of their future students. Not all graduate students have the opportunity to serve as teaching assistants, but a great many do, and for them the experience and wisdom of the established teachers, supplemented by such experimental and theoretical studies in education as may be relevant, could be used to provide guidance for those with talent and aid to those who could be assisted to attain competence.

SPECIALIZATION VERSUS BREADTH

The criticism of the graduate school's failure to provide adequate preparation for teaching within the traditional Ph.D. program is less serious than the attack on the Ph.D. itself as unsuited for the production of teachers by virtue of its crippling narrowness and overspecialization. The issue is breadth versus specialization, and the object of principal objection is the dissertation. It is significant that the most severe strictures on the Ph.D. in this connection are usually from humanists, to a lesser degree from social scientists, and this indication of differences in attitude is one of many warning signs that to talk about the Ph.D. without taking into account significant differences among the various disciplines is to invite distortion and confusion.

One reason why there is relatively little concern among the sciences about the usefulness of doctoral study for teachers is that a substantially smaller proportion of scientists go into teaching than do Ph.D.'s in other disciplines. At the other end of the scale are the humanities, in which the Ph.D. in most instances leads to teaching. There is, moreover, a basic difference in the nature of the disciplines themselves. Whereas breadth is desirable in any branch of learning and in any learned man, in the humanist it is more nearly demanded by the nature of the field. The humanist has an affinity with Bacon's bold claim to have taken all knowledge to be his province, for who can determine in advance what kind of learning the scholar in the humanities will not need or the teacher find it illuminating to draw upon? It is in large part for these reasons that, although criticism of the Ph.D. as preparation for teachers spares no discipline, it comes less often from scientists than from nonscientists, and the horrible examples are drawn usually from technical studies in the humanities and the more humanistically oriented aspects of the social sciences. The distinction was noted by a speaker at the A.A.U. conference in 1933: "The reason that the titles of some doctoral theses in the humanities evoke a smile is not that they are narrower and more minute than the subjects pursued by scientists, but that narrowness and minuteness seem so hopeless when compared with the vast expanse of the humanities themselves." And the same speaker concludes, "Humanistic research must have, like humanistic teaching, a far broader outlook than in the sciences."

Since it is the research aspect of the Ph.D. which seems to direct the program away from breadth, the requirement most vulnerable to criticism is that of the thesis. In the writings on the Ph.D. the word seems to attract a characteristic cluster of themes and ideas. The associations became established quite early. During a discussion at the A.A.U. conference in 1908 of the practice of requiring publication of the thesis, the representative from the University of Virginia said:

> I myself . . . am of the opinion that as "Doctor" means "teacher," the Doctor of Philosophy ought to be a man fitted to be a *professor* first and foremost, rather than an investigator of minutiae and publisher of writings which no one reads. I agree with the views published years ago by such men as Mommsen, Bluntschli, and Carl Vogt, that the German dissertation is in most cases pretentious humbug. The same is true of the American article . . . I do not believe in artificially luring men of mediocre ability into the publication of stupid monographs upon wholly uninteresting themes, and in persuading such men that they have been doing "original research."

Where breadth of learning is made the primary qualification for a teacher, the dissertation is usually characterized in pejorative terms, disparaging its pedantry, triviality, unreadability, and lack of synthesis and originality. A particular item of offense is the phrase "original contribution to learning," often preceded ironically by the adjective "so-called." Much of this criticism seems to imply that the young scholar enjoined to be original and contribute to knowledge is encouraged, perhaps necessarily driven, to search for new information, however trivial, and discouraged from more worthy aims. The pedestrian type of dissertation, sometimes described as "factual" research, is compared to its disadvantage with "scholarship," defined by Earl McGrath as "knowing his subject broadly, not narrowly, and being able to see the relationships and the philosophical significance of new knowledge, as it is produced."[4] In a characteristic passage, McGrath places the usual "factual" dissertation far below the products of the significant powers of the mind.

Much of the "original" factual research rewarded with the Ph.D. degree involves mechanical, pedestrian intellectual operations far below the level of those employed in philosophical synthesis of existing knowledge in new patterns of meaning. The conceptualization involved in Einstein's development of the relativity theory, for example, required an order of intellectual rigor and creativeness, a perception of integrating relationships far superior to the discovery of most of the factual data on which they were based.[5]

One can only agree with the last sentence, but one is then left wondering what this appeal to the most sublime products of human genius has to do with the value of a requirement intended as the first serious test of a graduate student's ability in independent research and about which even the most sanguine expectations must be modest by comparison. Perhaps because of a disinclination to become enmeshed in this sort of *reductio ad absurdum,* serious proponents of the thesis requirement tend to avoid the phrase "original contribution to knowledge." One is more likely to find such statements as that it "should exhibit thoroughly independent scholarly ability" (from the A.A.U. conference of 1908), or that it should embody the "results of individual research" (A.A.U. conference of 1912), or that it should be "a modest *specimen eruditionis"* (A.G.S. conference of 1957).

The most determined and severe critics of the Ph.D. as a standard preparation for college teachers give the impression at times that they would not regret the elimination of the dissertation as a fixed requirement. Such a radical revision is, at present, unlikely. The dissertation has always been a distinctive feature of a degree which leads up to an exercise in independent investigation toward which the course of study is a preparation. Former President Ray Lyman Wilbur of Stanford went so far as to recommend to the A.A.U. in 1924 "that the standard for the degree be so changed that the recipient of that degree would be freed from the necessity of taking set courses of any kind. It should be a degree conferred upon one who has done original research." The conditions of advanced specialized research today render this notion of the Ph.D. utopian, and course work constitutes a good part of the doctoral program, excessive in some fields. Nevertheless, the Ph.D. degree and the dissertation have become inseparable. The only serious question is whether the dissertation in its present form best serves the ends of the degree, and whether a degree program of which the dissertation is the culmination is the best possible preparation for college teachers.

The difference between the various disciplines becomes significant here. In the sciences the question of the value of the dissertation, whatever the student's professional goals, does not arise with any serious conviction. Research to an advanced student of science is what writing music is to a student of composition. A similar attitude of general approval exists in the behavioral sciences, especially those which have made the most determined effort to adopt the methods and attitudes of the natural sciences. When we come to the humanities—or to put the case more precisely, to those studies in which the research is not guided by mathematical models and techniques and is centered in the library rather than in the laboratory or the field—the case is different. It is here that the charges of narrowness, overspecialization, lack of significance appear most frequently and where the dissertation is attacked as perverting the habits and interests of prospective teachers. The humanities are unusual among the disciplines in that they study the products of man's creative acts—literature, music, art, philosophy, and even the products of scientific discovery. These present two aspects: they can be approached as objects of scholarly study, whether historical or technical, and they can be approached as mankind's timeless resources of wisdom with the power to arouse enthusiasm and provide inspiration. In their second capacity they are subject to judgments about their relative value and to critical appreciation and understanding.

As training for scholarship, the Ph.D. dissertation is more likely to concern itself with those aspects of humanistic study that lend themselves to scholarly discipline and control than to those which call for the most creative kind of critical judgment and esthetic and ethical discrimination—aspects, however, which a teacher of college students must consider if he is to convey to them an appreciation and critical understanding of the works of man. Hence the charge of triviality and pedantry that is brought against many humanistic dissertations. It is wrong, however, to fuse together the charge of triviality, which is a serious one, with the implication that all technical and scholarly studies ("factual research") of and relating to literature and the arts are menial and irrelevant to a future teacher. In particular, the common notion that they are a product of nineteenth-century scientism improperly applied to the humanities is seriously incorrect, because it fails to take into account that such scholarship has always been an important and useful part of the study of letters and arts ever since the Greeks turned their attention to Homer, the Renaissance to making classical literature and learning once more available and understood, and the eighteenth century to preserving Shakespeare from the ravages of time and the changes in language and taste. And it is also unwise to pass judgment on the value of some of these studies in advance. The application of critical textual methods to the Bible had extraordinary consequences; the laborious deciphering of trivial texts and the study of charred remains has altered our notions of early history; and the tedious reconstruction of Elizabethan theatrical practices has had far more to do with improving and revitalizing theatrical presentation of Shakespeare's plays in our times than most of the best criticism.

Putting the problem of triviality and research in a proper perspective is one thing, but it does not eliminate the problem of specialization or overspecialization. Triviality and uselessness may be merely a consequence of lack of talent and scope on the part of the student, but specialization is at the heart of the whole matter, for specialization is sometimes condemned as a danger not only to good teaching but to good research as well. Yet specialization is the inescapable condition of an advanced state of learning, as it is of an advanced culture. The complete generalist is to be found in the most primitive societies. All professional excellence demands some degree of specialization; and the more complex a society and a culture, the more specialization it will demand, and none has ever required more than our own. A program of study which has as its aim the advancement of learning cannot escape specialization. The only problem is whether it can escape its evils.

One of the defects in the arguments over this issue is that the specialization noted in doctoral dissertations is made the basis of the conclusion that the Ph.D. program is too narrow. In most cases, it will be found that the program of study was broad and comprehensive, and the general examinations demanding. In fact, one of the present criticisms of the Ph.D. is that too much is expected of the student in this respect. Admittedly, the dissertation will be specialized, since that is a condition of careful scholarship, especially if the time allotted is limited and the student is still not a master of his field. One of the paradoxes of the current debate is to find in one and the same discussion a recommendation that breadth and imaginative synthesis be required of a dissertation, and also a condemnation of the Ph.D. program for taking too long. A survey of the titles in *Microfilm Abstracts* reveals many dissertation titles which suggest problems that are not merely technical and that require synthesis and critical judgment, but such topics would still have to be limited in order to avoid superficiality and reliance on second-hand knowledge and opinion. One of the differences between science and the "library" disciplines is that originality and distinction often appear in the early works of scientists of ability, but it is otherwise in the humanities where the great syntheses and the profound insights are usually the work of maturity. This is a consideration not often taken into account when dissertations are criticized for narrowness of scope and recommendations are made that graduate students investigate subjects which would tax the knowledge, the scholarly sophistication, and the wisdom of mature and capable scholars.

The recommendation that interdepartmental programs should be used to avoid narrowness also needs to be carefully scrutinized. It should be noted, first, that many programs of study leading to the Ph.D. are already interdisciplinary. Biologists find it necessary to study mathematics and chemistry; students of literature have to become familiar with philosophy and history and linguistics. Interdisciplinary research for the dissertation becomes useful in certain cases, but is not in itself a panacea. Interdisciplinary studies have to grow out of a natural or inevitable association of disciplines, where two or more branches of knowledge fuse to create a new one, as in biochemistry, or where an area becomes interesting in a new way and requires the attention of more than one approach, as in current programs on Africa, centers for the study of materials, the associations of engineering and biology, and aerospace science. But to urge interdisciplinary problems in order to enforce breadth may result in purely artificial confrontations of two areas (as in some artificial comparisons in two literatures) or in placing added jeopardy upon the student by adding to his already heavy program the need to master two subjects rather than one.

Since specialization is an inescapable condition of serious scholarship and research, we must look for breadth in the preparation which the student brings to the graduate school and in the program of study which precedes the dissertation. We must try also to inculcate breadth in the research program, not by impossible and grandiose types of subjects, but by a proper approach to specialization itself, by providing the student with a broad theoretical foundation for his studies and by enabling him to see the relevance of what he is doing to the large possibilities of his field. The graduate student working on his dissertation should "be made to understand that his specialty is Loki's cat, that what he sees of it above the surface may appear small and easily manageable but that in reality it is necessarily bound to the universe."[6] No one would contend that we accomplish anything like this degree of comprehension and intellectual wisdom with most of our Ph.D.'s, and this may well be our most serious failure.

The Ph.D., with an extended period of advanced study culminating in a research dissertation, has produced many excellent scholars. There are also many excellent teachers at every level of college and university work who have acquired the Ph.D. degree, and so it can at least be said that the Ph.D. has not prevented them from becoming ornaments of their profession. A considerable number of these may not engage in continuous research which is published, but the criticism of the Ph.D. program on the grounds that many who go through the research and writing for a dissertation never publish or undertake another such exercise is the weakest argument against the dissertation and the least worthy of serious consideration. No one attacks the writing of compositions by advanced students of music because few of them will ever have their works performed by any major orchestras, or the writing of novels by ambitious undergraduates because most of these novels will never be published and because few of those that are will be read by anyone a decade later. In the kingdom of the mind, many are called but few are chosen. There appears to be an unavoidable waste in the preparation for worthwhile creative achievement, suggesting the prodigal efforts of nature to

assure the survival of existing species. A case could even be made
out that the experience of the dissertation has given those who have
undergone it an understanding of the way knowledge grows, of the
difficulty of establishing fact and truth, and of the drudgery as well
as the excitement of finding something new or giving new insight to
old data, and that such an experience can be nothing but valuable
to one who will teach at an advanced level though he were never to
undertake a program of research of similar scope again or publish a
line.

POSSIBILITY OF AN INTERMEDIATE DEGREE

It cannot be proved, however, that the dissertation is absolutely essential to bringing out the best gifts of the individual as a teacher.
In a talk before the A.A.U. in 1925, Wilbur Cross, confronting op-
posing demands—on the one hand that the graduate school center
its training on research, and on the other that it place its primary
emphasis on the training of teachers—said:

> These are the two voices—the one of the university, the other of the
> college. We may decide to listen to but one voice—it may be the voice
> of Jacob—but we shall surely feel the hands of Esau. There is no es-
> cape from the dual character of the graduate school, though the
> conflict between its two purposes may be mitigated and perhaps re-
> moved altogether, without making either purpose primary or secon-
> dary.

It is common to say that research and good teaching go together,
but everyone knows that the two are not invariably found together
in that relationship like a binary star, and it might be better to say,
and truer, that continuous study in the most interesting materials
available to one's field is essential to good teaching. It may therefore be possible to question seriously and honestly, whether for
some graduate students and for some careers in teaching, especially
in colleges and junior colleges where the advancement of learning is
not an essential responsibility of the faculty, the time which went
into the dissertation were not better spent in gaining breadth, in
studying auxiliary and cognate areas, and in expanding one's horizons. In a well-planned course of study for such students, seminars
would provide an initiation into the experience of research and the

meaningful organization of results. A comprehensive examination would terminate the program, and could also serve the secondary purpose of qualifying those with the requisite ability and motivation who underwent a change of mind about their career to proceed to the Ph.D. by fulfilling the dissertation requirement. Such a program would meet the objection that no teacher at the college level should lack some firsthand experience of what research means in his discipline, as well as the further objection that an intermediate degree would create a category of second-class academic citizens who would be forever excluded from a university career. It would, above all, discourage from a demanding and rigorous academic exercise those who do not have the taste or the requisite talents for it, but who do have the other qualifications for careers for which this exercise is not an absolutely essential preparation. One thinks of all the lost souls who wander today in an academic limbo because, though they have successfully completed a serious and demanding course of study, they have no respectable academic symbol of identification because their teaching position neither permits the time nor provides the incentive to meet the dissertation requirement for the Ph.D.

That this approach has not found favor and that a special program of this sort for future teachers has been vigorously opposed by most graduate deans and even most college presidents does not invalidate its logic nor eliminate the possibility that the pressing demands of our times will force this alternative upon us.[7] But if such a program does get established, it will not, and should not, be crowned by the Ph.D. degree simply on the assumption that the graduate school is a teacher-training institution and that the Ph.D. is a teaching degree. A degree which from its start has been associated with scholarship and whose traditions derive from research and the advancement of learning will not be easily captured and made to apply to something quite different in the expectation that the prestige of the degree will carry over to its new application.

PERIOD OF STUDY REQUIRED FOR THE PH.D.

Among those who accept the philosophy and traditions of the Ph.D. degree, a principal concern at the moment is to make the degree program more orderly and predictable. The issue upon which this reform is focused is the duration of the degree program. Surveys have revealed that the number of years between the bachelor's degree and the Ph.D. varies greatly and that the completion of the degree requires for many students an inordinate amount of time in comparison with established professional degrees. As with so many questions relating to the Ph.D., this one has a deceptive simplicity. A distinction has first to be made between the number of years which may have elapsed in any given case between the bachelor's degree and the doctorate and the number of years actually spent at a university in pursuit of the Ph.D. A far greater number of Ph.D. candidates interrupt their program of study than is the case in medicine or law.

A major reason for delay in completing the work for the Ph.D. degree is financial. The average Ph.D. comes from a less affluent socioeconomic group than does the lawyer or physician, and since he often goes into a less lucrative profession, he is less likely to continue his education by means of loans. Moreover, the medical or law student cannot practice his profession before he has earned his degree, but in many cases, especially in teaching, the prospective Ph.D. can. Many graduate students are supported by teaching assistantships, which in themselves prevent a full-time program. Again, many of them, when support runs out or is inadequate, can readily find teaching positions which give them financial independence and professional responsibility before the completion of the degree. This may be imprudent of them, but they are aided and abetted in their imprudence because their services are needed by universities and colleges faced with the problem of staffing undergraduate instruction. Any reform that enabled all students to complete their graduate studies without teaching assistantships or interruption of their studies to take full-time teaching positions would find a number of colleges and universities confronting a crisis.

Particularly serious is the interruption of the degree program at just the moment when the work on the dissertation is about to get under way; for, once separated from adequate research facilities, from other students, and from the dissertation adviser, and burdened by new full-time professional duties, the student finds himself drifting away from his final academic goal. In this situation the humanities and some of the social sciences are less well off than the rest: there is less support available for these disciplines, there is almost no support for study during the summer, and there is no equivalent for the research assistantship in the sciences which pays a student while he is doing his research.

Aside from these external circumstances, there are difficulties inherent in the nature of the degree itself. The Ph.D. can be earned in almost any branch of learning, and so there is no established program of preparation and no established curriculum for it, sometimes not even within a given department. Moreover, at a time of unprecedented growth and change in the world of knowledge, when old disciplines are being modified, new ones coming into being, and unusual and fruitful associations of disciplines being encouraged, it is not easy to make each program of study tidy and predictable. The sheer bulk of available knowledge is growing rapidly, and in those branches of learning which are cumulative, there is little disposition to reduce the field (a student of literature does not leave out Chaucer because James Joyce has become important, he merely adds Joyce; and a student of history is not free to leave the French Revolution out of consideration because of the Russian Revolution, he merely is asked to know also about the Russian). The student is at a loss sometimes when to terminate his formal course of study because he is not sure just how much he will be expected to know.

The dissertation is a further complication. It is misleading to compare the Ph.D. with other professional degrees because, in addition to all other points of difference, it is an open-end degree. When a student enters a graduate school he does not, like the student of law or medicine, enter a class with which he hopes to graduate; he enters upon a degree program whose end is not precisely known. It is not possible to predict in advance just how long the research will take, what unexpected difficulties will arise, and just how much time will be required to organize and write up the results. Here again the differences between disciplines become important. Mathematicians seem to have the best record of completion within the ideal time span of three and not more than four years for their best students; but mathematics is the least interdisciplinary of all the established doctoral subjects and the most neatly organized. The sciences are generally better off than the non-sciences. They are better supported, but, just as important, the student is usually part of a research project and his research receives some of its impetus from the tempo of the project of which he is a part. The student in the humanities is more isolated. Moreover, the dissertation in the humanities requires generally more time for the period of study before the writing, and it also takes more time in the writing itself, not only because it is longer but because in other disciplines the significant distinctions are made by means of symbolic systems like mathematical demonstrations, statistical tables, and charts, whereas in the humanities the discriminations must depend on language itself. In all disciplines, however, there is an unpredictable element represented by the dissertation which interferes with a uniform and fixed time scheme for the Ph.D.

And there are also those subtle and unanalyzable complications which do not figure conspicuously in the discussions of this problem—the special relationship between student and adviser, the different responses of students to intellectual independence, the reluctance of some to leave familiar and lively surroundings for something perhaps not so good and to accept finally the responsibilities of maturity and freedom from supervision, and all those other uninvestigated factors which make up the Penelope's web syndrome and delay the final moment of completion.

The very special nature of the problem, however, merely places greater responsibility on those who administer graduate programs to see that these inherent difficulties do not result in academic anarchy or destroy the will and enthusiasm of the students. A great deal can be done to improve the administration of degree programs and to promote the student's progress. More systematic supervision of degree candidates by departments would greatly increase efficiency and student morale. More precise indication of what students should expect by way of examinations, and greater insistence on requiring students to take general examinations without indefinite delay would also help. There is reason to believe, too, that the spirit of independence is not sufficiently encouraged and may even be stifled in some instances by impossible programs and prolonged registration in formal courses designed to improve the student's organized knowledge of the field; and it would probably help if the practice in some sciences of having the student define the area of his research before entering his third year became common in other disciplines. The ideal, however, would be to have every student continue in graduate school full time until the completion of his degree program, as is normally the case in law and medicine. This would require some radical improvement in the support of students outside the sciences—a reform suggested on a small scale by the new Woodrow Wilson dissertation year fellowships—for under those circumstances systematic supervision of individual degree programs would be much more effective than it is now. It would also be easier under those conditions for departments and thesis advisers to distinguish between the Ph.D. degree and a student's life work. Under nearly ideal conditions, it would not be impossible to bring the degree program within the theoretical limit of three years for the best-prepared and most energetic minority, and four years for the rest.

Language requirement

It will appear anticlimactic that the item last to be considered is essentially a minor detail—the foreign language requirement. Yet in some ways nothing is more characteristic of the complications and anomalies which result from the necessity of adopting specific means to accomplish ideal ends than the long, unresolved, and joyless argument about the place of languages in the program. It is not difficult to guess how the requirement got there. The advantage of studying the modern European languages was pointed out as early as the late eighteenth century in several of the proposals for improving education which appeared just after the Revolutionary War. When, during the nineteenth century, American scholars began to go to Europe for their advanced studies, knowledge of French and German became essential. And in the early days of the development of a vigorous scholarly tradition in this country, the most up-to-date learning was available only to one who knew foreign languages. It is not too difficult to speculate on why the number required became two. French and German gave a student access to the best in letters and scholarship beyond English, and these have remained the basis of the language requirement. With the growing importance of Russian in science, most graduate schools now permit a choice among these three as the standard. But other languages are admitted, usually with the provision that the student must show their relevance to his field of study though often for no better reason than that he knows no other. And with the influx of foreign students difficult questions have arisen, such as whether it is quite fair to ask a student whose native language is not one of those required and who has already had to learn English, to learn two other foreign languages, or whether it is proper to accept his native language as one of the two languages required (illogical in most fields) or to substitute English for one of the foreign languages. In certain departments it is possible to "substitute" statistics or some other special essential tool for one of the foreign languages (the argument goes, "is not mathematics a language?"). What this device does is to enable a graduate school to maintain in its catalogue that two languages are required for the Ph.D. but to reduce the requirement to one in effect for those departments that wish to arrange it that way.

This gradual change represents a fundamental questioning of the language requirement, a movement which is strongest among the social sciences. The natural sciences have for the most part supported the full requirement, chiefly because the reading of scientific literature in foreign language journals is an actuality and in the present rapid growth of scientific knowledge a necessity, and also because reading of foreign scientific journals does not require the same degree of language mastery as in, say, economics. The principal objection raised against the requirement is that it is no longer functional for most students and thus becomes artificial if not punitive, and since there is so much that needs to be mastered in any field of learning today, the time spent in meeting the language requirement should be spent in acquiring tools and learning methods closely related to the student's work. This is the real purpose behind the device of substitution.

It is true that for many students the language requirement becomes a formidable or at best an irritating hazard. Their previous training in languages has often been meager; many have studied only one language, a few none at all. For the majority of graduate students, any proficiency once acquired is atrophied through disuse, the temptation is to defer the test in the hopes of getting ready for it, and so the moment when the student must prepare for it arrives just as he has begun to gain momentum in his studies and to focus on his research. Educationally, nothing could be worse. And where the student has been given no assignment that can be properly completed only by using a foreign language—a not unusual situation even in the humanities—he approaches the task of refreshing his memory or, more difficult still, of learning a new language from the start, with practically no motivation.

Many suggestions have been made and contrivances devised to reduce the frictions which the requirement produces. A few graduate schools look for evidence of language proficiency as a condition of admission, but if this policy were followed by all graduate schools the present outcry against their failure to produce enough Ph.D.'s would become even shriller. And in any event, it is perhaps better for the world of learning to select the most able among all applicants rather than to restrict admission to the ablest among those who were fortunate enough to have attended schools which enabled them to learn two modern foreign languages. Another device is to withhold financial aid for failure to meet the language requirement by the end of the first year, a means of creating motivation which many regard as punitive, especially in departments which are not enthusiastic about the requirement to begin with. There are also frequent suggestions that every seminar should require the use of at least one item to be read in a foreign language, an excellent suggestion, but one not likely to be heeded by many able teachers of seminars who are not going to take kindly to being told what they must or should do.

The proponents of the requirement are, however, in the majority, as is evidenced by the adherence of the major graduate schools to it in spite of modifications and liberalizations that may occur here and there, and there is little indication that the requirement will be eliminated completely. The chief argument used in its defense has been that elimination of the language requirements will result in a lowering of standards. This is an unfortunate line of defense, and nothing has done more to confuse the question of what standards mean for the Ph.D. and how a graduate school can preserve and improve standards than the regular association of this important matter with the language requirement. The requirement is also defended on cultural grounds. But if it is cultural improvement that we wish to promote, then we must consider whether some other use of a graduate student's time will not meet this purpose better than preparation for demonstrating a minimum ability to read one or two foreign languages. More important still, what a degree program requires of all students must bear a direct relationship to its primary aim; and, while it is true that any serious educational program will indirectly contribute to a student's cultural growth—however we define this elusive quality—the primary aim of the Ph.D. is not general culture. The best defense still remains that inability to read one or more of the foreign languages in which much of the world's important literature and learning are written is a serious handicap to a man who wishes to make a career of the pursuit of learning. As we have already observed, the sciences tend to accept this view. The humanities are by their very nature disposed to endorse it, though they do not have as good a record as the logic of their position requires in making the requirement functional for most students. This leaves the matter still open for discussion on the part of those who would prefer to see the individual department or field of study determine whether such a requirement should be demanded of its students at all.

To an impartial outsider, the discussions of the language requirement must have an air of high comedy about them. Bernard Berelson begins his survey of this issue with the preamble: "Somewhere in this country today, any day, another faculty committee is drawing up another report on the foreign language requirement for the doctorate."[8] A trace of illogic haunts the arguments, and the depth of feeling which the issue arouses seems out of all proportion to the importance of so secondary a feature of the Ph.D. One begins to suspect that something more important than the issues which rise to the surface lies behind the debate, and that beyond the practical necessities which originally dictated the requirement there lurks a second unexpressed aim which has survived into the present.

It has always been the hope of American educators that the products of our highest earned academic degree will be the equal of those produced by any other educational system anywhere. Compared with the best educated Europeans, who are usually able to manage one or more foreign languages with some ease, the American prod-

uct has often seemed provincial. With the great advances in scholarship in the United States and the extraordinary proliferation of
learned journals in English, the necessity of knowing French and
German to keep abreast of the important advances in knowledge
has become less than absolute. This indication of the strength of
American learning, while it has reduced the necessity for mastering
foreign languages in many fields, has not served to destroy the
image of the learned man as one at home and at ease among men of
learning anywhere in the world or to alter our expectation that the
best products of our educational system will be second to none by
any standard of comparison. And just at the moment when the Ph.D.
has gained the respect of other nations and the American man of
learning is becoming a truly international figure by travel to conferences, teaching at foreign universities, and entertaining his con-
freres from abroad in his own country, there is an understandable
reluctance to remove the one requirement which provides a modest
guarantee that provincialism will not be the mark by which the
American scholar will be identified in his new role.

The best hope for accomplishing this purpose, however, as well
as for resolving the long debate over the place of foreign languages
in doctoral study, is not the foreign language requirement for the
Ph.D. in its present form but the widespread new interest in the
study of foreign languages, which now can begin as early as the elementary school, and the encouragement given to foreign language
programs by Federal support. The present generation of graduate
students is the product of a period of uncertainty and discourage-
ment for language study in this country. Those of the next generation will enter graduate school without the same serious handicaps,
and the whole issue may then become irrelevant, as it generally is
in Europe and Russia where by the time a student is permitted to
enter advanced studies he has already acquired proficiency in some
useful foreign language. The present earnest efforts to preserve the
language requirement for the Ph.D. may be seen, therefore, as a
relic of the idealism which characterized the work of those who
were associated with the Ph.D. at its beginnings and which is
reflected in the present efforts to make the degree a symbol of the
man of learning at his best. To most of those associated with gradu-

ate study today, the total elimination of the language requirement at this juncture would seem like the removing of one of the props of an alluring myth or archetypal image that is always on the verge of becoming a reality.

THE CHANGING CHARACTER OF THE DEGREE

The Ph.D. is, in fact, continually in a state of becoming. It is unlikely that it will ever reach a final, fixed state or be free of the restless concern over its proper character. Tied to the vast and complicated treasure of knowledge and committed to its advancement, the Ph.D. has a tropism to irregularity and unpredictability. The degree is also closely associated with teaching in institutions of higher learning, an activity which calls for the kind of authority that comes from being a master of what one professes, and at the same time demands, among other qualifications, breadth and wisdom; and in this connection the degree seems to have a tropism toward narrowness. Both teaching and the advancement of learning at their best call for a measure of unselfishness and idealism, and in consequence the Ph.D. is almost of necessity a source of disappointment as we view the limitations of the actual products of our graduate schools against the model which we have in mind as the goal.

Today all the traditional and inherent difficulties of the Ph.D. have become magnified. Universities have been going through a difficult and confused period; and the graduate schools have been confronted with rising enrollments, increasing demands on their resources, changing conditions in national and local support of students, and revolutionary changes in the state of knowledge itself. It is not to be wondered at that this should also have been a period of vigorous and unremitting criticism of the graduate schools and of the quality and character of their most cherished product, nor is it to be deplored. If a time ever came when American universities allowed themselves or were permitted to become complacent over the state of their highest academic degree, the whole enterprise would have become moribund.

What the graduate schools are trying to do, however, is important and serious enough to ask for a responsible and informed level of debate concerning their problems and their activities; and it is perhaps not too much to hope that we have now reached a sober stage in our reflections about the Ph.D. when criticisms of its presumed failings will not sound like angry editorials, the issues will not be stated with such fierce rigor as to place the choice between unacceptable extremes, and it will be easier to determine when the question is one of means or of ends. It is the high purpose of a university to preserve and make available what is valuable from the past, to interpret the intellectual and artistic innovations of the present, and to advance knowledge. The Ph.D. has been the academic symbol of the efforts of American universities to provide capable, dedicated, and well-trained men who will carry these endeavors into the next generation. The preservation and improvement of what the degree stands for is a responsibility which the graduate schools cannot assume lightly, or renounce—deliberately or by default—with a clear conscience.

NOTES

1. In addition to the criticisms of the Ph.D. by American educators as reported in the preceding chapter, "The Rise of Graduate Education," there have been criticisms from abroad. For example, *The Times Literary Supplement,* in its June 28, 1963, issue, published a double-barreled attack on the American Ph.D. in a review of a book by an American professor of English which originally served as a doctoral dissertation and was subsequently issued by an American university press. The review took the form of a leader entitled "Doggerel Displayed" (p. 476), and the moral of the attack was underscored by an editorial, "Tangible Results," on the opposite page. The attack went beyond criticism of an educational program which rewarded such trivial and pretentious exercises in scholarship with a degree to comment also on the evils of a system of academic preferment which encouraged their publication. It has all the air of a well-planned Dunciad—the victim was carefully selected and was made to bear the onus of an ill vastly greater than himself, and the issue was kept alive in the correspondence columns for several weeks.
2. There is no better method of surveying the development of graduate study in the United States and of the controversies which have accompanied it than to go through the *Proceedings of the Association of American Universities* from 1900 to the present and, after 1950, the *Proceedings of the Association of Graduate Schools*. In this essay I have not provided page references for passages cited from this source but have identified them by the date of the particular volume and the speaker or topic of the report.
3. Earl McGrath, *The Graduate School and the Decline of Liberal Education* (New York: Bureau of Publications, Teachers College, Columbia University, 1959), p. 12.
4. *Ibid.*, p. 40.
5. *Loc. cit.*

6. "Specialization and the Pursuit of Excellence," *Journal of the American Medical Association*, May 16, 1959, p. 294.
7. The *Proceedings* of the A.G.S. for 1962, pp. 45 ff., will illustrate how solitary one can be made to feel who revives such a proposal before the profession. It does not seem to me that the annual exhortations to improve the master's degree and extend to two years the normal period of study for it are likely to succeed in changing the nature of that degree, and I can therefore see no hope in that direction for providing a respectable advanced degree suitable for college and junior college teachers who in all likelihood will not ever become productive scholars. The University of Toronto has recently announced a new intermediate degree, the Master of Philosophy (Phil.M.), beyond the master's degree and below the Ph.D., which will not require a dissertation and will be offered in fields other than the natural sciences.
8. Bernard Berelson, *Graduate Education in the United States* (New York: McGraw-Hill Book Co., 1960), p. 196.

Other Doctorates

JOHN W. ASHTON

OTHER doctorates offered by American universities have been for the most part an American creation designed to meet the needs of the professional schools. The older universities—those established before the beginning of this century—were, with few exceptions, essentially liberal arts colleges designed to prepare teachers, to offer the necessary preprofessional work for prospective lawyers, doctors, and clergymen; and to develop "cultured gentlemen," whatever at any particular time that phrase might mean.

But in this century the idea of a university education has been broadened to encompass in addition preparation for responsible positions in business, industry, and other vocations. The broadened concept resulted eventually in the creation of those other profes-

JOHN W. ASHTON, recently of Indiana University, is a native New Englander. Born in Maine in 1900, he attended Bates College, receiving the A.B. in 1922. He then moved westward and began teaching English at the State University of Iowa where he remained until 1940 except for three years, 1923–26, during which he did graduate work at the University of Chicago. He received the Ph.D. from Chicago in 1928. From 1940 to 1945 he was professor and chairman of the Department of English at the University of Kansas. Since 1945 at Indiana he has served as professor of English and dean of the College of Arts and Sciences, vice-president for student and educational services, and vice-president and dean of the Graduate School. As a member of numerous graduate school organizations and of national fellowship selection committees, Dr. Ashton consistently voices concern for high academic standards. Despite his administrative duties, Dr. Ashton has written extensively on literary subjects and on graduate education. In 1952 Bates awarded him "another doctorate," the LL.D. On February 1, 1965, Dr. Ashton, having retired from Indiana, accepted a new assignment as director of title II, Higher Education Facilities Act, U.S. Office of Education.

sional schools that now make up a considerable portion of the work and enrollment of our full-fledged universities. At first, the new programs took the form of greater stress in the undergraduate years on professional studies as a part of the baccalaureate work. As these professional curricula (note that these were not thought of as pre-professional, as was the undergraduate work in law and medicine) developed, separate undergraduate schools were formed both because the central college of liberal arts was often unsympathetic to, and often intolerant of, the special needs of these programs and because their sponsors felt that only a separate division of the university could command the prestige that would enable them to meet these needs. Hence developed schools of business, of education, of music, and the like. Thereafter, consistent with the pattern of university development generally, graduate courses were added from time to time to the offerings in these specialized, professional areas. The question arose inevitably of offering graduate degrees, first on the master's level and eventually on the doctorate level.

Problems that had accompanied the development of the under-graduate programs were generally intensified as graduate work was added. The graduate schools, many of them not long separately organized, were still essentially graduate schools of arts and sciences, with the majority of their faculty (if, indeed, they were separately organized from the arts and sciences faculty) drawn from the academic areas that had often been unsympathetic to the creation of professional school patterns. Furthermore, they were committed to a type of graduate work which the new professional schools often felt either did not meet their needs or included requirements that had little or no relevance to their students' professional development and plans. The discussions, sometimes acrimonious, centered on the Ph.D.—curriculum, language requirements, and nature of the research and dissertation required.

The established graduate schools feared that a curriculum full of applied or clinical courses would fail to give graduate students that depth of understanding considered essential to the doctorate. If a student in one of the newer professions were expected to spend most of his time in the mastery of techniques, it was felt, his work from course to course and from year to year might be largely repetitive, rather than progressive from one level of understanding to another. At times this was so much an *idée fixe* that a newly proposed professional curriculum was assumed to be guilty until it could be proved innocent of being merely practical work. Too often the argument for high standards was used as a defense against innovation and experimentation in new fields of graduate work and new needs in professional fields. I am reminded of a remark of a colleague at Shrivenham American University in England at the end of World War II who said of his home university, "The School of Education is a part of the graduate faculty, and whenever they want to set up a new program, we simply all turn out and vote it down." This may have been efficacious but hardly indicated a reasonable or objective attitude for the consideration of new graduate programs.

Fears of and objections to the development of new programs have long been common at every level of higher education. Often they are based on budgetary considerations. Funds are never limitless, and inevitably new programs compete with old for the almost always scanty amounts available. A major administrative problem is whether to put all the money into the well-established programs—strengthening them, attempting to bring them to pre-eminence—or to provide opportunities for the development of new fields and areas. New degrees have often had to fight against the well-entrenched programs. Nor has the competition always been for budgets alone. In the days before the influx of students at the end of World War II, any department or program was likely to guard jealously its prior claim to students. The gambit, sometimes by innuendo, was that the new program was clearly inferior in content and standards to the already established ones.

The opposition was not merely selfish or venal nor even often so motivated, for faculty and administration could in all honesty see and fear a departure from tradition in the new professional and vocational programs, particularly in the last fifty years. Abraham Flexner saw chaos in the proliferation of courses and programs a generation ago.

CHARACTERISTICS OF OTHER DOCTORATES

In spite of these conflicts, it has been one of the great achievements of American graduate education that it has expanded, especially

since World War II, into new fields, and curricula have been re-
vised and altered to take into account new areas of knowledge and
new social and intellectual needs. Incidentally, this adaptability of
graduate—and undergraduate—education is usually conveniently
overlooked by critics of the graduate schools who are intent on
seeing them only as rigid, self-centered structures. That the expansion has not all taken place within the pattern of the Ph.D. may
demonstrate some rigidity, but it also signifies that different ends
may best be served by different programs and different degrees. The
issue is put fairly by a professor of business administration:

> We, of course, believe that if a man wishes to teach from a liberal
> arts point of view and in a liberal arts school, he should, by all
> means, take the Ph.D. If his goal is to teach in a professional school
> of business, or business subjects in a liberal arts school, to serve as a
> business consultant or as a business or public administrator, then he
> logically should take a professional business degree. This, we know,
> does not make him any less socially conscious or narrow than if he
> sought the degree, Doctor of Philosophy. Indeed, we think he may be
> broader and he needs to be broader. This is because the business man
> is often a leader in social and political as well as economic affairs. He
> must have an awareness of his social responsibilities and it is our in-
> tent that those future professors who fall under our suzerainty at any
> level of study will get this and pass it on to their students.[1]

In the establishment of new doctoral degrees, the distinctions
among programs have not always been clear nor valid. In many instances the wedge that finally split a program off from the Ph.D.
was the requirement of a reading knowledge of two foreign languages. Many graduate schools have debated the functions and usefulness of the language requirement, how the language skill should
be tested, the use of the language in the research toward the doctorate. Some schools have permitted the substitution of a tool course,
such as statistics, for one of the languages. But whatever the discussions and justifications, the requirement stands as a barrier between
the established Ph.D. pattern and that desired for the newly developing professional programs, many of which exhibit no fundamental need for proficiency in a foreign language.

Another element contributing to the creation of new or other
doctoral degrees has been the nature of the research and the dissertation. To oversimplify: the research for the Ph.D. has traditionally

been pure or fundamental, whereas that in the professional fields has tended to be applied. Theoretically, the student in economics might concern himself with a research problem in economic theory or history, but a candidate for a business degree would investigate the application of economic or management principles to a particular business situation—in one sense, a case study. A student might do research in the history or theory of music for the Ph.D., but if he wished, say, to create a sonata or perform a significant type of music, he would do so in the pattern of the Doctor of Music. Again, in education, the Ph.D. candidate might do his research in the history or philosophy of education, but for the Ed.D. degree he would make a practical study of an educational problem, perhaps by surveying a school system or a national or regional curricular pattern, or would draw up a testing program.

This was—and is—the theory. Particularly in the contemporary world, however, the boundaries between pure and applied research are constantly being lost, and many distinctions, once valid, break down. A casual reading of dissertation titles in a commencement program may lead even the initiated to ponder the real difference between the research done for two degrees with different names.

I exaggerate somewhat, of course, for in a field like music the distinction remains quite clear, as it is largely for the D.B.A. as well. But in the case of education, both curriculum and dissertation might in many instances be interchanged for the two degrees, and the only significant difference would be that the holder of the Ph.D. satisfied the foreign language requirement and the Doctor of Education did not.

A MULTITUDE OF DEGREES

So much for the background. When we turn to an examination of the actual offering of doctoral degrees other than the Ph.D., we are in a thicket of names and characteristics that gives an impression of riotous freedom, if not chaos. Members of the Association of Graduate Schools, which until recently have given most of the doctorates in this country, offer no less than 27 doctoral degrees other than the Ph.D. This is a small number, however, in comparison with the roughly 250 doctoral degrees, including the Ph.D. but not the M.D., D.V.M., or D.D.S., that have been offered at one time or another by American universities.[2] What is even more striking is that 64 doctorates, including the first professional degrees in medicine and dentistry, are now being awarded. Certainly these figures are indicative of a breakdown of doctoral programs into narrowly limited segments of subject matter.

The variations are not so great as they appear to be. Some of the multiplicity results from narrow definitions, for instance, the naming of a degree for each field of engineering or the insertion "of Science" in a title (Doctor of Science in Geological Engineering). At some time there have been four landscape doctorates: Doctor of Landscape Architecture, Doctor of Landscape Design, Doctor of Landscape Engineering, and Doctor of Landscape Management. Some titles appear to have been chiefly exercises in ingenuity—Doctor of the Art of Oratory, Doctor of Education in the College Teaching of the Humanities, and a similar one in the social sciences. There have been Doctors of English Divinity and of English Literature, of Expression, of Family Life, of Hebrew Letters or of Hebrew Literature, of Hospital Administration, of Household Economy or of Household Science, of Industry, of Languages, of Literary Interpretation—the list grows the more fantastic the longer it is made. Probably many of the more curious examples grew out of special, or supposedly special, situations where enthusiasm for a new program sought expression in a distinctive title, or where a new program, on only the fringes of established academic respectability, was denied access to the Ph.D. and sought its own designation.

Others represent an attempt to supply a general education at the graduate level, either to make up for the deficiencies of undergraduate work or to prepare college teachers for general courses in the humanities, the social sciences, or the natural sciences. In the doctorate in humanities, the danger has been that the student would never get beyond the knowledge of things in general nor attain that deep penetration of a subject that ought to characterize any doctorate, whether pure or applied. Admittedly these examples are the exceptions, each appearing in only one institution and most of them no longer given, but collectively they are the antithesis of rigid adherence to the Ph.D. pattern.

The more nearly standard non-Ph.D. programs are the Doctor of Engineering, the Doctor of Education, the Doctor of Business Administration, the Doctor of Music, the Doctor of Public Health, the Doctor of Social Work or of Social Welfare, and a variety of law degrees: Doctor of Judicial Science, Doctor of Civil Law, Doctor of Common Law, Doctor of Talmudic Law, and Doctor of Jurisprudence, which are commonly awarded as research degrees in law beyond the LL.B. and LL.M. The engineering doctorate is still broken up occasionally into the various fields of chemical, civil, and so forth, but the tendency is to give the one degree for all fields.

In addition, a few institutions award degrees that are true research or professional degrees at the highest level. These include the Doctor of Architecture, the Doctor of Forestry, the Doctor of Public Administration, the Doctor of Science (very largely conferred now only as an honorary degree), and a group of medical research degrees: Doctor of Medical Sciences, Doctor of Clinical Science, Doctor of the Science of Hygiene, and in one institution the Doctor of Veterinary Science, which is a post-D.V.M. degree and calls for a dissertation that is an "original contribution to knowledge." There are also the advanced degrees in religion: the Doctor of Theology, the Doctor of Sacred Theology, the Doctor of Religious Education, and the Doctor of Sacred Music. In the field of the fine arts and music there are doctorates of fine arts, of musical arts, and of music, and to these we shall return. There is even a Doctor of Physical Education degree and one of Recreation.

ARE THERE REAL DISTINCTIONS?

This list of what we might think of as standard degrees is long, but a paradox lies in the fact that many of the areas of study and research in which they are given are also represented in Ph.D. programs. Of the members of the Association of Graduate Schools mentioned earlier, thirteen give only the Ph.D. Of course, many of these institutions offer doctoral work in the fields listed above, although other institutions have apparently considered some of these fields to be inappropriate for the Ph.D. degree. Are we to suppose that the work toward the degree differs substantially in kind in the two institutions? I think not. Perhaps in institutions offering a mul-

tiplicity of doctorates, the Ph.D. candidate is required to show reading proficiency in two foreign languages, whereas in the institution
that gives only the Ph.D., no language, or only one, may be required
in special professional fields. But this is not a safe generalization. It
is not even safe to say that the Ph.D. candidate generally is required
to be proficient (however "proficient" is defined) in two languages
for in several instances—as mentioned earlier—a course in statistics
or some other tool may be substituted for one of the languages. And
in some of the non-Ph.D. programs two languages are required: the
Doctor of Forestry at Duke, the Doctor of Medical Sciences and
Doctor of Public Health at Harvard, the Doctor of Music Arts at
Illinois and at Cornell, to mention only a few. The Doctor of Education almost never requires proficiency in foreign language,
though at Clark University there is a catalogue requirement of two
foreign languages, with the loophole that a minor in a field closely
related to the major may be substituted for the language requirement, subject to the approval of the Graduate Board. Thus, at
Clark the Ed.D. candidates are expected to satisfy all the requirements for a Ph.D. if we may take at face value the board's statement.

Graduate school bulletins do not disclose any striking difference
between the research and dissertation for the different degrees. Almost every institution speaks of expecting a dissertation to be "an
original contribution to knowledge," whether it be for the Ph.D.,
the Ed.D., the Doctor of Engineering, or any other degree. In the
case of Johns Hopkins, indeed, it is specified that the research for
the Doctor of Engineering be "fundamental in nature" and "lead to
an original contribution to engineering science."

In practice there is a clear difference between the Ph.D. and the
"other doctorates" in this matter. I have already indicated that in
the case of music the lines can be sharply drawn between the Doctor of Music as a performer's or composer's degree and the Ph.D. as
one which calls for research in musicology or in music history. The
same clear distinction might be assumed to prevail in a field like
engineering, where the development of a design would be the appropriate work for the Doctor of Engineering, whereas fundamental
research would be appropriate for the Ph.D. But here the lines are
not always easy to draw. A theoretical physicist may not be much

concerned, if at all, with hardware, but an engineer interested in nuclear reactors may need to do a good deal of research into theoretical physics. This is a middle ground. At the opposite extreme is the Ed.D. where, as indicated earlier, any theoretical difference between it and the Ph.D. has long since been lost, and the only real difference is that the former seldom requires knowledge of a foreign language. This is a pity, for there are two distinct areas of professional endeavor which could be recognized as differentiating the degrees. The Ed.D. might well be designed for those planning to go into high-level administration in school systems or into statistical and planning analysis. The Ph.D. could then be utilized for those who are going into college and university teaching in schools or departments of education and are interested in the history, philosophy, and theory of education. Such a division of labor might dissolve the notion, justified or not, that the Ed.D. is an inferior degree and enable it to stand securely on its own feet, as does the D.B.A.

Admittedly this is too neat a packaging of the fields, but the schools of business administration have made great strides in accomplishing such a distinction. They focus attention in the master's degree on the preparation of future business executives; in the D.B.A. the intent is to prepare researchers and teachers in the various fields of business administration. For persons interested in the theoretical aspects, leaders in business education may recommend study for the Ph.D. with a major in economics or perhaps a combined major in economics and one of the fields of "applied" business. Even here I would not suggest that all the distinctions are clear and that no angel—or dean—muddies the waters, but at least the D.B.A. has achieved a distinctive significance.

The confusion evident is a product in part of the confusions and animosities out of which many of the "other doctorates" grew. But it is a product also of the complexity of American higher education and the recognition of the validity of a great many areas of study that were not recognized in the tradition of a century ago. It is a product also of the great changes that have taken place in the world of knowledge, particularly the sciences and the professions, breaking down barriers between fields, creating new interactions among them, calling for new specializations.

We recognize in a general way a real difference of mode between fundamental and applied research, between theory and practice, between scholarly research and creative artistry. It is when we try to confine graduate programs for the doctorate within compartments that we get into trouble, for research and, for that matter, artistic creation have a way of breaking through boundaries, not only between established disciplines such as physics and biology but also, and even more readily, between fundamental and applied research and between scholarly and professional goals.

I think we cannot hope for exact distinctions between the Ph.D. and other doctorates; for one thing, the other doctorates are too well established in their present patterns. But at the same time the differences—whatever they may prove to be—ought to be significant, rather than based simply on an unwillingness to meet the standards of the Ph.D. For a student to say he wishes to take an Ed.D. because he doesn't want to meet any language requirements is as insufficient as for an engineer to work toward a Doctor of Engineering in order not to avoid becoming proficient in mathematics. To put the difference on that basis and on that scale would make the Ed.D. degree inferior, as it is sometimes accused of being.

In summary, the other doctorates have a valid place in American higher education as long as they see for themselves a significant function and are not created as an escape from the requirements of the Ph.D. Ideally they are oriented to the profession which gives each its name and are designed to meet the needs of that profession on the highest level of education. At their best they serve a function that is parallel but noncompetitive with the Ph.D.! The sad fact is that the ideal situation does not always exist, that ends are not clearly seen, that ways are not clearly defined, and that professional goals are not clearly achieved.

THE CREATIVE ARTS

This study would be incomplete without brief attention to the problem of the place of the creative arts in doctoral programs. Music has settled the matter satisfactorily for itself, but what of the writer or painter or sculptor? For the most part such persons have, if they concerned themselves at all with academic degrees, been content with a Master of Fine Arts or an M.A. But with increasing numbers of practicing artists and writers becoming faculty members, there is a growing disposition for them to seek the prestige, real or imagined, of the doctorate. For many years the State University of Iowa has awarded the Ph.D. for the writing of poetry or fiction or drama in place of a research dissertation. When the possibility of wider acceptance of this substitution was discussed at a meeting of the American Council of Learned Societies a few years ago, it was howled down by those who insisted that the essence of the Ph.D. was a research thesis.

Obviously, the mathematicians have been embroiled for some time in a debate of whether anything but a creative piece of work is acceptable for the Ph.D. in mathematics, and some have urged the development of a new degree to provide for historical studies and the like. "Creative" is used in slightly different connotations in these two cases, but the difference is not as great as might be supposed. In each case the student is expected to build a solid foundation in his subject; he is also expected to strike out pretty much on his own, drawing on the resources of his creative, rather than necessarily analytical, powers. But the attitude of the mathematicians is the opposite of that toward creative work in literature and the arts. The mathematicians insist—or many of them do—that only creative work is worthy of the Ph.D.; the opponents of the Ph.D. for creative writing insist that this degree is only for research, and creative work doesn't qualify.

Must we have a new degree for each category of candidates? Or must we simply say that neither belongs in the range of doctoral work? Or is it conceivable, in view of the many interrelations and overlappings of Ph.D. and non-Ph.D. degrees, that the creative writer or artist and the student of the history of mathematics might both find shelter under the wide umbrella of the Ph.D.?

It is appropriate to end on this questioning note, for our study has shown that the problems of other doctorates are closely related to the question of the nature of the Ph.D. itself. History implies that each institution will settle the matter to suit itself. If this means a Doctor of Literature for the creative writer (parallel to the Doctor of Music) and a Doctor of Mathematics (or whatever names might be decided upon) for the noncreative mathematician, such action will only emphasize the rigidity in the definition of the Ph.D. and will add to the already confusing and sometimes meaningless variety of other doctorates.

A RATIONAL PATTERN

In the best of all possible academic worlds, freed from the ambitions of particular groups and programs or from desires to build empires, order might be introduced into the present chaos of doctoral programs by establishing just three doctorates (aside from the standard medical and dental degrees), whose areas could be pretty well defined. One degree, presumably the Ph.D., would be awarded for basic research—whatever the field—that to some extent enlarges or redefines the present boundaries of knowledge. It should be, more truly than it now is, a doctorate in the love of learning or, more accurately, in the love of wisdom. A second degree, equally significant for its own purposes, would be awarded for applied or technical studies—the engineering designs; the merely quantitative studies, drawn from the hosts of questionnaires that report on the present state of health education in the ninth grade, or the prevalence of some sociological characteristic in communities of a certain size; the survey of business practices, and so on. And the third doctorate might recognize creative work of high quality that has been developed through vigorous training and experimentation.

But this is not the best of all possible worlds, and there are years of tradition and sometimes of conflict behind many of the "other doctorates" that have made a place for themselves in American higher education. Perhaps the best we can hope for is that the tendency toward greater particularity in the name of the doctorate may reverse itself and that the other doctorates will become fewer in number and broader in scope or at least in inclusiveness. And certainly we should strive vigorously toward making any doctorate call for high standards of performance and provide strenuous intellectual and practical experience for the doctoral student.

NOTES

1. L. L. Waters, "Graduate Study in Business: Indiana University, 1948–1963" (Unpublished ms; Indiana University).
2. Walter Crosby Eells and Harold A. Haswell, *Academic Degrees: Earned and Honorary Degrees Conferred by Institutions of Higher Education in the United States,* OE-54008 (Washington: Government Printing Office, 1960).

The Master's Degree

JOHN L. SNELL

T HE master's degree, it has been said, is "a bit like a street-walker—all things to all men (and at different prices)."[1] Whatever the quality of the merchandise or its price, a high and rising demand for the master's degree exists. In the academic year 1962–63 almost 88,000 persons earned the master's in the United States, thus taking 17 percent of all degrees earned in institutions of higher education. The popularity of the master's degree among teachers in the schools and its tangible value to them are well known. Because of the shortage of Ph.D.'s, it is often the highest degree held by college teachers, though it is not regarded as adequate. In 1953–54 it was the highest degree held by half of all college and university faculty members. It was the highest held by 60 percent of all new faculty in 1962–63.[2]

In recent discussions of graduate education some critics have suggested that the master's is of such diverse (and even small) significance that in many fields it scarcely serves a useful purpose. Paradoxically, others have called for development of the master's into a really reputable degree for college teachers in order to alleviate the present and increasing shortage of Ph.D.'s. But if the past and the present of the master's render its elimination unlikely, past

JOHN L. SNELL, a native North Carolinian, is one of the country's youngest graduate deans. Born in 1923, he took the A.B., the A.M., and the Ph.D. at the University of North Carolina. Since 1953 he has taught European history at Tulane University. His published works include five books on the origins of World War II and the Nazi regime. In 1958–60 Dr. Snell was a principal investigator of the graduate study in history sponsored by the American Historical Society. The study, *The Education of Historians in the United States,* has been widely used. Dr. Snell became dean of Tulane's Graduate School in 1963.

and present also pose obstacles to attempts to "rehabilitate" the master's degree.

THE WAY TO THE PRESENT

Late medieval scholars in Europe earned the master's degree, but in England by the seventeenth century the master's had become an honorary degree. It was commonly awarded to any college graduate who wanted it three years after earning the baccalaureate. This practice was exported to the American colonies and continued until well after the Civil War. Several universities, including Harvard, the University of the City of New York (later to become New York University), Columbia, the University of Virginia, and the University of Michigan, attempted to establish programs for earned master's degrees before 1861 but generally were unsuccessful; the lack of financial assistance for students unquestionably was a major cause of the stillbirth of these pioneer graduate programs. Such master's programs as were inaugurated before the Civil War were largely extensions of undergraduate curricula; they offered additional breadth but little specialization or research.[3]

In the 1870's a new interest in the earned master's degree developed. The rapidly growing popularity of the Ph.D. stimulated many universities to offer work leading to the M.A. and M.S., and the number of persons earning these degrees increased. The contrast with the pre-Civil War years was made possible by five major developments in addition to the offering of fellowships.

First, by the period of 1870–90 there was work to be done that demanded graduate training. Teaching positions in colleges awaited those who earned the master's, for the number of Ph.D.'s did not approach the demand for faculty members. In 1884 only 19 of 189 Harvard professors and only six of 88 members of Michigan's faculty held the doctorate. Second, the rapid expansion of high schools and colleges prepared larger numbers of students for graduate study than could have been imagined before 1861—larger numbers than any nation in history had ever known. Eventually the high schools, like the colleges, would also provide a large demand for teachers with the master's degree, though this would come chiefly in the twentieth century. With only 7 percent of its youth age fourteen to seventeen in high school in 1889–90, the nation would see the percentage rise to 15 percent in 1909–10, to 51 percent in 1929–30, and to 77 percent in 1949–50; by 1961–62 the figure would stand at 90 percent. Third, the elective system in the colleges, widely adopted by the 1890's, encouraged a degree of undergraduate concentration that better prepared student tastes and abilities for the specialized work in the graduate schools.

Fourth, American women, demanding equal rights in every kind of activity, swelled the numbers of candidates for the master's degree. Only half a dozen colleges had admitted women before the Civil War, but by 1900 more than two thirds of American colleges and universities opened their doors to them. By 1894 one sixth of those who annually earned master's degrees were women, and in subsequent years the percentage followed the rise of the feminist movement: one fifth in 1900, one fourth in 1907, and one third in 1913—at which point the rising curve began to level off. In the whole period 1870–1958 women were to take 34 percent of all master's degrees awarded by colleges and universities in the United States.

Fifth, the development of summer schools enabled increasing numbers of public school teachers to continue their studies at the graduate level while simultaneously earning a livelihood. Summer school enrollment stood at 132,500 in 1919, rose to 388,000 in 1929, was up to 456,700 by 1939, and reached 943,000 in 1949.

Other developments may have been at work, but these five alone—plus fellowships—were enough to cause a powerful upsurge in the output of master's programs. As early as 1880, 879 master's were being awarded annually in the United States. Since then every decade has seen a sharp increase, ranging from 34 percent in 1890–1900 to 242 percent in 1920–30. Between 1870 and 1962 roughly 1.5 million master's degrees were awarded.[4]

THE PRESENT AS PROLOGUE

A most striking fact about the current output of master's degrees is that almost half of all awarded from 1870 to 1962 were granted in the decade 1953–62 (670,152, or 45 percent). Yearly output had risen to 85,000 in 1961–62, and reached 87,900 in 1962–63.

TABLE 1: *Award of Master's Degrees by 621 Institutions, by Type of Institution, 1961–62*

TYPE	NO. OF INSTITUTIONS		NO. OF MASTER'S AWARDED	AVERAGE
	Total	Awarding Master's		
Universities..................	143	143	56,660	396
Liberal arts colleges............	751	218	13,084	60
Teachers colleges..............	194	122	10,794	88
Technological schools...........	51	28	3,021	108
Theological or religious institutions......................	89	59	593	10
Schools of art.................	41	26	375	14
Other professional schools.......	40	25	362	14

Source: Wayne E. Tolliver, *Earned Degrees Conferred, 1961–1962*, OE-54013-62 (Washington: Government Printing Office, 1963), p. 7.

Accompanying the increase in the number of master's degrees awarded has been an increase in the number of institutions awarding them; from 1958 to 1962 alone the increase was from 569 to 621.[5] Currently, nearly 30 percent of the liberal arts colleges, about 63 percent of the teachers colleges, and all the universities in the United States award the master's in one form or another. Universities continue to account for a large majority of the degrees annually awarded, averaging 396 degrees each in 1961–62 (Table 1). The average number per awarding institution (all types) was 137.

Recent growth has not been steady in all types of institutions. The most dramatic shift—and one of importance—has been the markedly larger increase in the output of public institutions since 1947–48 as compared with that of private institutions (Table 2). Then almost 60 percent of all master's degrees were awarded by private institutions. By 1952–53 the balance had shifted to the public

TABLE 2: *Award of Master's Degrees by Public and Private Institutions, Selected Years, 1947–62*

YEAR	NO. OF MASTER'S AWARDED			PERCENT PRIVATE
	Total	Public Institutions	Private Institutions	
1947–48..........	42,449	17,696	24,753	58
1952–53..........	61,023	31,113	29,910	49
1961–62..........	84,889	50,663	34,226	40

Source: Tolliver, *Earned Degrees Conferred, 1961–1962*, pp. 2–5.

institutions, and in 1961–62 no less than 60 percent of all master's degrees were awarded by them; the relationship of 1947–48 had been reversed. Although the private institutions' share of degrees awarded at all levels has declined (to 43 percent of all baccalaureate degrees and 46 percent of all doctorates), the swift decline of their

TABLE 3: *Award of Master's Degrees, by Regions, 1961–62*

Region, by State	No.	Region, by State	No.
East (34 percent)	*28,842*	*Midwest (30 percent)*	*25,306*
Connecticut	1,732	Illinois	4,763
Delaware	186	Indiana	3,835
District of Columbia	1,858	Iowa	1,088
Maine	219	Kansas	1,368
Maryland	843	Michigan	5,312
Massachusetts	4,956	Minnesota	1,244
New Hampshire	202	Missouri	1,783
New Jersey	1,852	Nebraska	607
New York	11,734	Ohio	3,500
Pennsylvania	4,100	Wisconsin	1,806
Rhode Island	269		
Vermont	283	*West (17 percent)*	*14,760*
West Virginia	608	Alaska	27
		Arizona	933
South (18 percent)	*15,673*	California	7,228
Alabama	973	Colorado	1,814
Arkansas	730	Hawaii	96
Florida	1,272	Idaho	206
Georgia	826	Montana	274
Kentucky	887	Nevada	54
Louisiana	1,004	New Mexico	578
Mississippi	665	North Dakota	263
North Carolina	1,715	Oregon	1,052
Oklahoma	1,349	South Dakota	328
South Carolina	333	Utah	603
Tennessee	1,592	Washington	1,119
Texas	3,586	Wyoming	185
Virginia	707		
Puerto Rico	34		

Source: Tolliver, *Earned Degrees Conferred, 1961–1962*, pp. 16–36. In addition to degrees shown, 308 were awarded by U.S. service schools.

share of master's degrees from 58 to 40 percent within fifteen years is especially notable. The trend seems well established, for the percentage of master's awarded by private institutions declined each year except two between 1947 and 1962.

Regional output of master's degrees is also markedly uneven, with the predominance lying in the East (Table 3). In 1961–62, that area produced slightly more than a third of the national total, while the South, with about 28 percent of the nation's population, awarded only 18 percent. Two states in the East (New York plus either Massachusetts or Pennsylvania) awarded more master's degrees than the entire South. In the West, awards in 1961–62 typically reflected the lopsided distribution of population in the region, with California accounting for 49 percent of the regional total. California was the second most productive state in the nation, exceeded only by New York.

A large part of the annual output is accounted for by a few of the largest institutions. The thirty-five largest producers in 1961–62 granted 32,656 degrees, for an average of 933 each. Thus 5.6 percent of the institutions awarding master's degrees in 1961–62 accounted for 38 percent of the total. Table 4 lists the 118 institutions that awarded more than 200 degrees each in 1961–62. As Berelson has noted, the major producers tend to be: (1) those with large teachers college components; (2) urban institutions with a large clientele of teachers seeking advanced degrees; and (3) state universities with obligations to the public schools of their states.[6]

Table 4 quickly suggests that significant numbers of master's degrees are being awarded by institutions that command only modest academic reputations. Conversely, a number of the better institutions in the nation are not among the major producers. Princeton, generally included among the top ten universities, ranked only 109th in production of master's in 1961–62, awarding 233; neighboring Seton Hall University awarded more. Three of the six Southern members of the Association of American Universities and the Association of Graduate Schools awarded fewer than 200 master's degrees each in 1961–62. Appalachian State Teachers College awarded more than Duke (165) and East Texas State 57 percent more than Tulane (196); George Peabody awarded four times as many as Vanderbilt (140). Los Angeles State College of Applied Arts and Sciences awarded four times more than the California Institute of Technology (129); Ball State Teachers awarded more than the University of Chicago.

The preponderance of education as the field of award is made explicit in Table 5. All other master's, whatever the professional or academic concentration, are being earned in much smaller numbers.

TABLE 4: *118 Institutions Awarding More Than 200 Master's Degrees Each, 1961–62*

Institution	No. Master's Degrees	Institution	No. Master's Degrees
New York Univ.	2,437	Florida State Univ.	351
Columbia Univ.	2,294	Fordham Univ.	351
Univ. of Michigan	2,093	San Jose State Coll.	351
Indiana Univ.	1,520	Univ. of Nebraska	348
Univ. of Illinois	1,486	Long Beach State Coll.	344
Univ. of Wisconsin	1,360	St. Louis Univ.	344
Univ. of Southern California	1,157	Univ. of Kansas	341
Univ. of California, Berkeley	1,082	Western Michigan Univ.	334
Michigan State Univ.	1,070	Brooklyn Coll.	329
Univ. of Minnesota	1,013	Univ. of Pittsburgh	328
Harvard Univ. (incl. Radcliffe Coll.).	991	Univ. of Denver	319
Ohio State Univ.	915	Eastern Michigan Univ.	316
Univ. of Pennsylvania	908	Rensselaer Polytechnic Inst.	309
Stanford Univ.	899	East Texas State Coll.	308
Purdue Univ.	841	North Texas State Coll.	308
Univ. of California, Los Angeles.	822	Johns Hopkins Univ.	304
Wayne State Univ.	818	Xavier Univ. (Ohio)	300
George Washington Univ.	806	Univ. of Rochester	296
Boston Univ.	788	Univ. of Kentucky	295
Pennsylvania State Univ.	773	Washington Univ.	292
Mass. Inst. of Tech.	714	Univ. of Virginia	289
Syracuse Univ.	653	Miami Univ.	285
Univ. of Missouri	649	Boston Coll.	283
Yale Univ.	614	Kansas State Univ.	281
State Univ. of Iowa	611	Univ. of New Mexico	278
George Peabody Coll. for Teachers..	561	Univ. of Cincinnati	276
Univ. of North Carolina at Chapel Hill	560	Auburn Univ.	275
Univ. of Colorado	545	Indiana State Coll.	275
Univ. of Washington	537	State College at Boston	274
Ball State Teachers Coll.	533	Univ. of Georgia	273
Catholic Univ.	531	Kansas State Teachers Coll. (Emporia)	272
Los Angeles State Coll. of Appl. Arts and Sci.	530	Univ. of Detroit	269
Colorado State Coll.	527	St. Johns Univ.	266
City Coll. of the City of N.Y.	511	Univ. of Connecticut	264
Temple Univ.	507	East Carolina Coll.	262
Univ. of Chicago	498	Univ. of Utah	261
Rutgers—The State Univ.	486	Southern Methodist Univ.	259
Oklahoma State Univ.	464	State Univ. Coll. at Albany (N.Y.)..	257
Univ. of Texas	458	Iowa State Univ.	256
San Francisco State Coll.	453	American Univ.	251
Univ. of Florida	450	Marquette Univ.	250
Cornell Univ.	444	Seton Hall Univ.	247
Louisiana State Univ.	441	Duquesne Univ.	245
Univ. of Alabama	428	Univ. of Mississippi	244
Univ. of Oregon	428	Loyola Univ. (Ill.)	243
Arizona State Univ.	423	State Univ. Coll., College of Education, Buffalo (N.Y.)	241
Univ. of Notre Dame	421	De Paul Univ.	238
Western Reserve Univ.	407	Northern Illinois Univ.	237
Univ. of Arkansas	402	Lehigh Univ.	235
Univ. of Arizona	397	Princeton Univ.	233
Oregon State Univ.	392	Texas A&M Univ.	223
Hunter College	389	University of Miami	222
Univ. of Tennessee	387	Marshall Univ.	221
West Virginia Univ.	387	Drexel Inst. of Tech.	214
Kent State Univ.	384	Univ. of Houston	210
Southern Illinois Univ.	384	Hillyer Coll. (Conn.)	209
Univ. of Maryland	383	Univ. of Maine	207
Hofstra Coll.	381	U.S. Naval Postgraduate School	206
Univ. of Oklahoma	356	Appalachian State Teachers Coll.	201

Source: Tolliver, *Earned Degrees Conferred, 1961–1962*, pp. 16–36.

THE MASTER'S DEGREE IN THE MARKET

Of what use is the master's degree to the man or woman who earns one? For what professional or cultural functions does it prepare one? What demand will there be for persons who earn master's degrees during the years just ahead?

For persons who expect to earn the Ph.D. degree, the master's program may simply be a valuable part of doctoral training. A great majority of Ph.D.'s earn the master's on the way to the doctorate. In the field of history, which is more or less representative in this matter, one fourth of the Ph.D.-training departments require students who aspire to the doctorate to take the master's degree; only 7 percent are indifferent or discourage them from doing so; the others encourage it. It appears that seven-eighths of all new Ph.D.'s in the South from 1950 to 1958 earned the master's degree along the way to the doctorate.[7]

Whether or not Ph.D. candidates should earn the master's continues to be debated. The master's was bypassed by slightly more than half of the first Ph.D.'s who completed their programs within three years while holding National Defense Education Act title IV fellowships. Those who earned the master's disagreed about the value of doing so; half thought that it was "a waste of time."[8] If the master's program is not a rigorous one, the promising graduate student will probably gain by proceeding directly to the Ph.D. If the master's program is demanding, involving the writing of a substantial thesis, it may slow one's progress toward the doctorate. Thus, one analyst of graduate programs concluded in 1959 that "for students who are going to take a doctor's degree, the master's degree serves no real purpose."[9]

But this advice overlooks at least three factors that should urge would-be Ph.D's to earn the master's degree. First, no student in his first year of graduate study can *know* that he is "going to take a doctor's degree." Whether he will be allowed to progress toward the doctorate depends on his performance over at least two years of graduate study, and usually longer. Graduate students are well advised to think of the master's as a form of insurance against the possibility that they may not be granted a Ph.D. Second, in deciding whether or not to allow a student to continue graduate study beyond a first or subsequent year, graduate faculties need to base their judgment on the quality of the student's research, writing, and examinations for the master's degree. Third, most students need the education that the master's program can afford before fully plunging into the independent research and writing expected of them in preparing a doctoral dissertation. It is noteworthy that although half of the first group of title IV Ph.D.'s who earned the master's thought it "a waste of time," the other half acknowledged that writing the master's thesis had provided valuable experience.

In this, as in most other issues in graduate education, consideration of the needs of individual students appears to be the best rule to follow. If a first-year student distinguishes himself in research and writing in the judgment of two respected faculty members, both of whom believe he should work toward the Ph.D. without taking the master's, the student should be allowed to do so. If more time is likely to be lost than gained in bypassing the master's, as is likely with the average student, the student should be required to grow while earning the master's. A carefully planned master's program need not unduly delay the progress of an able graduate student toward the Ph.D. If the master's requirements are fully met as late as the end of the second year of graduate study and if the student has continued to take courses during his second year in residence, little time will have been lost. Second-year courses usually are in excess of those required for the M.A. and the M.S., and in many universities all formal courses for the Ph.D. can be completed in two years of graduate study. None of this denies, of course, the importance of finding ways in most fields of study to make the master's a one-year degree. If this can be managed, the master's will certainly not delay the progress of Ph.D. candidates toward the doctorate. On balance, most of them should earn the master's before going far toward the Ph.D.

Although most Ph.D.'s do (and should) earn the master's degree, the majority of persons who earn the master's do not become Ph.D.'s. What professional future awaits the person for whom the master's is the highest degree earned?

Table 5 tells a good bit about the current supply of master's and thus indirectly suggests variations in demand among the various fields in the recent past. The master's, it is quite clear, is chiefly a degree for teachers. Two fifths (42 percent) of those who earned the degree in 1961–62 carried out graduate study in departments or schools of education; in 1947–48 only 30 percent did so.[10] These quite clearly were preparing themselves for careers in elementary or secondary teaching or administration. In addition, large numbers of those who earned the degree in a subject-matter field (for example,

TABLE 5: *Variations in Productivity of Master's Degrees by Fields:** *First-Year Graduate Enrollment, Fall 1961, and Number of Master's Degrees Awarded, 1961–62*

FIELD	MASTER'S AND SECOND-LEVEL DEGREES, 1961–62			FIRST-YEAR ENROLLMENT, FALL 1961	DEGREES AWARDED PER 100 ENROLLED
	Men	Women	Total		
1. Education	19,838	16,094	35,932	80,967	44
2. Engineering	8,869	40	8,909	21,551	41
3. Social sciences	5,667	1,652	7,319	24,253	30
4. Business and commerce	5,128	175	5,303	19,092	28
5. Physical sciences	3,544	385	3,929	12,245	32
6. English and journalism	1,899	1,866	3,765	9,520	39
7. Fine and applied arts	1,858	1,293	3,151	6,774	46
8. Mathematical subjects	2,179	501	2,680	7,851	34
9. Biological sciences	1,982	660	2,642	7,699	34
10. Psychology	1,269	563	1,832	5,655	32
11. Foreign languages and literature	781	815	1,596	3,985	40
12. Agriculture	1,072	35	1,107	1,783	62
13. Home economics	21	522	543	981	55
14. Library sciences	101	420	521	1,217	43
15. Philosophy	372	59	431	1,175	37
16. Architecture	296	15	311	479	65
17. Forestry	249	1	250	333	75
18. Geography	212	30	242	656	37
All Fields	55,337	25,126	80,463	206,216	39

* Does not include law, medicine, theology, and general curriculum enrollees.
Source: Adapted from *Digest of Educational Statistics*, 1963 ed., OE-10024-63 (Washington: Government Printing Office, 1963), pp. 64–70.

in the social sciences and English) found or returned to positions as high school teachers.

Those who earn master's degrees in education and subject-matter areas may expect the demand for their services in elementary and secondary schools to remain high during the years ahead, especially since no surplus has been built up in recent years. While high school enrollments have increased 71 percent (1949–62), the number of master's degrees awarded has increased only 67 percent.[11] It is hoped that school systems will increasingly employ secondary teachers who have concentrated their studies—whether graduate or undergraduate—in a subject-matter area rather than in the pedagogically oriented education programs.[12]

Many teaching positions will be open in the expanding junior colleges during the next several years for persons who earn master's degrees in subject-matter specialties. In 1962–63, as during the last several years, junior college administrators have reported shortages of qualified teachers in several fields. In those in which shortages have been most severe—especially mathematics, physics, chemistry, English,' and foreign languages[13]—high demand may be expected to continue for several years to come.

Many positions, at least temporary positions, will be available in four-year colleges, but no graduate student should content himself with the terminal master's on the assumption that he will readily find promotion, substantial salary increases, and tenure as a member of a college faculty. But of this, more later.

Persons with master's degrees are increasingly needed for other than teaching positions. Need exists for them in all of the performing arts. In 1961–62 only 3,151 master's degrees were awarded in the fine and applied arts (Table 5). Yet, in the period 1952–62 the number of little theater and similar groups grew rapidly; the number of symphony orchestras in the United States increased from 800 to 1,252; performing opera groups increased from about 300 to some 780; and attendance at the Metropolitan Museum of Art rose about 200 percent.[14]

More masters in the professional fields are also needed. It is noteworthy that only 521 persons earned the master's degree in library science in 1961–62 (Table 5). A shortage of professionally trained librarians already exists in our colleges and universities and promises to become more acute. Public libraries also need more trained personnel; between 1956 and 1962 the number of books borrowed from public libraries in the United States increased from 500,000 to 800,000.[15]

It appears clear that the demand is large for additional numbers of masters in social work. As Dean Walter L. Kindelsperger of Tulane University noted in October 1963, "we have more social problems [than in the past], we are doing more about them, and we are doing it in a way that requires more social workers." One estimate contends that the number of "fully trained" social workers should be increased from the 1,700 of 1962 to 28,000 by 1970. Some 38,000 persons were employed in public assistance programs alone in 1962; it is expected that by 1970 about 83,000 will be needed. The expanding enrollments of the schools of social work in the nation (5,370 students in 1959, 6,039 in 1962, and an estimated 8,800 by fall 1965) are encouraging.[16]

The demand in the engineering fields for masters also should continue at a high level. In 1961–62 about 13,000 master's degrees were awarded in engineering, mathematics, and the physical sciences; of these 8,909 were earned in engineering (Table 5). Though the annual output has increased to this level from 4,904 in 1950, the industrial, technological, and teaching demands for such persons are far from satisfied. The President's Science Advisory Committee in December 1962 predicted that by 1970 some 30,000 master's would be needed annually in engineering, mathematics, and the physical sciences; probably two thirds of them will be needed in engineering. In the decade 1951–60, the four fields of engineering most popular among those who earned the master's degree were electrical (25 percent of all engineering master's degrees awarded), mechanical (17 percent), civil (15 percent), and chemical (11 percent).[17]

The Master of Business Administration programs of the nation have not nearly satisfied the existing demand for persons ready to step into teaching and managerial positions. Though 5,303 persons earned the master's in business and commerce in 1961–62 (Table 5), more are needed in the immediate future.

A special word should be said about opportunities for women who may earn master's degrees. As Table 5 shows, some professional areas tend to be "women's areas" and some are almost exclusively areas for men. Table 6 (adapted from Table 5) shows the pattern.

Though education is shown as a mixed area rather than one predominantly for women, it offers more opportunities than any other for women who earn the master's. More than three fifths of all master's awarded to women in 1961–62 were in education. While women earned 31 percent of all master's degrees in 1961–62, they earned 45 percent of all master's degrees awarded in education.[18] This is hardly surprising in view of the fact that four fifths of all elementary teachers and at least half of all high school teachers in the United States are women. Of all new college and university faculty members appointed, 24 percent in 1962–63 were women.[19] Women with master's will be needed for the teaching professions in increasing numbers in the years ahead, and more might well find positions in the "male professions" if they break out of the patterns of specialization of the past.

WHAT IS THE MASTER'S DEGREE?

Karl Marx in his later years, amazed at the variety of persons who by then called themselves "Marxist," once exclaimed: "Marxist? Ich bin kein Marxist!" The recipient of a master's degree, knowing the

TABLE 6: *Variations among Fields of Master's Degrees, by Sex*

Almost Exclusively Male	Predominantly Male	Mixed	Almost Exclusively or Predominantly Female
Engineering Business and commerce Agriculture Architecture Forestry	Social sciences Physical sciences Mathematical sciences Biological sciences Philosophy Geography	Education English and journalism Fine and applied arts Psychology Foreign languages and literature	Home economics Library sciences

variety of content, requirements, and quality of master's programs among institutions even in a single field, might similarly be tempted to repudiate his identification with others who exhibit the same label.

What *is* the master's degree? The question cannot be answered simply, because there is no single master's degree. In 1960 no fewer than 121 varieties of the Master of Arts alone were offered in colleges and universities of the United States, and to these were added 272 types of Master of Science degrees. The M.A. (so designated in 258 institutions; 41 prefer "A.M." from *Artium Magister*) and the M.S. have been the most prevalent, followed by the Master of Education (M.Ed.). An incomplete list of others would include the Master of Business Administration, or M.B.A. (offered in 1960 by 111 institutions); Master of Music, M.Mus. (83), Master of Fine Arts, M.F.A. (54); and the Master of Religious Education, M.R.E., M.R.Ed. (41).[20]

Variety in nomenclature has its counterpart in programs. Diversity makes it impossible to discuss a "typical" master's program. Even among the professional degree programs there is great heterogeneity. One of the few generalizations possible is that several of the professional degrees commonly and explicitly require two years of graduate study. The following descriptions of specific programs may be suggestive of programs in the fields noted:

> The *Master of Social Work* program at Tulane University includes four semesters of postgraduate classroom courses accompanied by four semesters of field instruction and an acceptable research project; no foreign language examination is required.

> The program for the *Master of Business Administration* at Stanford University is briefly described as follows: "The M.B.A. Program stresses the *general* management approach and is designed for students who as undergraduates majored in the social sciences and humanities, sciences, and engineering. The 'case method' is the primary tool of instruction, although other techniques, such as lectures and discussion, are employed whenever desirable. During the second year, M.B.A. students may take 15 quarter units (10 semester units) in other Schools and Departments. . . ."

In general, students entering the better M.B.A. programs without undergraduate courses in economics or business subjects will face a two-year program. At schools such as Stanford, Chicago, Tulane, and Harvard, fewer than one-third of recent M.B.A. entrants had undergraduate backgrounds in business. Those who have majored in liberal arts and engineering subjects as undergraduates are welcomed. The emphasis in the M.B.A. programs usually is on the making of managerial decisions.

> Indiana University describes its *Master of Fine Arts* program as follows: "a minimum of sixty (60) [semester] hours of work is required. In lieu of a thesis, the student is required to present an original work executed in his specific medium, such as painting or sculpture. . . ." From nine to fifteen hours of courses in the history of art must be taken, depending upon the candidate's previous training. Obviously, this is a two-year degree program.

> The *Master of Engineering (M.E.)* degree at Harvard is based upon the following requirements: Two years of residence, during which sixteen half-courses are taken. Up to four half-courses may be devoted to completion of a research project under faculty supervision. No thesis, foreign language, or general examination is required for the degree.

The requirements at the University of Illinois for the *Master of Education* degree are as follows: At least eight units of course work, including four units in education. At least two units are taken in fields other than education. The residence requirement may be met by participating in two eight-week summer sessions as a full-time student or in four summer sessions of four weeks each.

The residence requirements for the professional master's thus range from a total of sixteen weeks (of summer school) in education up to two years in more demanding programs.

It is understandable that variations appear among requirements for the master's in different professional fields, but the great variations within a single field are more difficult to understand and to justify. Divergencies in programs leading to the Master of Arts in the single discipline of history are illustrative. The following highlights emerge from a study of requirements for the M.A. in history in 77 universities and 87 colleges.[21]

1. *Admission of students:* An average undergraduate record of C satisfies the minimum standards of some graduate programs, while a few that can afford to be most selective regularly exclude students who have achieved A— undergraduate records in obscure colleges. Usually an undergraduate B average is the stated minimum.

2. *Grading standards:* In the nation at large, 88 percent of the Ph.D.-training departments and 85 percent of the colleges require minimum grades of B in graduate courses. But only 69 percent of the Eastern colleges state this as a minimum requirement.

3. *Hours:* Thirty semester hours, or an equivalent number of quarter hours, are normally required in programs that do not require a thesis or that give six semester hours of credit for the thesis.

4. *Thesis:* Often an institution offers the student the option of taking the master's with or without a thesis. In the nation as a whole three fourths of the colleges and universities require a thesis, but the range of practice is puzzling. Only 50 percent of the universities in the Midwest (but 94 percent of the colleges) report that a thesis is required. In the East only 62 percent of the colleges, but 83 percent of the universities, require a thesis. Many institutions that do not require a thesis of all candidates for the master's do demand it of those who wish to work toward the doctorate; but others say it is unnecessary. In many institutions the thesis requirement has been dropped simply because the faculty is so overburdened with large numbers of students that it cannot devote time to the demanding task of directing master's theses. It is indicative of the pressures of work that in 12

percent of the universities only one faculty reader of a thesis is sufficient to pass on it, although two readers are required in a third of the universities and three readers in 54 percent of them. The length of the thesis varies from a low of 56 pages to a high of 358; three fourths of the theses are under 160 pages in length.

5. *Linguistic ability:* Forty-eight percent of the institutions require the candidate in history to pass a foreign language examination. It is regrettable that slightly more than half do not, but the situation in the field of history does not quite support Berelson's conclusion that the language requirement at the master's level "was typically discarded some time ago."[22] It is heartening to note that when a thesis is written on the history of a foreign area, 90 percent of the Eastern colleges require the student to use sources in the language of that area.

6. *Courses outside the department of history:* In 25 percent of the departments the candidate is *required* to take other than history courses; in 21 percent he is *discouraged* from doing so; in a slight majority of departments the student is *encouraged* to do so.

7. *General examination for the master's:* About 15 to 20 percent of the history departments require neither a written nor an oral terminal examination over the master's program; about half administer only an oral examination, and 30 percent require both written and oral examinations.

The history master's is not unique. The variations in requirements cited above are indicative of those that would be found in a comparative study of almost any other discipline.

The variations in master's programs have come about in some cases as pragmatic adjustments to the possibilities and necessities of local situations. Other variations reflect deep-rooted disagreements within faculties about the educational philosophy of the master's degree. These disagreements are manifestations in the 1960's of the dilemma that educators a century ago failed to resolve. Should the master's program be a continuation of broad, liberal arts undergraduate education (Virginia, 1831; Sewanee, 1860)—a natural outgrowth of the English type of college in America? Many say "yes." Should the master's, on the contrary, introduce the candidate to specialized courses and research in depth, in the style of the German universities? In the 1870's many said "yes," and the rapid growth of Ph.D. programs did not dissuade them. Many still say "yes."

Members of the present generation of graduate faculties, trained in the traditions of both groups of nineteenth-century contenders, consciously or unconsciously keep the faith and continue the struggle. Since both "broadeners" and "specializers" are found within single departments, the usual result is compromise in human relations and on requirements for the master's degree. Thus this degree, quite often, is not solidly of one character or the other. With rigorous seminars and the thesis required, the program is one for budding specialists; without either of these added to classroom instruction, it is a means of increasing breadth, of making up undergraduate deficiencies in the arts and sciences; and most typically it is a mixture of the two, with one or more of the research requirements. Both broadeners and specializers can claim the foreign language requirement as their own, the former in the name of humane studies and the latter as a tool for research.

Whatever the philosophy or the specific requirements of the Master of Arts and Master of Science programs, stated regulations usually suggest that the degree requirements may be completed in one year of graduate study. The first master's program to be announced by a state university—at the University of Nebraska in 1886—stipulated a minimum of one year of residence.[23] All too frequently this is misleading. A survey of 182 persons granted the master's in history by *colleges* in 1958 showed that the mean period required was eighteen months (two full academic years or one and a half calendar years); only 15 percent completed the degree in nine months of study.[24] Again, history is not unique. The median student who took the master's while earning the Ph.D. in universities in the South, 1950–58, required closer to two years than one year to complete the master's program, and there was little variation among fields (physical sciences, 1.7 years; biosciences, 1.8; social sciences, 1.7; humanities, 1.7).[25]

Probably the pursuit of the Ph.D. tends to create misleading averages. Since the candidates are going to be in graduate school anyway, they often ask, why worry whether the master's is completed in nine months or fifteen or even more? An analysis of the relationship of number of students enrolled in various master's programs in the fall semester of 1961–62 to the number who earned degrees in 1961–62 suggests (Table 5) that the time required for the degree does vary considerably among the disciplines. The rate of productivity in all fields for that academic year was 39 master's degrees for every 100 students enrolled in the fall semester. But the wide range among areas may be noted as follows:

Areas of low or slow productivity (fewer than 34 degrees per 100 students): Social sciences, business-commerce, physical sciences, and psychology.

Areas of high or rapid productivity (more than 44 degrees per 100 students): Fine and applied arts, agriculture, home economics, architecture, and forestry. Note that every one of these is an "applied" subject area.

Areas of average productivity (34–44 degrees per 100 students): Education, engineering, English-journalism, mathematical subjects, biological sciences, foreign languages and literature, library science, philosophy, and geography.

Much has been made in recent years of the need to accelerate Ph.D. training, but too little has been said about the problem of prolonged master's study. After all, it is at the master's level that the delay of Ph.D. candidates begins, and here society's loss owing to prolonged programs is great because of the large numbers of persons involved.

Why do students so often require more than one year—or even two—for the master's? In May 1963 at Tulane University, the chairmen of several departments advised the dean of the Graduate School why certain students who were just then being awarded the master's had required more than two academic years to graduate. The reasons most often cited seem to be typical of those at graduate schools nationally.

Weak background of the student: Miss —— "came here in the fall of 1960 with a record of undergraduate work taken more than ten years previously in a teachers college and mediocre results in the Graduate Record Examination. Despite the good recommendations from her superior officers in the USPHS Communicable Disease Center (where she had been working), we anticipated she would have some difficulty in adjusting to the level of work required here. . . . She thus spent about two and a half years total time, somewhat longer than is usual in our Department for students planning to take the M.S. degree."

Difficulty with foreign languages: "The reasons for Mr. ——'s slow progress toward his M.A. degree are varied. He is a slow worker, and I suspect that this was the principal contributing cause. Another reason was his difficulty in passing the reading examination in Spanish. He worked at it over a period of several years, but seemed to make little progress."

Lack of zeal for research: "In short, the reason why Mr. ——— received his master's degree after more than two years is his initially dilatory research effort."

Part-time study: "We frequently have practicing engineers from the New Orleans area enrolled as part-time graduate students. Normally these men take only one course per semester and, hence, as much as four or five years is not unusual or out of place. This is the case with Mr. ———."

Financial need requires periods of full-time work: Mr. ——— "was compelled to do manual labor for one summer in order to support himself, and from the academic point of view that summer was wasted."

Marriage and work: "Mrs. ——— was admitted to the Department as Miss ——— in February 1959. A very good student, she took 27 hours of graduate courses between February 1959 and May 1960. She also attended the Université Laval in the summer of 1960. In 1960–61 she taught at St. Mary's Dominican College while attending a seminar at Tulane and working on her thesis. She married and now has a child. With all this she fulfilled all her requirements and carried her thesis to completion, under the direction of Professor ———. She took her final oral this May. She has done creditable work and intends to teach in a local institution."

Graduate faculties, the graduate dean, and students—working together with a will to remove unnecessary delays—can remedy some of these causes of prolonged master's study. Some of them, known in graduate schools all over the nation, will be difficult to avoid even with the best will and effort of all. Whatever the remedies, these appear to be the most common causes of delayed master's programs, the problems to which solutions are needed.

CRITICISMS, PROPOSED CHANGES, EXPERIMENTS

Uncertainty or contention about the requirements of master's programs and differences of opinion about the function of the master's degree have been echoed since graduate study was successfully begun in the nineteenth century. The master's was up for discussion on several occasions within the Association of American Universities in the first half of this century. The following questions and criticisms were among those aired: *1902:* Should the master's be treated as a terminal degree or simply as a step toward the Ph.D.? *1910:* (1) It is offered by many institutions that cannot be trusted to maintain high standards; (2) a thesis is not always required; (3) the degree is stronger in departments that do not concentrate on the Ph.D.; (4) it is mainly a degree for secondary teachers. (But in the same year both Johns Hopkins and Yale were advocating a two-year master's as a degree for college teachers.) *1921:* Comments on "existing confusion" in master's programs. *1924:* The degree should be regarded simply as an extension of undergraduate education. *1935:* More comments on "evident confusion" about the master's degree. *1936:* The master's should be regarded simply as an extension of undergraduate education.[26]

More recently Berelson has concluded that "Master's work today is not graduate in character but more nearly on the order of a fifth year of undergraduate work."[27] On the other hand, in 1962 a committee of the American Historical Association, noting that the master's usually required considerably more than "a fifth year," recommended that "work for this degree should not require more than one calendar year of study."[28]

Considerable concern has been expressed in recent years about master's training for teachers. Several prestigious institutions, disturbed about the need for secondary teachers well grounded in subject-matter areas, have inaugurated programs leading to the Master of Arts in Teaching (M.A.T.). Among them are Harvard, Yale, Wesleyan University, Brown, Colgate, Johns Hopkins, Duke, Vanderbilt, and Tulane. The requirements for the M.A.T. already vary widely among institutions. The degree commonly requires more hours of course work than the M.A. or M.S., divides them between education and one subject-matter discipline, requires no foreign language examination, usually requires no thesis, and sometimes requires no terminal examination. In some programs it can be completed in nine to twelve months of full-time graduate study.

Concern about master's-level, as well as undergraduate, preparation of prospective teachers in elementary and secondary schools found a powerful spokesman in James B. Conant, former president of Harvard and author of important books on the schools. In his 1963 report on *The Education of American Teachers,* Dr. Conant called for more rigorous but more flexible master's programs for teachers, with more work in subject-matter disciplines than many master's programs in education have provided in the past. His major suggestions follow:

> The graduate schools of education or their equivalent (in universities organized without such separate degree-granting schools) should devise a program for increasing the competence of teachers as teachers with the following characteristics:
>
> (1) It should be open to any graduate of the same institution in the same field of endeavor (e.g., elementary education, secondary school social studies, etc.).
>
> (2) Courses should be allowed for credit toward the 30 semester hours whether or not the courses are of an elementary nature, provided they are clearly courses needed to increase the competence of the teacher.
>
> (3) No credit toward the degree should be given for extension courses or courses taken on campus while the teacher is engaged on a full-time teaching job.
>
> (4) Passing of a comprehensive examination should be required for the master's degree, as is now the case in some institutions.
>
> (5) The summer-school sessions should be arranged so that four summer residences will complete the degree requirements, or two summers plus one full-time semester residence.
>
> (6) If the offering in the arts and sciences is not wide enough to provide meaningful work in the summer session (as it would not be in some state colleges), arrangements should be made for the transfer of credit from a university summer school with a good offering of courses in subject-matter fields.
>
> (7) For elementary teachers, the degree should be master of education in elementary education; for secondary teachers, master of education in English (or science or social science or modern languages or mathematics).[29]

A major topic in recent discussions of the master's has been the possibility of rehabilitating it as a degree for college teachers. Spurred on by knowledge of the approaching shortage of Ph.D.'s, the Committee on Policies in Graduate Education of the Association of Graduate Schools in 1957 proposed a year-and-a-half program that would not necessarily be terminal:

> The first year should be exactly like that of the candidate for the Ph.D., since the difference between the degrees should pivot on amount and not on quality. In the third term (the first of the second

year), each candidate should take a course directly concerned with the teaching of this subject. This course should be taught only by members of the student's department. . . . In this same term the student would write an essay of 75 to 125 pages, preferably stemming from his seminar of the second term, which need not be the original contribution demanded of the Ph.D. Finally, the student's subject should be named on the Master's diploma.[30]

In November 1957, the trustees of the Carnegie Foundation for the Advancement of Teaching, citing the report of the four A.G.S. deans quoted above, called for "a rigorous effort" to "revitalize the Master's degree and make it a terminal degree for teaching."[31] Then in 1959 Oliver C. Carmichael, consultant to the Fund for the Advancement of Education and former president of the University of Alabama, proposed with enthusiasm, tenacity, and geniality a program that would prepare masters for college teaching positions and at the same time recruit graduate students for the Ph.D. and accelerate graduate study by achieving closer articulation of undergraduate and graduate study.

In 1960, supported by grants from the Fund for the Advancement of Education, several pilot programs such as Carmichael advocated were inaugurated in various parts of the nation. These programs carried into effect some or all of the following principles that Carmichael spelled out in 1961: (1) selection and advice of potential master's candidates and college teachers from among "the upper 15 to 20 percent of the student body" during the first two undergraduate years; (2) treatment of the junior, senior, and fifth years of study as a unit, thus creating a "three-year master's"; (3) a limited amount of teaching experience during the senior undergraduate or postbaccalaureate year of study; (4) closer faculty supervision of the especially selected students, and much more work of the graduate type during the junior and senior years, with emphasis on wide reading, the writing of research papers, and solid grounding in foreign languages; and (5) preparation of a master's thesis. The degree to be awarded at the end of the program should be called the Master of Philosophy to distinguish it from the Master of Arts or other degrees not regarded as satisfactory preparation for college teachers.[32]

Carmichael believed that the programs he advocated would help recruit Ph.D. candidates. Inaugurated in a number of colleges and universities after 1960, they undoubtedly have. He also believed that they would equip their graduates "to do satisfactory college teaching, at least in the first two years of college." It appears certain that many junior colleges will be fortunate in the years ahead if they can attract persons with terminal master's degrees such as Carmichael envisioned.

But these proposals and others will not produce faculty members that will satisfy the demands of four-year colleges and universities in the United States. The point should be made here emphatically that the movement is, in reality, not one to rehabilitate or revitalize the master's degree, but one that hopes to make it something it never has been since Ph.D.'s began to be regularly awarded in the 1880's and 1890's. The master's, based on one year of graduate study has not been, will not be, and should not be developed into a degree that will place its bearer in good standing on a four-year college faculty although, according to Berelson, two thirds of all graduate deans and college presidents favor the bolstering of the master's degree toward that objective.[33] As Berelson added, the preference of college presidents for the doctorate is well known. It should be noted in this connection that the annual output of Ph.D.'s has increased 130 percent between 1949 and 1962, while the master's output went up only 67 percent and college enrollments 71 percent.[34]

Despite this increase in the production of Ph.D.'s they will be in short supply during the coming years and critically short in some fields. Persons who hold no degree higher than the master's will be given temporary positions on college faculties, but they will usually be, as they have been in the past, persons who have: (1) earned the master's in the more reputable Ph.D. programs; (2) studied at least a year beyond the master's. Many will be "ABD"—All But Dissertation—master's. And their opportunities for advancement will be circumscribed.

To test the point, the author of this essay asked in one of the sections of the meeting of the American Council on Education in October 1963 whether the smaller colleges might not solve their problem of recruiting faculty members in the sciences by appointing persons with master's degrees. He pointed out that administrators of small colleges frequently lament the preoccupation of Ph.D.'s with research, allegedly at the expense of their teaching, and suggested as tactfully as possible that master's degree faculty members might serve the small colleges well. The suggestion was made after several administrative officers of small colleges had sharply called attention to the difficulties of recruiting Ph.D.'s. Still the response to the suggestion was negative. It was clear that the college presidents would not happily settle for the master's degree.

One major reason why the master's cannot be made fully reputable for four-year college faculty members is that requirements for it vary so widely. It is generally known that many who hold terminal master's degrees have been awarded them as consolation prizes when they were found to be insufficiently promising for Ph.D. candidacy. And one of the most basic reasons the master's cannot be bolstered into a fully reputable degree for tenure and advancing college faculty members is implicit in the statistics reported in this essay, especially in Table 4: the degree is too widely awarded in too large numbers. It appears that the top twelve universities of the nation have provided about 35 percent of the faculty members in American colleges and universities.[35] These professors with degrees from the most prestigious universities will not be content to approve the appointment to permanent positions and to recommend promotions to colleagues who hold master's degrees from one or another of 621 or more institutions, many of which they view as weaker institutions than the colleges in which they teach. And the regional accrediting agencies will back them up; they continue to look for Ph.D.'s on college and university faculties before giving them a satisfactory rating.

In the final analysis college faculty leaders and administrators will not settle for colleagues with only the master's because they know that they *should* not. The struggle to make the Ph.D. *the* acceptable degree for college teachers—the struggle for recognition of the principle that college teachers should have had intensive research training and are better teachers if they continue after graduate study to carry on research—was not easily or quickly won. Such victory as has been accomplished should not be surrendered. A wiser, if colder, course will be for the better colleges to appoint the best person with a master's they can find when they cannot recruit a good Ph.D., to make the appointment temporary, to assist the appointee in every way possible to earn the doctorate if he is an excellent teacher, and if he is not a potential Ph.D. to replace him after a relatively short period of service.

Several conclusions may be drawn from this survey of the present state of the master's degree. They might be called the "Fourteen Points" for the master's degree:

1. Financial support of graduate students was essential for the successful inauguration of master's programs and graduate study in general in the nineteenth century, and it remains essential today. The idea of providing fellowships from public funds is as old as the American Revolution of 1776–83. Implementation of the idea since the mid-1950's, especially through NSF, NIH, and NDEA programs, has played an important part in increasing the number of master's awarded annually from 56,823 in 1953–54 to 87,900 in 1962–63. A National Humanities Foundation is needed to provide financial support for master's as well as Ph.D. programs in fields that have had little support from Federal funds up to the present.

2. Private institutions awarded almost 60 percent of all master's degrees in 1947–48, but only 40 percent in 1961–62. They should take steps to check this decline. Both public and private financial support will be needed in larger amounts if they are to do so.

3. Regional output of master's degrees is grossly inadequate in the South, and in the West it is highly concentrated in one state, California. The South itself must do more to remedy its shortcomings.

4. Only 5.6 percent of the 621 institutions awarding master's degrees account for 38 percent of current output. Those engaged in mass production should rigorously review their standards. Even if the prestige of the master's degree cannot be bolstered, it is important to prevent its decline. It is in the national interest that the high concentration of master's output in a few institutions be somewhat lessened, but this does not mean that any four-year college should offer the master's degree without due regard for its preparedness.

5. The master's degree involving preparation of a thesis and re-

quiring reading knowledge of one foreign language (passed early) is useful to Ph.D. candidates. But little is to be gained by asking Ph.D. candidates to earn the master's unless a thesis or equivalent research and writing are required.

6. The master's is chiefly a degree for elementary and secondary teachers. Yet, too many (42 percent) master's degrees are being awarded in education. It is in the interest of effective teaching in the secondary schools that more prospective teachers at that level earn the Master of Arts or Master of Science degrees in academic disciplines.

7. In the years just ahead the demand for persons with master's degrees probably will exceed the supply in several teaching areas at the high school and junior college levels (especially in mathematics, physics, chemistry, English, and foreign languages); persons with the master's in the arts, library science, social work, engineering, and business administration should be able to find positions that call upon their graduate training.

8. Currently about 31 percent of all master's degrees are awarded to women. This proportion represents a decline in the last twenty years, probably because of a trend toward early marriage. Women of ability should be encouraged to earn the master's degree, and on the basis of past experience it can reasonably be hoped that they may receive up to one third of all master's awarded annually.

9. Admission to master's programs should be limited to students who have achieved undergraduate records of at least B grades unless especially high scores on the Graduate Record Examination or other evidence of unusual ability warrants their admission. More rigorous standards of admission should make possible the award of more than the present 39 master's degrees per year per 100 students enrolled in the fall semester.

10. Requirements for the master's degree vary widely. It is probably necessary that several professional fields require two years of study for the degree, but it is desirable to work toward more systematic programs for the M.A. and the M.S. Improved guidance is needed, especially early in the student's graduate study. Programs of no more than one calendar year should be the norm, hopefully with more uniform content, at least within a single discipline. The re- quirements should include a foreign language examination, semi-

nars, a thesis of limited scope, and a general examination. More emphasis should be placed on quality of work than on quantity.

11. It is not in the interest of good undergraduate instruction in most disciplines for master's candidates to do practice teaching in the institution in which they seek the degree, though all those who go on toward the Ph.D. should do a limited amount of teaching with supervision and constructive criticism from members of the graduate faculty before being awarded the doctorate.

12. The master's degree is not on the way out. The statistical evidence of burgeoning expansion makes this obvious. The evidence of demand for persons with master's degrees also makes it clear that the degree *should not be* on the way out.

13. Yet, the limitations of the master's degree need to be clearly recognized. Rooted in its history, they have been reinforced by developments since World War II. Even at its inception as an earned degree, the master's was caught between the bachelor's and the Ph.D. Never having a chance to win the prestige of the Ph.D., it added an uncertain quantity and quality to the baccalaureate degree. Its prestige has been diminished as it has been awarded in ever-larger numbers.

14. Many persons who have earned the master's degree must be employed at least temporarily as faculty members in many of the four-year colleges during the years just ahead. But effort and money can be better spent in bringing larger numbers of able students through accelerated Ph.D. programs than in trying to develop the master's into an adequate degree for college teachers.

A long dialogue over graduate education has continued, does continue, and shall continue. And the debate *should* continue, because even the debaters who know what has been said before need to think through the arguments and decide for themselves what to endorse and to preserve, what to condemn as outworn and to discard. If any major feature of the debate is to be cause for sorrow, it is that too few have engaged in it. Only if departmental faculties are concerned about the issues will discussion be translated into action and some of the less intractable problems of the past and present give way to solutions. It is to be hoped that more concern will be felt in the future about the master's degree. It is to be hoped that faculty members will establish rigorous M.A. and M.S. degrees which can be obtained in one year, and that they will not pursue the illusion that the master's can be made into a respectable degree for college teachers by prolonging programs already too long.

NOTES

1. J. P. Elder as quoted in Bernard Berelson, *Graduate Education in the United States* (New York: McGraw-Hill Book Co., 1960), p. 185.
2. Wayne E. Tolliver, *Earned Degrees Conferred, 1961–1962: Bachelor's and Higher Degrees*, U.S. Office of Education Circular No. 719 (Washington: Government Printing Office, 1963), p. 7; Ray C. Maul (ed.), *Teachers Supply and Demand in Universities, Colleges, and Junior Colleges, 1961–62 and 1962–63* (Washington: National Education Association, 1963), p. 13.
3. Richard J. Storr, *The Beginnings of Graduate Education in America* (Chicago: University of Chicago Press, 1953), pp. 7–8, 26–28, 33–34, 105, 123, 134; Frederick Rudolph, *The American College and University: A History* (New York: Alfred A. Knopf, 1962), pp. 126–29, 234, 337.
4. Rudolph, *American College and University*, pp. 322–23, 395; *Digest of Educational Statistics*, 1963 ed., OE-10024-63 (Washington: Government Printing Office, 1963), pp. 11, 71; and Mary Irwin (ed.), *American Universities and Colleges* (8th ed.; Washington: American Council on Education, 1960), pp. 15, 1144–45.
5. Berelson, *Graduate Education*, p. 35; Tolliver, *Earned Degrees Conferred, 1961–1962*, p. 7.
6. Berelson, *Graduate Education*, p. 94.
7. Dexter Perkins, John L. Snell, and others, *The Education of Historians in the United States* (New York: McGraw-Hill Book Co., 1962), p. 86; Alexander Heard, *The Lost Years in Graduate Education* (Atlanta, Ga.: Southern Regional Education Board, 1963), p. 10.
8. Gustave O. Arlt, "The First Ph.D.'s under Title IV," *Journal of Higher Education*, May 1963, pp. 244–45.
9. Hayward Keniston, *Graduate Study and Research in the Arts and Sciences at the University of Pennsylvania* (Philadelphia: University of Pennsylvania Press, 1959), p. 43.
10. Berelson, *Graduate Education*, p. 36, for the 1947–48 percentage.
11. *Digest of Educational Statistics*, 1963 ed., pp. 11, 71.
12. See also the recommendation offered by James B. Conant, *The Education of American Teachers* (New York: McGraw-Hill Book Co., 1963).
13. Maul, *Teacher Supply and Demand . . ., 1961–62 and 1962–63*, p. 39.
14. From *Mass Media and Mass Culture*, lecture by Frank Stanton at Dartmouth College, Nov. 26, 1962 (New York: Columbia Broadcasting System, Inc., n.d.), pp. 9, 11, 13, 15.
15. *Ibid.*, p. 13.
16. New Orleans *States-Item*, Oct. 8, 1963.
17. The President's Science Advisory Committee, *Meeting Manpower Needs in Science and Technology: I, Graduate Training in Engineering, Mathematics, and Physical Sciences* (Washington: Government Printing Office, 1962), pp. 6–7; Clarence B. Lindquist, *Degrees in the Biological and Physical Sciences, Mathematics and Engineering*, OE-54029 (Washington: Government Printing Office, 1963), p. 18.

18. Tolliver, *Earned Degrees Conferred, 1961–1962,* pp. 2, 8–11.
19. Maul, *Teacher Supply and Demand . . ., 1961–62 and 1962–63,* pp. 26, 63.
20. Walter Crosby Eells and Harold A. Haswell, *Academic Degrees: Earned and Honorary Degrees Conferred by Institutions of Higher Education in the United States,* OE-54008 (Washington: Government Printing Office, 1960), pp. 26, 61, 248–69. The often puzzling abbreviations for the master's—and other—degrees are identified in alphabetical order, *ibid.,* pp. 274–318.
21. Unless otherwise indicated, the information given in points 1–7 is from Perkins, Snell, and others, *The Education of Historians,* pp. 88–97.
22. Berelson, *Graduate Education,* p. 196.
23. Byrne J. Horton, *The Graduate School: Its Origin and Administrative Development* (New York: New York University Bookstore, 1940), p. 74.
24. Perkins, Snell, and others, *The Education of Historians,* p. 95.
25. Heard, *The Lost Years,* pp. 15–17.
26. Reported by Berelson, *Graduate Education,* pp. 18, 21, 30, 185.
27. *Ibid.,* p. 186.
28. Perkins, Snell, and others, *The Education of Historians,* p. 203.
29. Conant, *The Education of American Teachers,* p. 216.
30. *Journal of Proceedings and Addresses of the Association of American Universities, 1957* (Columbia, Mo.: n.d.), pp. 35–41.
31. Grayson L. Kirk and others, "The Education of College Teachers," in *Fifty-third Annual Report,* The Carnegie Foundation for the Advancement of Teaching (New York: The Foundation, 1958), pp. 13, 18.
32. Oliver C. Carmichael, *Graduate Education: A Critique and a Program* (New York: Harper & Bros., 1961), pp. 159–77.
33. Berelson, *Graduate Education,* p. 188.
34. *Digest of Educational Statistics,* 1963 ed., pp. 59, 71. The need for a master's program for college teachers is more acute in Canada, where in 1963 one was under consideration at the University of Toronto. See American Council of Learned Societies *Newsletter,* October 1963, pp. 9–10.
35. Berelson, *Graduate Education,* pp. 115–16.

Administering Graduate Education

ROY F. NICHOLS

THE administration of the graduate schools in American universities that offer the degree Doctor of Philosophy presents one of the most intriguing problems in the realm of higher education. The position of the graduate school, whatever the university, defies brief definition. A most revealing statement is that in no two institutions does the graduate school occupy the same position and have the same functions. It may be not much more than a registrar's office, or, again, it may be denoted by an impressive building. In one or two instances it has no more existence than a group of faculty with their students whose joint interests are made a matter of record in a place whence, on recommendation of the faculty, diplomas are issued at appropriate intervals. At the other extreme, its dean may serve on budget, appointments and promotions, and other administrative committees, rank other deans in the hierarchy, and attend trustees' meetings. Each university has a history that

ROY F. NICHOLS (A.B. and A.M., Rutgers; Ph.D., Columbia) typifies the graduate dean par excellence—an active teacher, author, and administrator. Since 1925 he has taught history at the University of Pennsylvania and, as visiting professor, at Columbia, Cambridge, and Stanford. In 1962 he was Fulbright lecturer in India and Japan. To date he has published eleven books, chiefly on nineteenth-century American history. His *Disruption of the American Democracy* won a Pulitzer prize in 1949. As dean of the Graduate School of Arts and Sciences and as vice-provost at Pennsylvania for a dozen years, he has won the respect and confidence of faculty and administrators. He has been a trustee of Rutgers University since 1950. His urbane manner, ready wit, and deftness as a presiding officer have brought him elected offices in a half-dozen historical societies and national organizations. He was president of the Association of Graduate Schools in 1962–63. Last December he was elected vice-president of the American Historical Association.

103

places its graduate school in the unique position it holds. There is no uniformity.

FOREIGN ORIGINS

As the historical essay in this volume reveals, the graduate school concept has never really fitted into the American educational pattern. It was, I believe, unfortunate that the program of graduate studies was called a "school" and that a dean was appointed. Had a school been truly created and its dean granted substantial responsibility, all would have been better. But in universities having from five to twenty-five schools, each with its own faculty, budget, curriculum, and defined functions, the establishment of a "nest of freedom" without independent faculty, budget, curriculum, stated term, or authority was bound to create what resulted.

In effect, graduate study had been developed as part of a European system, in which its position was logical, recognized, and provided for emotionally, psychologically, and financially. But then it was imposed upon the American sprawl of the college and other schools, without any system, without preparation, and without any real provision for it institutionally, financially, emotionally, or psychologically. Although the new Ph.D. was in a sense European, the need and desire for it in this country were genuine. Not American in origin, it was introduced in response to American needs.

It must be further borne in mind that a university in the United States is usually not a university in the German sense. It is a series of schools or colleges that have generally been attached to an older undergraduate college. This college and these schools have evolved as more or less self-contained entities, each with an organization that requires some sort of thoughtful faculty planning. Each has a staff that has been recruited, a curriculum that was planned and put into operation, a budget that must be calculated, secured, and spent. All these responsibilities require a sense of group identification and action. These elements the various other colleges and schools in the universities have had. But when a so-called school at the graduate level is imposed upon the established academic units, without curriculum, budget, or direct recruiting responsibilities, the essential ingredient is omitted and too little motivation is provided for carrying on a real group enterprise.

The result has been a minimum of thinking about graduate affairs. So little has been required. The little that was needed initially had been supplied by those whose thoughts were chiefly elsewhere. What had been considered a well-nigh perfect system was, in truncated shape, imposed on another operation that had never thought of it as more than an adjunct concern. Decision making and judgment were left to undergraduate departments whose collective thinking—curriculum making, recruiting, and budget—was by long custom not Ph.D.-oriented. Thus, it received surprisingly little thought. The graduate school, so-called, is practically as it was when it was imported. And now, when new schools are created, they too frequently are unblushingly copies rather than creations, although nearly a century has passed, the world is different, and the pace of change is vastly accelerated.

But no matter how incongruous or how irrational the position of the graduate school is, those administering it have had to face a variety of problems, procedures, and responsibilities with whatever administrative competence the universities might achieve.

The general pattern of organization, if there can be said to be one in a graduate school of arts and sciences, has been variously defined. This school offers the degrees of Ph.D., Master of Arts, and Master of Science in the traditional liberal arts and science departments. But it may also include in its jurisdiction the postbaccalaureate degrees in education, engineering, fine arts, medicine—the professional schools—so that in some institutions it also administers the Ed.D., the Sc.D. in engineering, and other research and professional doctorates. In contrast, certain professional schools prescribe the requirements for their own doctor's degrees and grant them without reference to the "Graduate School"! In still other schools there are accidental or planned variations.

FACULTY APPOINTMENTS

The organization, function, and control of graduate schools is subject to a similar infinite variety. In some schools the faculty still legislates in meetings of the whole body. In others, the faculty is organized in three or four divisions, whose members hold legislative meetings. With increasing size and complexity of interest, however, has come a practice of turning legislative powers over to an elected council, which exercises the real power. Sometimes power is assigned to the council to an extent that the faculty may be said to be superseded and the dean functions merely as a presiding officer.

Whatever the pattern of administration or the mechanism of control, the educational program of a graduate school is the responsibility of the faculty, and upon their competence and reputation depends much of the success of the program. The general process of recruiting and rewarding graduate faculties demonstrates some of the typical incongruities. The principal anomaly is that the dean of some other school, generally an undergraduate school, rather than the dean of the graduate school, has the means and the responsibility. Some dean who has a budget supervises the graduate dean's departments in the recruiting of the teaching staff; he authorizes them to proceed and indicates the money available. This must be the procedure because the graduate dean seldom has a budget or the authority to appoint. The primary moves, therefore, must be made outside the graduate school.

When authorization to negotiate has been secured from some other source, a department usually does the recruiting. At this point the graduate dean may be consulted, and names brought to him for advice, and sometimes for consent. If the scholar under consideration visits the campus, an opportunity for the dean to meet him is usually, though not inevitably, arranged. If the dean is a member of the central agency of appointments, he contributes his views to the discussion. In the process he may be able to block an appointment that he considers undesirable. In some instances his suggestions and recommendations may stir a department to take up a field or a scholar and may persuade the dean of an undergraduate or professional school or the administration to allot the sum required and to seek the man or woman in question. Rarely, however, can the graduate school administration feel that it has any responsibility for building a faculty save as it consents to appointments or accepts faculty designated by departments to give graduate instruction. Rarely can a graduate dean determine that this or that department needs strengthening or that a new department is required, and then allot the funds and prepare the specifications. There may be influence but there is seldom authority.

Rank, promotions, salaries and their increases fall into the same category of so-called administration. Recommendations for all these phases of faculty appraisal are handled elsewhere. The dean of the graduate school may have nothing to do with these matters; he may not even hear of such discusions until they are completed. On the other hand, he may be consulted and given opportunity to suggest or recommend. If he sits on any budget or other financial review committee, he may be able to suggest changes in decisions already made or cause new ones to be incorporated, but his is hardly a controlling voice. If it is persuasive, he may develop power but he cannot assert it as a prerogative. Faculty quality may be sighed for, and pleaded for, but not requisitioned. Fortunately, most administrative agencies in the university recognize the need for quality. If they have the knowledge and the force to acquire it, all is well. But if not, the graduate dean has little power of positive action to alter the situation. He must work through propaganda, politics, and personal influence.

CURRICULUM

An important administrative responsibility of any university division or school is its curriculum. In this matter there are normally two agencies, the departments of the faculty and a committee, often called a "curriculum committee" or "committee of instruction." The function of curricula in graduate schools is different from that in undergraduate schools. The plan of instruction in the graduate area is to assemble a group of research specialists, each of whom gives a seminar and/or a lecture course in his particular field. The formula further calls for a quasi-coverage of the recognized fields in the discipline. In history, for example, there are usually specialists on ancient, medieval, and modern European history, on various epochs and phases of American history, and on the history of Latin America, the Far East, and so on. The function of the committees on instruction, or their equivalent, is usually to pass upon the capacity of the faculty and the proposed courses rather than to prepare programs or project them. The graduate dean's function frequently is very significant because he often appoints these committees, presides over them, and prepares their agenda. Further than this, the extent of his influence is limited only by the breadth and depth of his imagination, knowledge, and influence. He is hampered often by the lack of a free budget with which to initiate and encourage new enterprises and appointments. The curriculum of the graduate school (if such a usually amorphous program can be so called) is in the main the creature of the departments, which can operate at the graduate level untrammeled by such controls as undergraduate colleges usually impose. The dean generally feels that he is presiding over a group of distinguished experts whose teaching is designed to recruit and advance those who are capable and motivated to make significant research efforts, rather than administering a program of instruction which has been worked out in the fashion of sequences current in baccalaureate schools.

Admitting and advising students

Another center of administrative coordination is the graduate student body, and it is this group which frequently absorbs a large proportion of the dean's time. In fact, their interests are generally his chief concern. The logical beginning is, of course, admissions. Here the criteria range from rigorous selection of only A students to admission of any applicant who holds a baccalaureate degree from an acceptable undergraduate school. The machinery can be as simple as the dean's signature of approval or as complicated as screening credentials in the dean's office and sending them to the departments for consideration by a departmental subcommittee, approval in a department meeting, and submission of departmental recommendations to a graduate school admissions committee or a vice-dean. At their simplest, credentials may consist of only an undergraduate transcript. If, however, the Graduate Record Examination is prescribed, arrangements must be made for those who have not taken the G.R.E. to do so, which may be no mean task. Then follows the need for interpretation of the G.R.E. scores.

When the record is complete for each applicant, questions still remain: Where does the dean draw the line? If the school could be filled with A students, is this desirable? Does not the B student contribute what is needed to show an A student what he is and why? Does not society require highly trained B students as well, and could it survive if completely dominated by A students?

Once students are admitted, the responsibilities of the dean's office become various, ranging from almost none, for it is generally held that the charge is now upon the departments. The departments prescribe, or at least approve, the proposed courses, and it is from them that advice must in large measure proceed. The quantity and quality of advice varies. At the worst, the student stands in a long line with a registration card made out, and the "adviser" gives his program a hasty glance and signs it and then passes on to the next student. In the most elaborate plans, the student is assigned to an adviser or even a committee, which discusses his plans and takes account of his interests and record to help him arrive at a program tailored to his needs and abilities. In many instances advice is also available in the dean's office (it would be interesting to know how much is given by clerks—experienced and capable, new and ignorant).

The chief problem often is that, because of the multiplicity of faculty duties, too few advisers are available to first-year graduate students, and there is little the dean can do to help unless he has budget resources. Happily, once the admissions process is past and the students find themselves in seminars, the situation is self-righting. But counseling is needed, seemingly now more than formerly, and advisers to students (including some psychiatrically trained) are established in some graduate offices.

When the students have been advised, the next step used to be uniform: the signed card was delivered at the graduate office, and thereafter the procedure was repeated at the beginning of each semester. At the end of each term the grade sheets were sent there by the departments and recorded. All records of this kind were the responsibility of the dean's office. In recent years, however, many universities have established central registration officers and central offices of record. In some instances, the graduate school has continued as a self-contained unit. In others, registration and grades are turned over to the registrar, with a duplicate of the records in the graduate school office so that data may be at hand upon which to determine whether degrees are to be granted and when.

One of the most significant functions of graduate school administration is the supervision of the appraisals in the three stages which have become traditional, whatever the contemporary agreement about their essential worth.

FOREIGN LANGUAGE REQUIREMENT

First is the matter of the foreign language requirements. Among the universities, the responsibility of the dean's office ranges widely. In some institutions the department in which the student is working examines the students and files the certificates of proficiency when the department is satisfied. The dean's main concern then is that the certificates be filed within the time prescribed (this date too varies, though in no case do I know of such certificates being accepted after the doctoral diploma has been issued). Again, the control may lie in the dean's office, including arrangements for the tests to be administered by the foreign language departments, which report the results directly to the dean, and sometimes including also provision by the graduate school for tutoring courses in the languages, financed from the dean's budget. The old requirement of French and German for everyone has been adjusted in various instances so that substitutions of other languages for either or both or statistics for one of them may be permitted. It is the dean's task to oversee the substitutions.

EXAMINATIONS

A second type of appraisal of progress is what used to be the examination determining admission to candidacy. One pattern of this test is a general examination—oral, written, or both—which may come later rather than earlier in the student's career. In this form it may be general, covering the whole waterfront, or may be administered in selected fields. The dean's responsibility for the general examination ranges from merely receiving and recording the result to appointing the examining committee and presiding over it in person or by deputy. It is also the responsibility of the dean's office to see that the test is given within whatever time limits the school prescribes. Practice regarding examiners varies: in some instances all the examiners come from the student's department; in others, a varying number of outsiders, chosen either by the departments or the dean, participate.

This examination has tended to come later and later in students' residence, a timing that encourages them to concentrate on lecture courses as a means of cramming and thus frequently delays starting on the dissertation. If students are frightened into waiting through three years of course work to take the examination, they are also likely to have little motivation to get on with their research until this hurdle has been cleared. To remove this blockage and also to avoid having to flunk any who have persevered so long in cramming, some schools give the examination at the end of the first year as a qualifying exam; some use the master's examination for this purpose. In effect, the successful student is admitted to candidacy. The qualifying examination has the great virtue of enabling committees to detect weakness early and save later wear and tear on the conscience. In some cases, there is no further examination until the final, which is held when all the student's course work is over.

The final appraisal, the defense of the dissertation, has undergone a variety of changes. The old formal defense of the printed dissertation and the requirement of publication have both been abandoned. The formality still exists in some universities, where visitors are invited and a small gallery may appear. The defense itself may be conducted entirely by members of the department concerned, or members of the committee may come from other departments, either by invitation or by the dean's appointment. The dissertations themselves may be under the charge of a supervisor or a committee, which may or may not be appointed by the dean's office. This committee may or may not include faculty outside the candidate's department. The appraisals range from imposing ones from which even the supervisor may be excluded to those directed and accepted by what amounts to the judgment of one man, the supervisor. The introduction of the early qualifying examination and the more comprehensive final subject-matter examination have led in some cases to abandonment of the dissertation defense. Thus, the German concept is giving way occasionally to an English practice of submitting the dissertation to referees, including representation from outside the university and excluding the supervisor. The judgment of the referees becomes the final evidence which the dean files.

The supervision of dissertations brings with it administrative chores. The original concept called for a printed book, but with the advent of microfilm the dean has had to become an expert on this form of reproduction. He or someone in his office must determine whether the manuscript is in shape for microfilming, whether the footnotes are in order, whether the index is adequate and in the right place, and whether the title page meets the form prescribed. At this point he may develop a clear but unprintable opinion of the capacity of graduate students to read, understand, and follow directions. What does the administrator do when a manuscript is submitted on the latest possible day and he finds that it really requires retyping, at considerable expense and with the penalty of a year's delay?

FINANCIAL AID

Another phase of administrative responsibility, and one of the most significant duties of the graduate dean, is the assignment of financial aid. The award of aid is becoming increasingly important in a time when graduate students can be competed for as vigorously as though they were football players. The sums available may be as low as a few hundred dollars in cash, and/or free tuition, or they can mount as high as $7,500; currently $2,000 and free tuition is a good life-supporting figure for the unmarried student. The awards are generally the sole responsibility of the graduate school, but the mechanics of distribution are no simple matter. The basic condition is that few, if any, universities have sufficient aid funds to warrant assigning quotas to the various departments. Not only are there not enough fellowships available for quotas, but also the applicants to the several departments vary in quality from year to year so that, were quotas assigned, some excellent students might be disqualified while others of inferior quality would be certified.

In the award of fellowships, how are the best to be chosen from applicants recommended by the departments of the graduate school, sometimes sixty in number? This presents the age-old problem of deciding between apples and pears, mathematics and English. The first step generally is for the graduate dean to submit the applications to the respective departments for ranking and eliminating.

There on out comes the variety. Sometimes there are divisional committees, sometimes committees of large size representing many interests; in other instances the task is given to a small committee charged with reading and rating all applications endorsed by the departments. Various experiments with rating scales are constantly under study, in the hope of finding more objective, impersonal methods of drawing the line between the fortunate and the rejects. The need is all the greater as the competition becomes keener, both among departments and among institutions.

Another administrative function concerns the process of appointing, paying, and assigning graduate students to salaried teaching positions. These are graduate students who teach in undergraduate schools. Who appoints them; who supervises them; who pays them? To whom are they accountable? In a number of instances the dean of the graduate school has nothing to do with the arrangements except to be reasonably grateful that these students are paid and subsidized by free tuition. But there are problems. Some assistants are merely graduate students not recommended for the fellowships which require no duties. Others may have no connection with the graduate school. Questions then arise: Should teaching fellows be required to be students of the same caliber as those given other awards? Should all assistants or teaching fellows be required to be registered in the graduate school? Should the graduate dean be required to approve these appointments? Should he have them on his budget? The answer in most cases is "No," but the problem needs further study if the interests of the graduates, the graduate schools, and the undergraduates are to be best served.

In addition to the academic functions described above, the dean may be a building administrator, a dormitory supervisor, the operator of dining rooms and cafeterias, a ceremonial officer presiding at high table in a vaulted hall. Likewise, he may run a library and a pool parlor with side lines in record booths and ping-pong tables. He may assign offices and meeting rooms in a graduate center and be the chief figure in a community of graduate students as homogeneous and well cared for as are the undergraduates dwelling in a house system. He may be asked to be a bill and rent collector and listen to the complaints of indignant landladies about the habits and morals of the students. He may have to determine whether gowns must be worn at dinner or whether smoking or Bermuda shorts will be tolerated in classrooms.

These are some of the programs and responsibilities that are the concern of the administrations of graduate schools and that are involved in the educational experience leading to the two master's degrees in arts and science and the Ph.D. There are problems as well related to the nature of the degrees themselves. The master's degree, long thought more or less permanently debased, is now a center of discussion. Can it be rehabilitated? Can a new, rigorous master's degree be designed particularly for prospective teachers as a means of lifting some of the pressure for the production of Ph.D.'s? Despite bold words and pious hopes, the master's degree is still looked upon as merely a step toward the Ph.D. or sometimes as a consolation prize awarded with the understanding, implied or otherwise, that the student is through with graduate work. The prudent seek it as an insurance policy, a diploma record of work done which can be forgotten when the Ph.D. is theirs; others work for it as a means of obtaining an increase in salary.

The discussion about the nature of the Ph.D. is even more fervent. The many candidates who pursue it only as a credential for obtaining a teaching position, as a union card, have given rise to the charge that the degree has been debased: its program, once designed primarily to provide training in research and discovery, has become a hazard to be surmounted if one is to have an opportunity to earn a living as a teacher, even in high schools. It is further alleged that the pressure for teachers with the degree has led to granting it to a number of border-line but persistent students who will never use their research training and who soon drop any pretense of doing so. This pressure carries with it administrative problems, for, in effect, deans are faced with an ambiguity about the purpose of and, therefore, the requirements for the degree.

Some proposals have been made to relieve the pressure on the Ph.D. degree by establishing some form of second degree, a Master of Philosophy, a Doctor of Arts, or a Ph.D. "in course," which would play down the dissertation as a definitive piece of research activity. These proposals if implemented would leave the Ph.D. as invented —a research training degree designed primarily to make students discoverers and only incidentally communicators. The opposition, however, is formidable, and at present there is no indication of imminent change. But with the growth of the number of graduate schools accelerating, those planning new programs, unfettered by local traditions, might well consider setting up requirements and procedures unclouded by ambiguities through which the dual purpose of the degree is recognized by the offering of two Ph.D. programs. Two forms of the Ph.D. would probably degrade the degree no more than some practices now tolerated.

CHANGES UNDER DISCUSSION

Finally, any discussion of graduate school administration must include a résumé of recent innovations. Two new functions are appearing on the graduate school scene. The first is the development and administration of research contracts between agencies of the Federal Government and individuals and divisions in the institutions. Again, variety characterizes the manner of administration. In some instances, there is little administration: individuals and departments, institutes and schools go out and make contracts with only nominal supervision save by the financial officers interested in costs and overhead. Then, again, a variety of directors, coordinators, and vice-presidents have been appointed to handle administration. In some places these duties are either assigned to or involve the dean of the graduate school. He may be a controlling official, a supervisor, or a coordinator; or he may share in the responsibility; or he may have no direct association with this snowballing function. Where he is directly involved, his functions may be so changed that he must alter his office arrangements and the apportionment of his time. There may also be more clerks and more associates. Undoubtedly involvement will take his mind off the intricacies of administering the language requirement and the time limit of students who seemed doomed by circumstances to take too long in their degree-seeking. And, if he is influential, the contract may include funds for research fellows. At many universities government contracts have made the graduate dean a figure of greater significance, wielding more power and influence.

Another development in the graduate school that is calling for administrative attention is the increasing number of postdoctoral scholars, especially in the sciences, who return to the university to refresh and update their learning. Formerly, the custom of granting Ph.D. courtesy to holders of the degree enabled those in the vicinity of a university to attend lectures and to work in the laboratories. Latterly, as the number has increased and industrial firms have encouraged this kind of refresher, several graduate schools have deemed it fairer to charge for the privilege and to develop, in a few instances, postdoctoral programs. Instead of the Ph.D.-holder filing an application for Ph.D. courtesy in the dean's office, he goes through registration and fee-paying procedure. If postdoctoral programs become more widespread, another new function for the graduate schools will have emerged. The dean may well open up new pages in the catalogue, and the various faculty divisions, curriculum committees, or committees on instruction may have an increasingly important responsibility. The dean's office will include in its concerns the needs of more mature, postdoctoral scholars. Hitherto few over thirty years of age have been registered, but now a growing number in their thirties and even forties are entering the ranks of registered scholars in the universities.

In brief, any survey of graduate school administration reveals the infinite variety. The graduate schools have certain elements in common: they all have faculty and students, they must have offices, and they may have deans. But there the community elements cease to be discernible. They do not have curricula, the faculty is usually paid by some other school, the students attend for no set term nor belong to classes designated by years. Often they have no building, no dormitories, no recreational or community center. The dean's office may be almost anywhere. In comparison with the precision of organization which characterizes practically all the other schools, the graduate school can scarcely be located and defined. A body of students scattered over the campus finds instruction where it may, and the graduate dean as an administrator is a good deal of an anomaly. He has records in his office, he keeps track of credits, he awards financial aid, and at a given point in time he certifies that students are ready for degrees. He presides over something called a faculty or a graduate council. He supervises admission of students and approves faculty to give instruction and the courses that students are permitted to take. He may be as powerful as any man in the administration save the president, chancellor, or provost, or he may be a combination of adviser and registrar. But whatever power he may have comes not from the university statutes but from his character and influence. His situation is unique in the university. It may be frustrating but it can be highly challenging and satisfying.

This American system of predoctoral education under such administration works, or at least it has worked. But do not the increasing numbers of advanced students demand a more effective means of supplying the doctoral training that a society and a body of knowledge, both constantly growing more complex, require?

The Graduate Student

LEONARD B. BEACH

Projections of graduate enrollment by the U.S. Office of Education estimated well over half a million degree-credit students in more than 650 colleges and universities by 1965, and close to a million by 1975. Even though less than half of this graduate-level population progresses at the recognized full-time rate of speed toward its degree objective, the massive character of the problem of training tomorrow's scholar-teachers becomes daily more apparent. Mass techniques will be employed, particularly in the large public universities; programs will be streamlined; students will be left increasingly to their own devices. The capacities of prestigious schools will quickly be filled. The newer schools will expand rapidly to meet the demand. As the degree mills grind faster, even though accreditation machinery proves to be desirable and attempts are made to regulate standards, it is hard to see how the Ph.D. can remain the same degree as in the past.

There is one substantial hope: the raw materials may be improving. The post-Sputnik years have been marked by a strong trend toward better preparation of our younger students in the areas of mathematics, science, and foreign languages. Radical changes in the basic curricula and in the methods of instruction in these subjects

LEONARD B. BEACH, a native of Connecticut, took his undergraduate work at Wesleyan University and the Ph.D. at Yale. He has taught English at Yale, Northwestern, Ohio State, Oklahoma, and Vanderbilt. In 1951 he was appointed graduate dean at Vanderbilt. His interest in the national problems of graduate education brought him the presidency of the Association of Graduate Schools and of the Conference of Deans of Southern Graduate Schools in 1957–58. His long experience in graduate education admirably prepares him to write about the problems of today's graduate student. Dean Beach has written articles on literary subjects.

have substantially accelerated the early stages of training for the technical professions. The social sciences and humanities are slowly following suit. Moreover, the prospects of rapid preferment and competitive salaries are serving to lure an increasing number of young people from entering professional schools of law, medicine, and business and into graduate schools of arts and sciences. A recent important study reveals that 83 out of 100 graduating seniors in American colleges have a high orientation toward further study, and 77 actually "expect" to continue formal education at some time in the future.[1] For whatever reason—social pressure, concern for the national defense, or long-range financial considerations—graduate studies are in fashion.

WHICH STUDENTS GO TO GRADUATE SCHOOL?

Where are these graduate students being prepared? Berelson has demonstrated that fewer than a hundred colleges and universities (out of 800) have produced three fourths of all the B.A.'s and B.S.'s who went on to take Ph.D.'s and Ed.D.'s. Moreover, a relatively small proportion of these came to the graduate schools from the detached liberal arts colleges. The universities themselves, especially the rapidly growing metropolitan and larger state universities, are the main source.[2] The National Academy of Science—National Research Council, in its December 1963 report, listed in order the fifteen leading sources of graduate students as City College of New York, University of California at Berkeley, Illinois, Harvard, Michigan, Wisconsin, New York University, Minnesota, Brooklyn College, University of California at Los Angeles, Cornell, Columbia, Chicago, Masssachusetts Institute of Technology, and Yale. (Thirteen of these are also among the top twenty producers of Ph.D.'s.) It is clear, moreover, that the university is better able than the small college to attract its undergraduates into advanced studies. Especially in the sciences and engineering, the research establishments of the larger institutions act as magnets to draw bright young scientists into the academic orbit. The vast book collections and unique treasures of the larger libraries perform similar functions in other fields. Without these advantages, the smaller colleges can provide instead more intimate relationships of teachers and students, often more stimulating competition in peer groups, and fewer distractions from the major disciplines. A minority of the outstanding leaders in each generation of graduate students will continue to demonstrate the vitality of our small-college tradition.

Which students actually go to graduate school? Given the strong pull toward further study existing among our college graduates, it is startling that only a fourth of them actually enroll in professional and graduate schools immediately upon graduation. The preponderance of evidence in many studies, however, suggests that the strong expectation mentioned above is not mere wishful thinking. Rather, delay for one cause or another has become embedded in the pattern of higher education in the United States. Each new generation of graduate students is a blend of raw and more or less seasoned candidates. Obstacles to continuing study over which the student himself has little or no control are obvious: insufficient financing, obligatory military service, and poor academic credentials. But the commonest explanation for deferred study is the desire "to get some practical experience first." The multiple opportunities for jobs in industry, dramatized by the on-campus recruitment and placement activities that increasingly encroach on senior year time and thought, tend to weaken motivation for graduate study even further. Marriage and a comfortable income make a tempting tandem. And many jobs hold out the promise of in-service training and university study without sacrifice of salary or seniority.

It is doubtful whether the present slight trend toward full-time enrollments in the graduate schools, from 40 to 48 percent in the past decade, can continue in the face of expanding programs in continuing, or adult, education. It is also doubtful whether the best interests of the nation and of the universities are served by the granting of the same degrees, especially the Ph.D., to the part-time "gradualist" and the full-time "professional" scholar.

Disturbing also are the findings of Davis in *Great Aspirations,* that "almost one-third of the highest API (Academic Performance Index) group are postponing their studies." Conversely, and equally disturbing, he tells us that "ten per cent of graduate students accepted and 22 per cent of those planning to attend are from the Bottom Half."[3] Assuming that the API, which takes into account the quality of the school as well as the grade score of the individual, is one of the most reliable predictors of performance in graduate study, a serious loss of brain power and an equally serious waste of graduate facilities are indicated in these two facts. Although it is true that the talent loss (and probable corresponding waste) is least in the medical and life sciences areas, the greater discrepancies in the humanities and social sciences, where one out of five Top Fifth males are not continuing their studies, highlight the failure of our society to give proper support to these two vitally important disciplines. *Great Aspirations,* while acknowledging the financial obstacle in the path of many aspiring students, points out that 73 percent of all those who applied for financial aid received some award. Furthermore, about 85 percent of all persons applying for admittance to graduate schools in 1961 (in a test sample based on 136 institutions) *were accepted* by one or more schools. The study suggests that "the decision not to apply at all is a greater screening factor than refusals of applications." The habit of postponement, coupled with the fear of financial complications, seems to be responsible for the low rates of application. The researchers of *Great Aspirations* arrive at the following conclusion:

> The great bulk of these students accept the desirability of advanced study, and the problem is not one of "selling" graduate school to them. . . . There undoubtedly remain, however, a hard core of genuine financial problems among the young fathers, students who are living where there is no graduate school, and students who have incurred debts during college. Financial aid programs perhaps can be developed and expanded to meet their needs. Our personal belief, however, and one which goes beyond the data, is that a great part of the problem lies in the fact that students are not well informed on the "facts of life" regarding graduate school, the economic costs of postponement, the availability of stipends, and the availability of schools; and that if a systematic attempt were made to counsel, during their junior year in college, all high API men with Arts and Science majors or career preferences, considerable improvement in these rates would result.[4]

More adequate information has indeed been emanating from the graduate schools, along with the annual tidal wave of broadsides announcing the availability of financial aid. Even more influential, however, in assisting the flow of undergraduate students into graduate and professional schools has been the rapid development of loan programs, both Federal and state, and the cooperation of local banks in liberalizing their plans for educational loans. The availability of large loan funds providing for long-term, low-charge awards based upon academic qualification *and need* will go far toward solving the economic problem of the graduate student.

Actual expenses of graduate students vary widely with circumstances, locations, and types of universities. L. J. Lins, coordinator of institutional studies at the University of Wisconsin, reports on a sample of non-commuters living away from their parental homes, weighted toward Ph.D. candidates. The following mean amounts were spent on living costs, exclusive of fees and tuition: "single men, $1,714.54; single women, $1,566.63; married men, $2,927.32." For the 1963–64 academic year, the annual fee charge for full-time resident students was $300 and the nonresident tuition was $1,000. The mean total expense for the academic year (excluding summer) is probably in the neighborhood of $4,000 for a married nonresident at most of the large state universities and generally more at the private ones. The chief sources of income are assistantships, scholarships, fellowships, and, in the case of married students, income from the work of wives (45.5 percent of the wives of Ph.D. candidates at Wisconsin in 1960–61 worked, averaging $2,265.44 in earnings; the mean number of hours worked per week was 29.4). Presumably most of the 61.5 percent with children could not afford the luxury of a working mother.[5]

The Wisconsin study reveals that nonresident students held a much larger percentage of the scholarship and fellowship funds (46 percent) than the in-state students (22.4 percent), a reflection of the strength of the university in attracting able students from many states and countries. Fellowships for married men ranged all the way from $435 to $5,375, for single men from $380 to $3,000, and for single women from $972 to $2,937. Only 21.8 percent of the scholarships and fellowships awarded came from the University of Wisconsin's own funding, 35.9 percent originated in a foundation (such as National Science Foundation or Woodrow Wilson National Scholarship Foundation), 11.5 percent in private industry, and 20.8 percent in miscellaneous other sources. Assistantships were more equitably distributed between in-state and out-of-state students, and single students (both male and female) were employed in larger proportion (67 percent) than married students (about 50 percent).

A recent study at Michigan State University, entitled "Graduate-School Talent Sold to the Highest Bidder" discloses the long-suspected truth that "whereas most universities seek graduate students with the highest potential for academic performance, the average graduate student chooses the university offering the highest stipend."[6] A partial census of students who turned down offers of admittance to Michigan State's Graduate School in 1962 shows 56 percent singling out the absence of financial assistance as responsible for their decision to go elsewhere, and 43 percent naming financial aid as the most influential factor in their selection of a graduate school. The reputation of the academic department and the good name of the institution were cited by only 13 percent and 7 percent respectively. The article concludes: "Only when the net income derived from a graduate assistantship or fellowship is no longer a variable, will the educational advantages offered become a primary factor in the student's selection of a graduate school." The most prestigious universities could probably withdraw from this war of stipends and still attract full quotas of top-level performers. But there is no sign of their willingness to do this. Harvard, for example, grants well over $2.5 million annually in scholarships and teaching fellowships. The dizzy upward spiral is likely to continue for several years to come.

The increasing importance of graduate school populations in the economic affairs of the universities and the communities containing them can be illustrated in the case of Ohio State University where, in 1961, the median income for well over 4,500 graduate students was $4,000, and the average income for married males was about $5,400.

NEED TO RE-EXAMINE THE PH.D. PROCESS

Ever-increasing financial aid to graduate students has a two-pronged purpose: to attract more and better students to certain fields where Ph.D.'s are in critically short supply; and to reduce the time of the degree process so as to lengthen the span of the scholar's productive life. The average age of married men working for the Ph.D. in 1963 was about 29 years. With all the conditions at their apparent best, as in the field of physics, for example, the age at which the average physicist takes his doctorate is still 30.5 years. At that, he is the youngest of the Ph.D.'s, as he was, at 23, the youngest of the B.A.'s. Clearly, the burden of proof is on the graduate schools to show why fewer than one in ten of over 150,000 carefully selected, well-supported, and expensively trained Ph.D. candidates manage to take the degree each year. It is not enough, in this writer's opinion, to explain that 70 percent of all graduate students come from white-collar families of modest social standing and income, that many of them have had to interrupt their studies to contribute to their own support, and that they have taken longer, therefore, to "get through school." Nor is it particularly relevant that only a fourth of the fathers of all persons awarded Ph.D.'s in 1961 had college degrees themselves and a third of them had not graduated from high school. The cultural lag has clearly and convincingly been compensated by the dedicated efforts of this upwardly mobile element in our society. As Berelson observes: "It is hard to overstate the importance of the graduate school to students of high talent but low origin . . . or its contribution in this respect to the American dream."[7] No, the students cannot be held responsible for a world they never made.

Rather, we should examine the defects in the Ph.D. process, many of which have been pointed out to us by both professional and unprofessional critics: too many courses, too many meaningless hurdles, oversized dissertations, and all the rest. Perhaps, at the risk of seeming to pamper them, we should take more seriously than we have the suggestions of the students themselves. In his article, "View From the Underside," Ian Braley registered a sharp complaint against the "powers that be who control graduate schools." Writing as "one of the survivors," Mr. Braley charged that "the candidates who gave up look like more suitable material than those who stayed." Too many of the "industrious moles" persisted to the end of the course. Too many of the brilliant and inventive minds refused to accept the "shoddy teaching and research of low-grade programs" and dropped out of the race. Too frequently, even at big-name universities, a bright and **well-motivated candidate** was discouraged by the frustrations of red tape **and** busywork, of inaccessible professors, and of irresponsible advisers. In Mr. Braley's observation, even the faculty looked with suspicion and annoyance on the challenging nonconformists, and preferred the comfortable deference of the plodders. Mr. Braley submits that this "leak" will not be plugged by larger and larger stipends. It will require extensive shoring up from within the house of graduate studies before we are prepared to receive the candidates of such "intelligence, integrity, and creative promise" as we need.[8]

Unfortunately, even assuming that we can tighten up and improve our program, measurements of motivation and creativity and of intellectual integrity are hard to come by. The best predictor is still the Academic Performance Index (with an assist from Graduate Record Examination scores and reliable sponsors). Low-rated students drop out of graduate school twice as often as high-rated ones. But 25 percent of dropouts are persons of high ability, where the cause is not financial insecurity or personal maladjustment or any explicit criticism of the graduate program. Career drive and motivation are clearly in question. Research-oriented people have low dropout rates. Prospective teachers are somewhat higher in degree mortality. "Miscellaneous" are most vulnerable. Generally, students whose professional values are consistent with those of the graduate school will persist to the end. In the three main divisions of study, dropouts are lowest in mathematics and the sciences, highest in the humanities, and intermediate in the social sciences. Outside employment is a serious obstacle to the completion of a degree; full-time outside workers suffer severe attrition, as do middle-aged or older students, regardless of ability ratings.

With Mr. Braley, the present writer believes that "an excellent program is still the most potent attraction" to draw desirable students, and that no program is excellent without good teaching, whether it be inspired lecturing, well-planned seminars, well-designed research, or well-supervised dissertations. In the final analysis, something of all of these should go into the making of every new scholar. These are the prime desiderata in responses to every questionnaire, at Harvard, at Berkeley, and between.

Complaints of graduate students

The bigness and impersonality of our larger universities result in a common complaint: "There are too many graduate students; too many tired, harassed or blasé professors; [there is] too much pressure on everybody. . . . If I were to do it over again, I'd go to a smaller, less prestigious university where everybody is a little less tired and insecure." At Columbia, the greatest source of student dissatisfaction is in the area of faculty-student relations. At Berkeley, students complain that their professors are inaccessible, but then rationalize that this remoteness probably teaches them to be independent.[9] Everywhere, graduate students long for the role of junior colleague as opposed to that of unrecognized and solitary scholar. "I would gladly knuckle down if my adviser would give me just one sign that I, and my work, are acceptable as Ph.D. potential." Under the increasing pressure of numbers, it is hard to see how a more intimate, personalized kind of instruction will be possible in our graduate schools in the years ahead. Only at the smaller schools is it possible now.

Potential sources of teachers

The shortage of Ph.D.'s for college and university teaching posts may be met in part by two groups of students whose potential usefulness has not been fully explored. Foreign-born and women teachers may well be able to step in where they would have been less than welcome a generation ago. The number of "international" students in our country increases each year, as does the inclination of many of them to seek permanent employment and citizenship here. Eight thousand Ph.D.'s and Ed.D.'s were granted to foreign-born students in the decade 1950–60, a gain of 6,000 over the previous decade, aggregating almost 10 percent of the total production of these degrees in 1950–60. If more financing from American sources can be found for these visitors, they will add enrichment to the preparation of our own students and provide ultimately teaching manpower of a very high quality.

Although it is true that the proportion of women Ph.D. winners has remained static (about 10 percent) for a number of years, there are signs that the ratio may be inching upward. Dr. Eleanor Dolan has pointed out that "in 1959, 70 percent of the women 18 to 24 years of age, married or single, with four or more years of college education, were in the labor force."[10] She estimated, because of this strong new motivation to share in the world's work, that by 1980 the total number of women at the undergraduate level in colleges and in universities may equal that of men. Since the jobs open to women are "all too often not commensurate with their intellectual potential," Dr. Dolan makes a strong plea for a reappraisal of higher education for and by women. Recent polls of college presidents indicate an almost universal willingness to consider appointment of women Ph.D.'s to their faculties. Especially in the humanities and the social sciences do their prospects appear bright.

The graduate student of 1965 finds himself at the very frontier of university life. He enjoys the best that the university has to offer, whether of physical support or intellectual opportunity. If he has accommodated himself properly, he has found a professor who likes him and who will see that he gets a good start in his scholarly career. If he has applied himself, he has developed powers of penetration and discrimination and independent judgment which will be his chief resources in professional life. Whatever his chosen career, he will always be at home among books and scholars.

NOTES

1. James A. Davis, *Great Aspirations* (Chicago: National Opinion Research Center, University of Chicago, 1963), I, 317.
2. Bernard Berelson, *Graduate Education in the United States* (New York: McGraw-Hill Book Co., 1960), pp. 130–33.
3. Davis, *Great Aspirations*, pp. 339 ff.
4. *Ibid.*, p. 411.
5. L. J. Lins, "Student Expenses and Sources of Income, 1960–61 Academic Year, The University of Wisconsin" (Office of Institutional Studies, The University of Wisconsin, 1961), pp. 72 ff. For a valuable study of the financial circumstances of our graduate students, one should turn to James A. Davis and others, *Stipends and Spouses* (Chicago: University of Chicago Press, 1962), sponsored by the National Opinion Research Center. As the title of the book suggests, sources of income are fully treated. The possibility of loan financing is adumbrated, the effects of NDEA and other loan plans not having been felt to any large extent in 1960–61.

6. Allan Tucker and Lee Sloan, "Graduate-School Talent Sold to the Highest Bidder," *Journal of Higher Education,* January 1964, pp. 12–16.
7. Berelson, *Graduate Education,* p. 134.
8. *Liberal Education,* December 1960, pp. 499–503.
9. See Ann M. Heiss, "Berkeley Doctoral Students Appraise Their Academic Programs" (Unpublished; April 1964). Dr. Heiss, assistant research educator in the Center for the Study of Higher Education at the University of California at Berkeley, has prepared the most comprehensive and helpful study of its kind that I have seen.
10. Eleanor F. Dolan, "Higher Education for Women: Time for Reappraisal," *Higher Education,* September 1963, pp. 5–15.

Fellowships, Assistantships, and Traineeships

HENRY E. BENT

T HE WORDS "fellow" and "fellowship" are deceptively simple and hardly suggest the complexity of the problems and the disagreements which they have engendered. In the early history of universities all members of a college—students, teachers, and administrators—were called "scholars." Even today at Oxford, Cambridge, Trinity, and Dublin, students are called "scholars"; the governing body, some of whom constitute the teaching staff, are called "fellows." At Harvard, the term "fellow" is applied to the governing body, or Corporation. The teaching staff then became the faculty. For this essay, however, it is appropriate to use the modern definitions as adopted by the Association of Graduate Schools:

> *Be It Resolved,* that it is the sense of the meeting that the term "fellowship" as distinct from "post-doctoral fellowship" should be

HENRY E. BENT (A.B., Oberlin; M.S., Northwestern; and Ph.D., California) in time of service, is the senior graduate dean in the United States. Since 1938 he has been dean of the graduate faculty, University of Missouri. He has been an influential force in graduate education as an elected officer and important committee member of national associations. He was president of the Association of Graduate Schools in 1952–53 and the first chairman of the Council of Graduate Schools of the United States, 1961–62. He was instrumental in the organization of the council. Similarly his influence has been felt in the Council on Graduate Work of the National Association of State Universities and Land-Grant Colleges. As the second administrator of the NDEA Title IV Fellowship Program in 1959–60, Dr. Bent set up the major administrative policies of that significant fellowship program. At Missouri, he teaches chemistry.

used in those cases and only in those cases in which the following conditions are satisfied:

1. A fellow is a full-time graduate student proceeding toward a higher degree.
2. He was awarded this title in open competition rather than appointed to it.
3. The award being a gift made to the student rather than for the project, does not affect his freedom to select his own research project.
4. His responsibility is to prosecute his studies for his degree and the award of the fellowship does not obligate him to serve the university as an assistant in teaching or otherwise, nor does it commit him in respect to future employment.
5. The award does not merely cover the tuition but also makes a substantial contribution toward the living expenses during tenure.

The title "teaching fellowship" is therefore considered to be a contradiction in terms and its use is discouraged.

The stipend of a fellowship as above defined would appear to be exempt from income tax under present regulations.

Today, the variety and complexity of problems surrounding fellowships are sufficient to occupy many administrators on a full-time basis and to involve legislators, courts, income tax officials, university presidents, deans, faculty, and, finally, students in endless discussion and sometimes acrimonious debate. Before discussing these problems, it seems profitable to seek explanations for the wide variations of opinion and procedures that exist. These are to be found in the meaning of the term "fellowship," the purposes behind the award of the fellowship, and the motivation of those involved in fellowship programs. Realizing that there is danger in trying to look behind actions in order to determine motives, I hope that no injustice will be done by recognizing that, in general, there is no such thing as an ulterior motive. What we call an "ulterior motive" is simply an unwise emphasis in a situation where there is multiple motivation. I will not attempt a clear distinction between *meaning* and *motivation* since it is difficult to discuss the former without consideration of the latter.

In this essay I will consider first the meaning of the fellowship to the student who holds it, then to the agency supplying the funds, to the organization that administers the funds, to the institutions that receive fellowship money, and, finally, to the individuals who select the fellows.

MEANINGS OF FELLOWSHIPS

To the student who receives a fellowship, the meaning is usually quite straightforward. It is simply a gift of money from sources of little concern to him which will enable him to proceed with his graduate studies. His motives in accepting it are frequently complex; often pure enthusiasm for acquiring knowledge in a given field is dominant. As one gains years of experience in academic life, it is easy to underestimate this purity of motive and idealism. I am confident it is an important factor with many students. A second motive, often of equal importance, is, with the financial assistance of the award, the student may prepare for a career which he conceives as of great importance in our society and one to which he is devoted with a loyalty not much different from that which impels other persons to go into the ministry or foreign missionary work. Here again, the cynic will tend to underestimate the significance of the motive, and a student who is shy may be reluctant to stress its importance; still it is a powerful motive in the minds of many students.

There is the obvious motive that a degree will be an open-sesame to a career. Occasionally, a student's enthusiasm may be questioned and his idealism somewhat tarnished, and he is suspected of seeking the doctorate as his future "union card." We should not, however, ignore the possibility that a student entering a program with the most lowly or distorted idea of his career may eventually discover a higher ideal of his contribution to society.

For many students, it should be noted, the prestige value of an award is more important than the stipend. This is particularly true of an award from a renowned university. For these students, a fellowship is a symbol and an inducement to enter a given profession.

To the individual or agency supplying funds, the situation is much more subtle and complicated. At one extreme is the donor who is motivated simply by the desire to help a graduate student who is suffering from privation and worry. This motive perhaps should be described as compassion. Not very different is the donor who, observing students working hard and sacrificing many pleasures while pursuing advanced degrees, feels that some reward is appropriate for those who are industrious. This is an idealistic motivation that attempts to stimulate good behavior by appropriate rewards.

Some fellowships, established to honor deceased relatives or friends, result from affection and loyalty to an individual and the desire to preserve his name and to contribute to his reputation by identifying him with a public-spirited activity. Endowed fellowships of this kind were numerous during the last century and the early part of the twentieth century but had little impact on graduate education. They were, of course, of great importance to the few students who received them.

During the early part of the present century, corporate fellowship programs began to appear on the scene. The large chemistry fellowship program financed by the Du Pont Company was one of the first to utilize fellowships as a stimulus to attract students into a profession. Conceived in very broad terms by the Du Pont Company, awards were made to students without commitment that future employment was either intended by the company or expected by the individual. Unquestionably, this fellowship program was designed to add to the manpower pool from which the company could draw.

Another motive for corporate fellowship programs is found in the sense of responsibility of the companies to society. This broadening of the responsibility of the corporation has been accompanied by an even more rapid expansion of the activities of the Federal Government. As a consequence some companies, finding that they are competing with the Federal Government in the fellowship field, have decreased or discontinued this type of support to higher education. At the same time the expansion of the activities of the Federal Government in many fields has led to a belief that private initiative should demonstrate its ability to discover important needs and take some responsibility in seeing that these needs are met. This attitude tends to keep companies in the fellowship field even though they are competing with large Federal programs.

Finally, there is the public relations value of a fellowship program that helps create a public image for a corporation as one of integrity, of responsibility, and of civic leadership. Some corporations today frankly admit that they give fellowships only to those prestige institutions where they feel the public relations value will help them; to other institutions they confine their financial support to research contracts that pay dividends in research of an applied nature.

An illustration of contributing to the manpower pool in a given area of academic training is to be found in the fellowship programs financed by foundations. The Woodrow Wilson National Fellowship program is the most outstanding, beginning as a program sponsored by Princeton University, later supported by the Association of Graduate Schools in the Association of American Universities, and, finally, established as an autonomous body supported by the Ford Foundation. The Carnegie Foundation and the Rockefeller Foundation have also given support to this program. The original concept was to increase the supply of college and university teachers by carefully selecting those individuals who appeared to have the appropriate qualifications and by giving them guidance and counseling so that they would become college teachers. Thus has come about a gradual transition in fellowship support from the prime consideration of the welfare of the student to the prime concern of the welfare of society. This is not to say that the welfare of the student is ignored; certainly the Woodrow Wilson program has been meticulous in its concern that each student be treated fairly, with his best interests placed first.

No attempt is made in this essay to give credit to all corporations and foundations that have established significant fellowship programs; rather, a few examples are given.

A new influence came onto the fellowship scene when the Federal Government became interested in the nation's scientific manpower. Following Word War I, the National Research Council established postdoctoral fellowships to assist the country in establishing itself in the fields of science in a period when scientific education and many kinds of industry were pre-eminent only in foreign countries. The chemical industry, for example, scarcely existed in this country prior to 1914, and great effort was necessary in order to accumulate the know-how and personnel to make our economy independent of Germany in this field. But it was not until after the National

Science Foundation had been established in 1950 that funds were made available in amounts sufficient to have any major impact upon the academic life of our universities. The foundation was, in large part, designed to increase the number of scientifically trained persons required by the nation's industries and universities.

Scarcely a decade later two new factors became important in the Federal Government's concern for fellowships. One was the defense effort of the country, and the other, the political implications of fellowship programs. Although there has been discussion whether or not the word "defense" was appropriately included in the National Defense Education Act, it was an important concept in the minds of legislators and those responsible for the act, including the graduate fellowship program, title IV. In my opinion we need make no apologies for the element of defense in this fellowship program nor scorn it out of a conviction that higher education should receive Federal support for other important reasons. In this program, for the first time, higher education was assisted broadly in a variety of fields. This significant aspect of the program is of more concern to universities than to the Federal Government and will be referred to later. Because a country's greatest resource is its manpower, especially its trained manpower, the stimulation of students to take advanced training is a legitimate concern of the Federal Government.

The political motivation for fellowships is twofold. On the international scene, the National Science Foundation, the Fulbright, Smith-Mundt, and other programs have shown a keen awareness of the importance of enabling American scholars to travel abroad and of bringing foreign scholars to the United States. The motivation behind these fellowship programs is complicated, involving not only the strengthening of science (which is essentially nonpolitical), but also the creation of better international understanding and the education of individuals who will be experienced in the ways of foreign countries and who may become available for political appointments.

Within the United States, the political importance of fellowships has been most clearly recognized by the NDEA title IV program. Here the effort has been to strengthen graduate education throughout the country and to make the benefits of the program available to all sections of the country. Some parts of the South and the West which had been slow in developing graduate work have been materially assisted. Title IV has been of benefit to higher education in every state in the Union and has received enthusiastic support from every section of the country. A program which relies upon Federal appropriations must necessarily recognize the importance of the mechanism by which Federal support is achieved.

Finally, I come to what may be called "mission-oriented programs." These cover a wide spectrum of activity, from a fellowship whose objective is the solution of a problem in a narrow, specialized area to the broadest possible program aimed at training more persons in a given area who will be useful to an agency or organization with a specific mission. At one extreme are fellowships established for students who will work in the field of clay mineralogy, an area of obvious interest to the manufacturer of firebrick. In fellowships for investigators in, say, cardiac or cancer research, the interest of the donor is not primarily in training individuals but in the contribution they may make to knowledge in a specific area. Closely related to this latter type is the appointment of a student to work on a research contract or grant made to an individual faculty member to investigate a specified problem. The graduate student's appointment is as a research assistant; yet, to both faculty member and student, there is no essential difference between the student on this appointment and one on a university fellowship working close by on the same or a similar problem. In both cases, the student may be chosen on the basis of merit, and his selection of the problem may have been as free in the one case as the other.

At the other end of the spectrum of mission-oriented programs are those designed to train persons in given areas. Perhaps the best example is the Woodrow Wilson program.

In the category of mission-oriented programs are the traineeships of the National Aeronautics and Space Administration and the National Institutes of Health. Although they are not strictly fellowships, their nature requires discussion here. Their objective is to further the Federal programs in space and health. The NASA program is designed to increase the number of highly trained persons in engineering, mathematics, and physics. As such, the "EMP" traineeships are not simply gifts to worthy graduate students to work in any desired field but, rather, are confined to those areas that are of immediate concern to the NASA program. The benefit to NASA is twofold: information and discoveries valuable to NASA may result from the dissertations of the trainees and, to a larger extent, the increased number of individuals qualified for employment in the NASA program.

Next in importance to the granting agency is the institution, usually the university, which is host to the fellow. In the early part of this century there were few fellowships, but the postdoctoral awards which permitted the recipient freedom to choose his institution made an important contribution to the prestige of many institutions. So pleased was an institution to have a postdoctoral fellow that it would gladly contribute laboratory space and a limited budget for his research when this was needed. As predoctoral fellowships have increased in number, they have likewise contributed to the prestige of an institution when the fellowship allows freedom of choice to the holder. The value to the institution of having many such fellows has made some of the larger and stronger institutions reluctant to see fellows distributed by artificial methods such as restricting the number at a given institution or assigning fellowships to institutions that are in the process of developing graduate programs.

A more important concern of institutions is the influence of fellowships in strengthening a graduate program. A few fellows may contribute far more than might be expected from the numbers involved, for the stimulus to the whole research program provided by two or three active young investigators can be very great. Postdoctoral fellows and fellowship holders working for a doctor's degree increasingly constitute the active research group in a graduate school; a few decades ago teaching assistants were of first importance. Since in many fields almost all graduate students receive financial support from funds handled by the university, fellows and teaching assistants constitute almost the entire graduate-level student body. Take these away and the graduate program disappears.

More recently another important factor has come into the fellowship picture—the subvention that is given to a university to help support the research of a fellow and that often helps to pay for his instruction. This is a far cry from the days when the institution was happy to contribute several hundred dollars to support a fellow. At present, the institution is more inclined to claim that it cannot afford to accept a fellow unless money is assigned to the institution to support his education. As a result, industrial corporations as well as Federal agencies customarily contribute an amount which has grown from a few hundred dollars to $2,000 or more to support each fellowship holder. Since these funds are quite fluid, they may become an important source of income for the institution, comparable to tuition and other educational and general income. Increasingly, faculty appointments as well as the purchase of expensive permanent equipment are financed by such subventions. Examples are the NSF, NIH, NDEA, and Woodrow Wilson programs. While the $2,000 subvention in the latter program is used largely for fellowships, $500 is available for the institution to spend in support of its graduate program. Thus, the subvention gives fellowships an importance quite beyond the interest in the individual student or the purpose of the donor since it constitutes general support for higher education. This kind of support, with few strings attached, is a boon to institutions in expanding and upgrading their graduate programs.

Academic life would be complicated even with only the factors mentioned above, but the story is far from its end. We must still consider the point of view of faculty members and their concerns for fellows and fellowships. Here the important factor is the personal relationship between the graduate student and his adviser. On one hand, the adviser contributes to the education of the graduate student and, on the other, the graduate student contributes to the research program of the adviser. Hence, a student holding a fellowship is a great asset to a professor largely because he is able to devote a large portion of his time to research. It is not surprising, therefore, that many faculty members feel that a strong fellowship program is the most important single factor contributing to the strength of a graduate program. Such support assures that there will be not only students, but students of high quality who will carry on research and stimulate discussion in graduate courses. A department without fellowships is, indeed, in a precarious position; in some areas it cannot compete in graduate education.

The personal relationship between faculty members and students affects fellowship programs. Strong personal reactions to students, respect for their scholarly ability, and personal friendship or affection also bear on the awarding of a fellowship. These attitudes often create bidding among professors or between institutions and frequently bring about increases in the stipend far beyond that required to cover the minimum living expenses of the student. Thus, a faculty member may be in effect "buying" a service he needs in his research program as much as he is awarding a fellowship to a needy student.

But the value of fellowships does not stop with the assistance which they give to a departmental program. When an institution is attempting to develop its graduate program, initiate doctoral work in a new area, or attract staff, it may rely on fellowships to give support to these efforts.

This discussion of factors in the appropriation of funds, the planning of programs, and the awarding of fellowships may help us to see more clearly the answers to various problems and questions that are currently being debated.

CRITICISMS OF FELLOWSHIP PROGRAMS

Some of the matters just discussed have been interpreted as depriving a graduate student of his freedom of choice of area of study and of graduate school. Academic freedom is usually interpreted in terms of the rights and privileges of professors, but it may well encompass the equally important freedoms of graduate students to choose the areas in which they will study and the institutions at which they will receive their training. Obviously, restrictions placed on fellowship programs in these respects constitute a serious loss of freedom. This loss is one of the prices we pay for our continuing defense effort and the emphasis that is placed on the natural sciences and engineering.

In recent years many complaints have arisen about the imbalance between the humanities and the natural sciences. "Imbalance" presupposes that we know what the proper balance is, although there is little evidence to support such a point of view. Patently, we should not try to produce the same number of doctoral candidates in philosophy and astronomy as in English and chemistry; therefore, no one would suggest that all departments should have the same support. Yet by some mysterious mathematics we place several departments in a given category and then come to the remarkable conclusion that we should have equality of support for the various categories. To be specific, we include in the humanities four or five departments—philosophy, English, modern languages, part of history, and the fine arts—and then compare this category with the natural sciences, which include perhaps a dozen departments in engineering, half a dozen or more in basic sciences, a dozen departments in agriculture, and another half-dozen in medicine. If we based support on the number of departments involved, we might easily conclude that the sciences do not receive the support they deserve! The point I am making is that this reasoning is fallacious and only emphasizes that we have no basic philosophy or fundamental guidelines to suggest what a proper balance should be. Actually, we should have little fear that pressure on students will cause them to succumb to financial blandishments in choosing their life work. Although the Green Report states that 87 percent of Federal support for graduate students is in the sciences, a 1963 survey by *Time* magazine shows that private foundation and independent fellowship programs largely offset this imbalance, and that the total support for the humanities and social sciences is about half of the amount for all fields.[1] The recent study from the Brookings Institution gives additional evidence concerning the so-called imbalance.[2] Its conclusion is that there has been no significant change in the percentage of graduate students in the sciences over the last ten years and that the loss of students in the humanities is to be attributed to the increase in students in the social sciences. These observations, of course, do not imply that fellowships have had no effect on the number of students in the sciences, but rather that there might have been a decrease in number had not fellowships been available. A second inference from the Brookings study is that students are not as easily moved from one field to another as has been feared. To put it bluntly, a student who excels in classical languages is not likely to go into physics, regardless of inducement, nor is the reverse likely to take place.

Unquestionably, certain fellowship programs have influenced some students' choice of institution. Much has been said of the impact of the title IV fellowship program in establishing doctoral programs at "weaker" schools. Such criticisms ignore the fact that these schools are developing rapidly and will offer doctoral work with or without title IV support. Significantly, title IV enables this transition to be achieved without a long period during which the institution struggles to get faculty, equipment, and students. Any one of these three components of a sound graduate program can be more readily achieved if the other two are present, but an institution developing a graduate program finds great difficulty in attaining these three elements at one time. The title IV program makes it possible for the institution to obtain staff, equipment, and fellows simultaneously.

The criticisms that fellowship programs are restrictive have their counterpart in complaints that graduate programs are too limited in scope. State-supported institutions are continually besieged to establish new graduate programs of education, not to mention graduate schools of library science, colleges of dentistry, pharmacy, architecture, and other special areas for the sole purpose of reducing travel and living costs of students. Given finite resources—an obvious limitation on all educational activities—the kind of complete freedom that many individuals would like is plainly impossible.

My answer to the question of proper balance is set forth in the following section.

A DESIGN FOR A FEDERAL FELLOWSHIP PROGRAM

What is the ideal design for a Federal fellowship program for higher education? Two criteria are of overriding importance. First, in a free society, fellowship support should be available for students in all areas of intellectual endeavor with no restriction on field. Second, fellowships should be available in a number sufficient to ensure that every student of superior ability has the maximum training from which he can profit. These objectives are far from having been attained, but should be kept clearly in mind by the academic community. Every effort should be put forth to achieve them.

To the academic community, the first criterion of comprehensive support of higher education requires no justification. Every institution recognizes that to be strong in one department requires strength in related departments, that all knowledge is essentially one, and that neglect of any phase of scholarship can do serious harm to all others. In fact, the very concept of assigning students to departments or to fields of study is contrary to the spirit of a great university, which stresses, most importantly, freedom of thought.

When we consider the programs of the Federal Government that are related to this question, we find quite a different attitude. The record to date comes far from meeting the first objective here stated. Federal support has been largely mission-oriented. It was almost an accident that the NDEA title IV program developed considerable breadth. A certain degree of patience, however, is in order since only a little over a decade ago there were virtually no Federal fellowships. It is not surprising to find that those areas of human activity in which Congress has the greatest interest will receive special consideration. A Congress concerned with health problems will be generous to the fellowship program of the National Institutes of Health; a Congress fearful of our national defense will support basic science, engineering, and mathematics; and a Congress which has made large commitments to the space age will be sympathetic to engineering, mathematics, and physics.

Congress has gone far beyond these limited objectives, however, and recognizes in the NDEA the need for college teachers in all fields. Here we come close to having comprehensive support of higher education without restriction. During the first year of the program, not only did the sciences receive support but also education, the social sciences, and the humanities without restriction except as institutions making application for fellowships restricted their own requests. Before long there were rumblings in Congress, with criticism of programs in ceramics, folklore, church music, and so forth. Some of these criticisms may have been malicious since ceramics was obviously a field as central to scientific progress as any other area of physics or engineering. In the case of folklore, the attack may have resulted from lack of understanding of the nature of graduate work in this area. This points up an important factor in Federal support of higher education, namely, that it is impossible in any given length of time to explain to every congressman the importance of every piece of research in every field of activity in a modern university. Some things must be taken on faith, and the obvious suggestion is that Congress should have confidence that no respectable university will squander its resources in trivial activities. Such a faith implies responsibility on the part of the university. Certainly the singling out of folklore as a subject for criticism demonstrates the inability of Congress to judge graduate work, rather than lack of responsibility on the part of universities. Adequate safeguards are to be found in the careful selection of programs by experts and responsible educators. This we have had from the beginning of the program.

Granted that in time of war or serious domestic crisis some freedom must be sacrificed, the basic goal of complete freedom of choice is one which must consistently be kept uppermost in the minds of educational institutions as well as the Federal Government. Perhaps in the minds of some there may be a fear that complete freedom of choice may result in undue crowding in some fields to the neglect of others. Fortunately, evidence seems to contradict this point of view. The variation in abilities and interests of students is so great that, given sufficient freedom, it seems likely that there will always be students interested in every important form of intellectual activity, and, conversely, there is little danger that all students would want to go into archaeology or into theoretical physics. Further national restraints are limitation in equipment and shortage of future jobs. To sacrifice the principle of comprehensive support is to sacrifice the greatest single asset that any graduate student has in his work—his spontaneous interest and enthusiasm. We may expect only second-rate achievement when a student is forced to devote himself to a second-choice interest.

Although we are still far from achieving our first objective of free choice of subject matter for students, we are even further from our goal of making advanced training available to all qualified students. Since the top 10 percent of a college graduating class traditionally is regarded as superior, then out of the 400,000 graduating seniors each year we should expect about 40,000 to be qualified for graduate fellowships. But 10 percent is too small if we accept all students who can profit by graduate work. A study of graduate enrollments in the late 1940's showed that a large fraction of our graduate students came from the second quarter of their graduating classes. Thus it appears that currently more than 100,000 students annually could profit by graduate work and merit financial support.

Clearly, the present federally sponsored fellowship program fails to supply the nation's need for doctors. To meet the ever-increasing need, graduate school enrollments must be substantially increased to at least 500,000 or more. The full-time predoctoral students being supported by the various agencies must be materially expanded far beyond the 40,000 now receiving this assistance.[3]

Employment after receiving a degree is not likely to be a problem. The demand for teachers is increasing far more rapidly than the production of doctoral candidates, and the demands anticipated by industry and government are impressive. NASA alone is considering a need for Ph.D.'s which exceeds the present total production in all fields.

The administration of fellowship programs is frequently criticized. The most obvious single suggestion is that there should be greater uniformity in the various Federal programs and in those supported by large foundations. The present chaotic situation in which each program has a stipend slightly different from every other, a different dependency allowance, a different subvention to the institution, and a different method of selection seems difficult to justify. Any one set of rules and regulations would be an improvement.

The matter of stipend is frequently discussed and requires careful consideration. In the past the figure has been quite arbitrarily set with little except the graduate teaching assistantship stipend to serve as a standard. A guess of the cost of living and a general impression of what is fair to the individual frequently has determined the size of the award. Too few data have been available regarding the actual living costs of graduate students. Recently, James A. Davis' *Stipends and Spouses*[4] has provided much useful information. As a suggested principle, a fellowship should be large enough to enable a student to devote full time to his graduate studies for the entire calendar year without his seeking additional employment. There seems little excuse for interrupting a student's graduate work by forcing him to engage in manual labor or other unrelated employment during the summer in order to earn enough to carry him through the academic year. Certain fellowships at present are larger than necessary to cover living costs during the academic year, but, though generous, are inadequate to permit summer study.

Dependency allowances are also open to criticism. A question could be raised whether this allowance should be as large as at present since it undoubtedly contributes to the size of families at a time when the population explosion is a major concern in all countries. Assuming that a fellowship program can scarcely be used as a mechanism for solving the population problem, the magnitude of the present dependency allowances of $400 or $500 seems not unreasonable. The chief objection to the customary method of counting dependents arises when an employed wife is considered a dependent even though she earns approximately the same income as her husband. As soon as the first child is born, however, the family not only loses the income of the wife but also has the added cost of the child. The dependency allowance should recognize that a first child involves a much greater financial outlay than the second child. One suggestion is that no dependency allowance be given for the wife unless there are children. This would mean that a married graduate student would have a fellowship of the same size as a single man but double the dependency allowance when his first child is born.*

The process of selecting fellows is a matter of serious importance. Increasingly, this responsibility is being shifted to the institution where the fellow will be working. Often these awards are called "traineeships" rather than fellowships in order to make the distinction in the selection process clear. The National Science Foundation moved a step in this direction with its Cooperative Graduate Fellowships program, but because a NSF fellowship implies national competition, applications must finally be reviewed by a national committee. The procedure of review by a national body has worked effectively in the past, but we can hardly expect such an expensive and time-consuming review for all existing Federal fellowships, especially when new ones may increase the total number by a factor of five or ten. The only solution seems to be that followed by NASA with its traineeships or the NDEA title iv program, namely, that of allowing the institution to make its own selection. Assuming that proper procedures are established within the institution, this is an excellent method. A student whose academic record, letters of recommendation, and examination scores are reviewed by a depart-

* Beginning in the fall 1964 Woodrow Wilson fellowships paid $1,800 to a single or married fellow, an additional $1,000 for one child, and $250 for each additional child.

ment of instruction is not likely to receive unjust treatment in the distribution of awards. Anyone who has reviewed departmental recommendations knows that his list is not likely to be much changed subsequently by a large review committee, either local or national. Therefore, the investment of time and money in a second review is of dubious value.

Financially, the responsibility for administering fellowship programs is increasingly in the hands of universities. This arrangement seems desirable since the payment of student stipends can be handled expeditiously by the institution in which the student is enrolled and which presumably has close contact with his schedule and his needs. The subvention which supports the fellow in his work is now pretty generally assigned to the institution without elaborate accounting details. When both stipend and subvention are handled by universities, we will have a simpler operation.

THE ANNOUNCEMENT OF FELLOWSHIP AWARDS

This topic has attracted attention for so many years that it requires detailed treatment. The history of the subject goes far back into the early part of the century when the Association of American Universities adopted a policy by which its members, with a few notable exceptions, agreed to award fellowships on a given date, most recently, April 1. Students were given until April 15 to accept or decline. These dates were set to permit evaluation of a student's achievement during the fall semester of the academic year in which he will receive his baccalaureate or first professional degree. Additionally, they were set to avoid unfair competition among institutions by requiring a student to commit himself to an early offer even though later acceptance of an offer from another institution might serve his interests better. By the late 1940's other institutions, not members of the A.A.U., became increasingly important in the graduate field. Since they were not bound by the agreement, the competition for fellows placed member institutions of the Association of Graduate Schools at a disadvantage since non-A.G.S. institutions could make their offers early in the spring. Dissatisfaction with this situation led, in the early 1950's, to a serious effort to obtain wider acceptance of the traditional A.G.S. dates among other institutions. The April 1 date did not gain acceptance by any large number of institutions, but the April 15 date was generally accepted. The following resolution was adopted by over 200 institutions, constituting most of those that had awarded as many as five doctoral degrees in the previous year.

> In every case in which a graduate assistantship, scholarship, or fellowship for the next academic year is offered to an actual or prospective graduate student, the student, if he indicates his acceptance before April 15, will have complete freedom through April 15 to submit in writing a resignation of his appointment in order to accept another graduate assistantship, scholarship, or fellowship. However, an acceptance given or left in force after April 15 commits him not to accept another appointment without first obtaining formal release for the purpose.

The institutions agreed to send an announcement of this resolution with all fellowship and assistantship awards and thus placed the main reliance for enforcement upon the students, not the institutions. Thus, when students are asked to commit themselves at an early date to the acceptance of a fellowship, they know that they may resign up until April 15 without being stigmatized as irresponsible in their behavior.

This agreement has eliminated much of the friction among institutions about fellowships. Notably, it says nothing about the dollar value of a fellowship when a particular person is in great demand by two or more institutions. The suggestion has frequently been made that an upper limit be set for fellowships, but this has been equally vigorously opposed, with the following argument: There are mixed motives in awarding a fellowship, one of which (mentioned earlier) is the purchase of a skill that may be in short supply; correlatively, in a free society a student should have the privilege of commanding the maximum price that a university is willing to pay. The difficulty of enforcing an upper limit on fellowship stipends would be even greater than in the case of athletic scholarships; certainly the policing of such a regulation would be difficult. The most generally held opinion at present is that no such restriction can effectively be placed upon the upper limit of a fellowship award, even though Federal agencies may decide to adopt a stipend that covers only the essential living expenses of the graduate student.

The April 1 date has created a curious situation. It has not been recognized by all of the 203 institutions which signed the April 15 agreement, but still stands on the records of the Association of Graduate Schools. Most of the A.G.S. institutions still make the majority of the awards on April 1. Though general agreement on the April 1 date is not probable, it would appear that most university fellowships will be awarded on this date. To make awards earlier is difficult; to make them later will conflict with the April 15 date.

TAXATION

This brings us to a topic which has involved more discussion, heated argument, and time than any other aspect of fellowship programs. When should a fellowship be subject to income tax and when should it be considered a gift and, therefore, nontaxable? In the early 1950's Dr. Claude J. Lapp, of the National Academy of Sciences—National Research Council, suggested to the Association of Graduate Schools that institutions take the initiative in using the word "fellowship" only when the award was in the nature of a gift and use some other term to characterize those awards where an important service is rendered. This seemed a reasonable suggestion and likely to appeal to the Internal Revenue Bureau. But it did not solve the problem for a number of reasons. First, it was pointed out by Dean J. P. Elder of Harvard University that "teaching fellows" had existed at Harvard for decades, if not centuries, and that it would be no less than a major revolution to change the name at his institution. Obviously, Harvard fellows were rendering service and, under the regulations of most regional offices of the Internal Revenue Service, would be taxed.

A more serious problem arose as awards developed that were not called fellowships but had many of the same characteristics, such as grants from the National Science Foundation in the support of basic research. The Internal Revenue Service has argued that a grant is made to a member of the faculty who then employs a student to carry on research in fulfillment of the grant and, therefore, the student is rendering a service and his stipend is subject to tax. By contrast, the faculty member involved in this operation, and the university administration usually supports him in this, contends that there is no important difference between the NSF award and a fellowship. The purpose of the National Science Foundation is not only to support research but also to assist simultaneously in the training of graduate students. It is only because of a technicality that the foundation will not allow the professor to call his payment to the student a "fellowship," the technicality resting on the fact that the foundation already has a fellowship program and therefore cannot allow the professor who has a grant to compete with the NSF in the award of a fellowship. The professor contends that there is no difference between the student paid a stipend while working with him on a research contract and another student on a fellowship working on the same problem. In both cases, the professor has chosen a line of work which he considers appropriate for graduate students; the graduate student decides to work with him primarily for the purpose of obtaining the doctor's degree and not simply to earn a salary. That the problem happens to have been specified in a research grant application in the one case is of no significance. True, the student on a research contract does not have complete freedom of choice of his research problem. But then no student has free choice to work on any problem that he might select. These two students differ little, if any, in the freedom which they have in their research. Credit in the graduate school is given for research in both cases, and the nature of the problem is such as to develop the student as much in the one case as in the other.

Finally, many faculty members point out that the stipend is not a salary since the size of the award is frequently less than half what the student could obtain for the same type of work were he employed in industry.

Differences over the appropriateness of taxing students who have what the university considers "fellowships" but which the Internal Revenue Service calls "research assistantships" has lead to extensive litigation. In several cases, the Federal courts have found in favor of the student. The most frequently cited is that of a graduate student at the University of Tennessee.

The National Science Foundation made a grant of $19,700 to the University of Tennessee to support pure research in the field of nuclear physics. The university, in connection with this grant, gave a graduate research assistantship to the petitioner, Chander P. Bhalla, who was a candidate for a Ph.D. degree in physics at the university, and it allowed him, for his research work, a stipend of $175 per month for a period of nine months. Equivalent research was required by the university of all candidates for the particular degree for which Bhalla was a candidate. Bhalla would have been required to complete such a research assignment as a condition to receiving the doctorate, even if no stipend had been allowed to him. The university gave him credit toward such degree for the research and study that he performed under the above-mentioned graduate research assistantship. The primary purpose of his research and study, Bhalla maintained, was the furtherance of his training and education. Under the above circumstances, it was held, that the total amount of the stipend which Bhalla had received was excludable from his gross income under section 117 of the 1954 Code.*

One might have expected that because of the court's decision, the Internal Revenue Service would adopt a uniform policy which would permit students on appointments equivalent to fellowships to be tax-exempt. This has not happened. Either because of a desire to ignore the decision of the courts or because the Internal Revenue Service has allowed so much autonomy to each individual district that central control is impossible, the problem seems scarcely nearer solution now than it was five years ago. Legislation has been proposed which would take the matter out of the hands of the courts and the Internal Revenue Service, and would determine that an award that is essentially a fellowship, regardless of its name, would be tax-exempt. This may appear a trivial question since it is obvious that stipends can simply be raised sufficiently to take care of the Federal tax. The net result, of course, would be that tax money would go back into the Treasury. Institutions are not happy with this answer to the problem since a distinction is created between students who are identical for academic purposes. Furthermore, a student may frequently recover his income tax on appeal at a date a year or two after the award. This makes little sense since the student needs the money when he is in graduate school, and the fact

* Petitioner v. Commissioner of Internal Revenue, Respondent, Docket No. 83128, Filed Oct. 7, 1960.

that he may possibly recover his income tax years later simply introduces an element of uncertainty and inequality.*

LONG-RANGE IMPLICATIONS OF FELLOWSHIP PROGRAMS

One cannot leave the discussion of fellowships without considering questions regarding the implication of these programs. There are those who insist that we have too many fellowships, that we are moving toward a welfare state, and that life is becoming too soft for the graduate student while working for his doctorate. With this I wholeheartedly disagree since in my experience students are not being corrupted by such assistance. Life in graduate school is not easy for any student working for the doctor's degree, and to assume that there is any advantage in adding to his mental anguish and emotional strain by the addition of financial worry is completely unrealistic. Students with whom I have had intimate contact—and these constituted a very considerable number while I was associated with the NDEA program—are, in my opinion, not only working hard but feel an added social responsibility because of the assistance they have received. Obviously, there are exceptions but they are few and far between. To assume that many students are being corrupted by financial assistance is about as realistic as to assume that our children are corrupted by free kindergarten or first-grade instruction. And it seems to me, there is more justification for supporting a graduate student than an undergraduate student working for his bachelor's degree. The graduate student has perhaps reached the limit of his or his family's financial resources; a few years earlier, as an undergraduate, he would have seemed an appropriate object for scholarship assistance. There seems to be a popular misconception that an undergraduate student is a subject for compassion, while the same student, several years later working for the doctorate, is a mature person who should be on his own resources.

A more important concern should be the effect of fellowships and

* The tax situation has changed since the above statements were written. The Bureau of Internal Revenue has accepted the decision of the court in the Bhalla case. Universities increasingly have discontinued withholding on stipends paid students, and there is discussion of legislation further to simplify this problem by eliminating some income of students from taxation regardless of the source of the funds.

the large amount of money involved in the competition between institutions and the competition among students for financial aid. The idea that an institution must prove itself superior in order to be respectable is perhaps an unfortunate carry-over from athletics where competition is of the essence and winning the game is the prime objective. Higher education is something more than a game, and a wholesome attitude toward the contributions of many institutions can be expected only when we minimize the idea of ranking them by an arbitrary standard of excellence. There is no doubt that fellowship programs contribute to this competitive aspect of higher education, which often produces an undue concentration of students and funds in a few centers of graduate work.

The effect of fellowships upon graduate students also requires consideration. Inevitably, awards are made to a large extent on the basis of grades obtained in courses, achievement on examinations, and letters of recommendation, all of which too often are personal reactions to the undergraduate behavior pattern of the student. Undoubtedly, students can develop skills in passing examinations and establish habits to ingratiate themselves with their professors. These are hardly the qualities which lead to rugged individualism and independence on the part of a scholar. Few students hoping to receive financial assistance can afford to disagree vigorously with their professors and go their independent way in the search of an education. If our graduate education consists of cramming for a certain type of examination, we will have lost the most important element in the training of a scholar—the desire to master a field of knowledge.

Finally, there are many who decry the concentration of funds in certain areas of scholarship that are of immediate concern to the Congress in providing for the health and welfare of the nation. The humanities have felt this neglect keenly, and there appears little immediate likelihood that the situation will change significantly. The establishment of a National Humanities Foundation may help. Many in the humanities feel that they will not be restored to their proper position of respect and influence until they are treated in exactly the same way as those in the sciences, that is, through an independent organization which will give them financial aid. Others believe that this is the wrong approach and that it would be better to have a single operation, such as the NDEA program, expanded to give support in *all* areas of higher education. Certain educational institutions object to such a solution because their experience with NDEA has been unfortunate; they fear that many subject-matter areas would continue to be neglected. Others express fear that higher education will suffer if too much power and control are concentrated in a single agency, and that it is advantageous to have Federal support diversified. The existence of many independent agencies would minimize the danger that a single wrong decision could produce serious consequences. This implies that smaller agencies are more subject to influence by universities and are more likely to be responsive to the needs of higher education.

In summary, I hope that I have demonstrated the tremendous complexity of fellowships caused by the wide variety of motives involved. There has been no attempt to trace in each problem the significance of the various kinds of motivation. Each is left to the reader for his own interpretation. The suggestion that I have tried to stress is that in future fellowship programs we should have two objectives. First, we should have faith in a free society and allow unrestricted fellowship awards as far as fields of study are concerned in order to utilize the best genius and enthusiasm of our students. Second, we should greatly expand our fellowship programs in order to make use of the nation's greatest asset, the intellectual capacity of our college graduates.

NOTES

1. *The Federal Government and Education* [report by Edith Green, chairman of Special Subcommittee on Education], Committee on Education and Labor, House of Representatives. 88th Cong., 1st Sess., June 1963, p. 33; "Graduate Fellowships: One of a Series of Special Reports for *Time* College Student Subscribers" (Oct. 11, 1963).
2. Harold Orlans, *The Effects of Federal Programs on Higher Education: A Study of 36 Universities and Colleges* (Washington: Brookings Institution, 1962), pp. 36–37.
3. *Federal Government and Education,* p. 33.
4. Chicago: University of Chicago Press, 1962.

Foreign Students

ROBERT S. FORD

A T THE very time when our colleges and universities are straining their facilities to the utmost to serve the soaring enrollments of American students, the number of foreign students continues to grow apace. The rate of increase has been particularly notable since the end of World War II, and in the past fourteen years the number has more than doubled—roughly, from 30,000 students in the academic year 1950–51 to 75,000 in 1963–64. If the trend continues at its recent accelerated pace, estimates are that by 1970, 120,000 foreign students will be studying in this nation's colleges and universities.[1]

In 1963 foreign students came from more than 150 countries and were enrolled in 1,800 institutions of higher learning in the fifty states, the Canal Zone, and Puerto Rico. In addition to students, 8,400 foreign professors, instructors, lecturers, and advanced research scholars were here on academic assignment, and 8,800 foreign physicians were residents or interns in hospitals. The grand total of foreign nationals here as scholars, students, and physicians came to 92,000.[2]

As a quick résumé, of the 75,000 students, 31,500 (42 percent) were enrolled at the graduate level as follows:

ROBERT S. FORD, associate dean, Horace H. Rackham School of Graduate Studies, University of Michigan, has dealt with the concerns of foreign graduate students since 1950. His administrative skill in handling these concerns attracted national attention and won him membership on numerous educational committees studying problems of the foreign student. As an economist (Ph.D., Columbia), he served on state and national commissions studying taxation and financial reforms. He has been a member of the Michigan Department of Economics since 1934 and has contributed to technical and professional journals.

	Percent
Doctoral candidates	30
Master's candidates	47
Unspecified	23

In the past five years the number of graduate students has increased faster (by 67 percent) than undergraduates (by 48 percent). Thus, any examination of graduate education should include discussion of problems raised by the presence of large numbers of international students. A brief statistical backdrop on countries of origin, fields of study, source of support, and the like may be helpful.

ORIGINS OF FOREIGN STUDENTS

According to the Institute of International Education, although almost all areas of the world have shown continuing increases in the number of students in the United States, relative proportions among areas have changed little in the last three years. During the past ten years, however, proportions have shifted because of the growing interest of Far and Near Eastern and African nations in sending their students here for training and because exchanges with the iron-curtain countries have been limited. The 1963–64 proportions were as follows:

	Percent
Far East	35.0
Latin America	17.2
Near and Middle East	13.2
Europe	12.5
North America (Canada and Bermuda)	11.4
Africa	8.2

Although the smallest proportion came from Africa, for the fifth consecutive year the African student population gained in its proportion, and the number increased by 23 percent (to 6,150) over the preceding year. About one fourth of the African students came from Nigeria and Kenya. In view of the increasing opportunities being provided for students from this continent to study abroad, still further rises are anticipated.

Among nationality groups, Canadians have constituted the largest contingent for several years, even though by 1963–64 their 8,500 represented only about 11 percent of the total. Ranking next were India, with 6,400 students, and the Republic of China, with 5,400.[3] Ranking below these were, successively, Iran, Hong Kong, Korea, the Philippines, Cuba, United Kingdom, Greece, Israel, Thailand, Mexico, Germany, United Arab Republic (Egypt), Venezuela, Nigeria, Turkey, and Jamaica. Each of these twenty countries, including the Crown Colony of Hong Kong, had more than 1,000 students here. It is noteworthy that the number of Cuban students declined to 837 in 1960–61 (half the number of the previous year), and rose to 2,179 in 1963–64.

Geographical origins reveal the heterogeneous character of our foreign student population. Often the term "foreign student" seems to imply a single, homogeneous group; in actuality, wide differences exist both among national and regional groups and between the 48 percent undergraduates and the 42 percent graduate[4] and special students, who are usually older and more mature. From an academic viewpoint, the 24 percent who come from North America and Western Europe have cultural backgrounds that permit them to adjust to life in an American educational institution with little difficulty. Standing in sharp contrast are the students from the other areas—three fourths of our international students—who have significant differences in cultures and educational backgrounds that are likely to engender needs and problems to be taken into consideration by faculty and nonacademic counselors.

CONCENTRATION IN THE UNITED STATES

Foreign students are largely concentrated in a few states and a small number of institutions. Prestige is an important factor in selection of institution, for in this matter foreign students resemble their American counterparts. In 1963–64, over 28 percent were concentrated in seven states:

	Number
California	11,705
New York	9,804
Michigan	4,757
Illinois	4,260
Massachusetts	3,833
Pennsylvania	3,170
District of Columbia	3,067

On the institutional side, 40 institutions reported a combined graduate-undergraduate foreign student population of more than 400 each, for a total of 33,654, or 44 percent, of the total (Table 7). The relative importance of foreign students, illustrated by the ratio of foreign students to total enrollment, ranges from 15.8 percent at

TABLE 7: *U.S. Institutions with More Than 400 Foreign Students, Fall 1963*

Institution	Number of Foreign Students	Percent of Total Enrollment
1. University of California	3,927	6.1
2. Columbia University	2,289	9.4
3. New York University	2,074	5.0
4. University of Illinois	1,383	4.2
5. University of Michigan	1,265	4.6
6. University of Minnesota	1,247	3.6
7. Howard University	1,077	15.8
8. University of Wisconsin	1,061	2.8
9. Harvard University	1,016	8.0
10. University of Pennsylvania	980	5.3
11. University of Southern California	947	4.8
12. Massachusetts Institute of Technology	893	12.9
13. Michigan State University	865	3.1
14. Wayne State University	850	3.8
15. Indiana University	730	3.8
16. University of Hawaii	659	6.1
17. Stanford University	646	6.1
18. Yale University	627	7.5
19. Cornell University	618	6.4
20. Purdue University	610	3.5
21. Ohio State University	606	2.0
22. University of Washington	587	2.8
23. Brigham Young University	569	3.7
24. University of Chicago	557	8.3
25. University of Missouri	541	2.3
26. University of North Carolina	537	7.2
27. University of Arizona	494	2.9
28. Kansas State University	494	5.4
29. University of Oregon	489	4.9
30. University of Texas	486	2.2
31. Oklahoma State University	482	3.4
32. Syracuse University	476	3.9
33. Georgetown University	475	6.7
34. University of Miami	475	3.6
35. American University	471	4.9
36. Louisiana State University	458	2.4
37. Catholic University of America	440	7.8
38. University of Kansas	438	3.8
39. California State Polytechnic College	412	6.5
40. San Francisco State College	408	2.6
Total	33,654	....

Source: *Open Doors, 1964* (New York: Institute of International Education, 1964), p. 8.

Howard University to 2 percent at Ohio State University. The proportions in the two institutions having the largest foreign student enrollment are 6.1 percent and 9.4 percent (Table 7). The graduate students too are concentrated in a small number of institutions; in 1960, three fourths (about 16,000) were in the 54 institutions that enrolled about one half of all foreign students.[5]

FIELDS AND LEVEL OF STUDY

In 1952, Kenneth Holland, president of the Institute of International Education, stated that "among the thousands of students from abroad studying in the United States, every field of study, no matter how esoteric, seems to be represented. It would be safe to say that every branch of learning taught in the United States has foreign students among the numbers doing research or taking courses toward a degree."[6] This situation prevails today, with much greater numbers in every field.

Engineering was the most popular area of study in 1963–64, for both graduates and undergraduates, with 16,600 students. Proportions among the major fields were as follows:

	Percent
Engineering	22.0
Humanities	19.5
Natural and physical sciences	17.6
Social sciences	15.1

Graduate students outnumbered undergraduates in the natural and physical sciences, the social sciences, and agriculture. Undergraduates predominated in the engineering fields (about 60 percent), the humanities, and business administration. In the medical sciences and education, graduates and undergraduates were about equally divided. The interests of students from the various regions in the major fields of study are shown in Table 8. Undergraduates predominated among the Latin Americans (64 percent) and North Americans (60 percent),[7] whereas graduate students outnumbered undergraduates among students from the Far East, Europe, and Africa.

TABLE 8: *Foreign Student Enrollments in Major Fields
of Study, by Geographic Area, 1964*

AREA	PERCENT			
	Engineer-ing	Natural and Physical Sciences	Humanities	Social Sciences
Far Eastern..................	21	22	16	14
Near and Middle Eastern......	36	15	12	14
Latin American*..............	22	12	22	13
European....................	18	15	30	16
North American†.............	11	14	26	15
African‡.....................	15	18	13	25

* An additional 10 percent were enrolled in business administration.
† In addition, business administration and education accounted for 10 percent and 11 percent respectively.
‡ In addition, business administration, 8 percent; education and agriculture, 5 percent each.

SOURCES OF FINANCIAL SUPPORT

Of the foreign students who come as undergraduates, many continue on to graduate or professional training, and the proportion doing so is likely to rise as increased numbers of undergraduates come from the developing countries of Asia, Africa, and Latin America. Currently, according to the 1963–64 Institute of International Education questionnaire, 37 percent of those replying had been here for three years or more—since 1961 or before. Of related significance, about 22 percent of foreign students were supported wholly or partly by U.S. colleges and universities.

Foreign students were supported in addition as follows: self-support, 46 percent; private organizations, both wholly and in part, 13 percent; U.S. government grants,[8] 10 percent; grants from foreign governments, 6 percent.

Regionally, students from North America (almost all from Canada) were the only group of whom more than half furnished their own support. The proportions of self-supporting students from other regions were as follows: Near and Middle East, 44 percent; Latin America, 42 percent; Far East, 38 percent; Europe, 28 percent; Oceania, 24 percent; Africa, 12 percent.

VISITING FOREIGN SCHOLARS IN THE UNITED STATES

Although, as a category, visiting foreign scholars do not have a direct bearing in a discussion of foreign students, they constitute a significant element of the international dimension of higher education in this country. Between 1955 and 1959, the number of foreign professors, instructors, lecturers, and research scholars more than tripled. Since that time, the same rate of increase has continued, with the number having risen from about 2,000 in 1958–59 to 8,400 in 1963–64. In this latter year the pattern of area representation was, in general, consistent with that of preceding years:

	Percent
Europe	40
Far East	32
Latin America	8
Near and Middle East	7
Canada	5

By nationality groups, the most numerous were the Japanese, 13 percent, and the United Kingdom sent almost as many. Twenty-one institutions, compared with 17 last year, reported more than 100 foreign scholars in residence. The University of California led, with 689, followed by Harvard, 423, and Massachusetts Institute of Technology, 416.

Also 1963–64, 8,800 foreign physicians came from more than 100 countries for training as residents or interns in U.S. hospitals. This was a considerable increase over the 7,250 of 1962–63.

ADMISSION REQUIREMENTS

The presence of large numbers of foreign students in this country creates problems for the educational institutions. Graduate schools are most immediately concerned with admissions policies and procedures, including standards of admission, evaluation of foreign university credentials, and proficiency in English. Some aspects of these problems will now be considered.

1. Admission Standards

A first proposition is that foreign students should not be encouraged to study in this country unless their undergraduate record shows clearly that they are qualified for advanced work. In a good many cases a student who develops difficulties probably should not have been admitted in the first place and may have been able to come only because some school was overgenerous in its evaluation of his record and did not adhere to the admission standards set for American students.

The maintenance of high standards operates for the best interests of the students themselves. Less difficulty and embarrassment ensue, both for the student and the college or university, if applicants with weak scholastic records are rejected rather than admitted with the probability of later academic expulsion or failure to meet degree requirements. Furthermore, to nurse along a poor student and ultimately award an advanced degree on lowered standards does not promote the prestige of American universities abroad and may lead to adverse foreign attitudes toward American higher education. This matter is discussed farther on in this essay.

As the number of foreign students increases, standards governing their admission tend to become more selective because they are competing with U.S. students, for whom standards are also rising under the pressure of bulging enrollments. The sharp competition for places among American students demands that foreign students be even better than average, particularly at the graduate level. Furthermore, the adjustment to a new cultural environment, a different educational system, and the need for proficiency in a language other than their native tongue exert such pressures on mediocre foreign students that they are likely to fall by the wayside. If they have been below average in their home countries, there is little basis for assuming they will show much improvement, or even be able to succeed, in an alien academic environment.

In addition to insistence upon a high scholastic record for admission, there must also be careful screening either to eliminate those whose undergraduate preparation has been inadequate or at least to require additional undergraduate work to build up their foundation for study at the graduate level. This leads into a consideration of foreign student transcripts and credentials.

2. Evaluation of Credentials

The core of the admissions process is the evaluation of an applicant's credentials, assuming his scholastic record is strong, to determine whether he has the equivalent of a four-year U.S. bachelor's degree, a problem that is often very difficult. Obviously, the evaluator should have some knowledge of foreign educational systems and some familiarity with the educational ladder in various foreign countries. Several studies on this subject have been published in the last few years, and standard source books and references should be made readily available to those persons concerned with admission and placement.

Most foreign systems are quite different from U.S. systems in organization, administration, equipment, methods of instruction, and conduct of examinations. Some foreign systems have been established on the theory that a student can obtain sufficient general education in secondary school and is prepared to specialize when he enters the university. Where this is the case, there is no real equivalent to an American bachelor's degree, and establishment of equivalency is arbitrary. A student coming from such a system will not have had preparation that would meet U.S. university distribution requirements in the humanities, sciences, and social studies in the freshman and sophomore years, although the work in his special field may be comparable to our junior or senior level. In such cases, it is generally desirable to require the student to work for a bachelor's degree, or at least to do about one year of additional work to make up deficiencies in preparation prior to accepting him in a master's degree program.

The name of a foreign degree may suggest the equivalent of a four-year American degree, but this may or may not be the case. There are some countries in which the lowest degree, and sometimes the only one given, is called a "doctorate" and it will probably be the equivalent of a bachelor's degree. In South American countries, the diploma, or title of *bachiller,* is given upon completion of secondary education and is required for admission to the university (as is also the case in universities of the French type, with their admission requirement of the *baccalauréate* II). The degree commonly granted by most South American universities, upon completion of the full course of university studies, is the *licenciado,* and a student should hold this degree or an equivalent professional degree, such as that of engineer, in order to be eligible for admission to a graduate school in the United States. The same is true of the French *licence* and *ingénieur* degrees. In Italy, the degree of *laurea* is conferred and the holder is called "doctor," but the degree is about the level of an American master's degree. In Scotland, the Master of Arts degree is comparable to an American bachelor's degree. The degree of *licentiate* in some countries, such as Iran, is at least one semester short of an American bachelor's degree, as is the A.B. awarded upon completion of the general course in some of the Canadian and other British Commonwealth universities. In those countries the B.S. honors degree is somewhat beyond an American bachelor's degree.

Another problem in admissions is evaluation of the quality of a student's undergraduate work. Universities in many foreign countries do not provide any kind of document comparable to an American college transcript. (Happily, more and more foreign universities are adopting an American type of transcript, among them the institutions of Iran, Iraq, Israel, Japan, Taiwan, and Turkey.) When a document shows only (1) the diploma or degree conferred, with a final specification of quality, (2) the degree or title conferred, a list of subjects studied, and a final mark of quality, or (3) degree or title conferred, list of subjects studied, and an average examination mark for each year, or (4) degree and type of honors or possibly only the degree, it may be necessary to obtain a statement from one or two of the student's professors regarding the class or division in which the student was placed, for example, high or low second class.

Often the university where a student did his undergraduate work is not listed in the standard reference sources, or it may be listed but has been awarding the bachelor's degree or equivalent for only four or five years. In such cases, when the student appears to be qualified from the standpoints of years attended, subjects studied, and grades obtained, it is advisable to require at least one semester of work to qualify for admission to a master's degree program.

3. Proficiency in English

An important factor in admission procedures is to determine the level of a foreign applicant's proficiency in English, assuming that his undergraduate preparation and scholastic record are satisfactory.

Careful scholastic screening is essential, and if a foreign student meets these requirements and has a competent command of English, he is not likely to have academic difficulties. Within the last few years, a number of institutions have become concerned over the problem of language competence and have adopted arrangements for testing the English proficiency of students who otherwise qualify for admission either before they leave their home country or after they arrive here but prior to actual enrollment. It is obviously preferable to require the test prior to the student's departure from his country. If the deficiencies are discovered after arrival here, the student must be provided with instruction in remedial English, which may require several months before he is prepared to engage in graduate work. The costs of graduate education for a foreign student may become excessively heavy if he must devote considerable time to learning basic English in order to understand ordinary classroom instruction and participate in seminars. Further, if he comes with a specific objective and his time is limited to the minimum period necessary—say, a year for a master's degree—his program will be full, with no time available for organized study of English.

Clearly, a satisfactory level of English competence is necessary if a foreign student wishes to study in the United States and attain a successful intellectual experience in the American culture.

An important step forward was taken in 1962 in coping with this problem on a nationwide basis. The National Council on the Testing of English as a Foreign Language was established, as a result of conferences on the testing of English proficiency of foreign students sponsored by the Center for Applied Linguistics of the Modern Language Association of America, the Institute of International Education, and the National Association of Foreign Student Advisers. The new council is associated with the Center for Applied Linguistics and has assumed responsibility for creating a testing program prescribed in the original conference. In 1963 the Ford Foundation made a two-year grant to assist in initiating the testing program, and the "TOEFL" tests were conducted by the Educational Testing Service, Princeton, New Jersey, at its established centers abroad, in 1964. More than 500 U.S. institutions endorsed the development of this program, and it gives promise of being used widely.

4. Finances

The financial support of individual foreign students is of paramount importance and must be given serious consideration by the admitting university. A nonimmigrant student must submit documentary evidence in applying for a visa that he will be able to support himself, from his own resources or with assistance from a sponsoring foundation or government agency, while pursuing a full course of study. The requirements differ among visa-issuing officers, but in general the student must submit evidence that he will have sufficient resources to support himself for a year. Likewise, a good many universities require a financial affidavit or statement certifying that an applicant will have funds for at least one year of study. If he has an official sponsor, verification or a financial guarantee can be obtained without difficulty.

The foreign student who stays on for more than a year often encounters financial difficulties. Family illness or death, crop failure, or some unforeseen disaster may affect his financial status. Under such circumstances, he will probably turn to his university for a loan or other financial assistance. The probability of such contingencies and consequent requests for emergency aid should be recognized by any university committed to the acceptance of foreign students. Admissions officers should probably give more attention to this phase of the problem, but certainly should forewarn foreign students about the difficulties of obtaining financial assistance, should they decide to stay longer than one year.

5. Academic Performance

Consideration of the foreign student problem would be incomplete without attention to the perennial question of academic performance. Much has been said about leniency in grading foreign students. In a questionnaire circulated among members of the Association of Graduate Schools in 1956, a majority of the graduate deans expressed the opinion that foreign students are not graded on an easier basis than American students. Some of the minority, however, were of the opinion that a double standard exists on a rather widespread basis. Of course, this is purely a subjective judgment and no conclusive proof is available.

In this connection the American Council on Education, disturbed about adverse foreign attitudes toward American higher education, through its Commission of Education and International Affairs appointed an *ad hoc* Committee To Insure a Better Understanding of American Higher Education Abroad, whose purpose was to study and identify the major cause of such attitudes. Interestingly, one of the causes, according to the committee, is the academic double standard, which operates when American colleges and universities admit, grant advanced standing to, or award degrees to foreign students by standards lower than those applied to American students.[9]

In 1953, the Committee on Foreign Students of the Association of Graduate Schools investigated differences in success of foreign students in member institutions of the A.G.S. For purposes of the investigation, the fields of study were grouped into five major divisions—biological, physical, and social sciences, engineering, and language and literature; the countries were classified into six major groups—Africa, British Commonwealth, Europe, Far East, Latin America, and Near East. The committee noted that, although a study by individual countries or universities might have been revealing, it appeared that performance was similar among students from areas of the world having similarities in systems of education and in language problems. The committee's report, with statistical compilations, was published in the *Journal of Proceedings and Addresses of the Association of Graduate Schools* for 1953.

Since student performance is intimately related to admission, the problem of academic success can probably be dealt with effectively only if colleges and universities maintain high admission standards and restrict acceptance to well-qualified students with adequate proficiency in English.

PROBLEMS FOR U.S. UNIVERSITIES

The foreign student problem is complex and involves both academic and nonacademic questions. The latter have been largely excluded from this chapter because they embrace such matters as counseling on personal and financial problems, housing and employment possibilities, immigration, social services, orientation, and so on, which fall more properly under the jurisdiction of the university international center or the foreign student adviser and do not involve the graduate school directly. The preceding section has dealt with those academic matters most likely to enhance the probability of a successful experience in graduate school. This concluding section will discuss two of the most pressing general problems, which will likely receive considerable attention during the next few years.

1. Increased Enrollments

A question of great immediate concern is how U.S. institutions can accommodate the anticipated increase in foreign students in the next few years. Indications are strong for an enrollment of 120,000 by 1970, if the present trend continues. It has been shown that one or more foreign students are enrolled in each of more than 1,800 U.S. institutions, ranging from our largest universities down to small technical schools. An offhand assumption might be that an increase of 40,000 students could be handled without overwhelming difficulty by such a large number of institutions. But the problem is not so simple. Almost one half of all foreign students are now enrolled in 40 universities. It seems probable that the impact of a sharp increase in foreign students will fall primarily on this small group of schools, because the foreign graduate student population is increasing more rapidly than the foreign undergraduate population,[10] and because these institutions are organized to handle large numbers of foreign students at both the graduate and undergraduate levels and are institutions that are for the most part well known outside the United States. In general, foreign students, like U.S. students, prefer to attend a large, well-known institution. Nevertheless, all applicants cannot be accepted by these universities, most of which have already been forced to limit admissions sharply, even for American students.

The needs of many of the foreign students could be met much more effectively by a wider distribution among qualified colleges and universities throughout the country. Greater numbers should be placed in smaller colleges as well as in community colleges and two-year technical institutes, where they could receive more personal attention and possibly obtain an even more satisfactory education. A foreign student coming from a rural community or from a small country whose economy is based primarily on agriculture or some other natural resource may not adjust easily at a large, prestigious institution in an urban area. In this connection, it should be noted that although agriculture is the basic industry in the countries from which many of these students come, only 2,294 foreign students were enrolled in this field in 1963–64.

The placement situation could be much improved through better guidance and counseling of foreign students in the selection of an institution in this country. They need advice and assistance in obtaining placement in the institution that can best provide what they need on the basis of their undergraduate preparation and also in light of their objectives upon return to their home country. Finally, even if better distribution is achieved, the institutions will still face serious problems and new concerns as more foreign students come to their campuses to study.

The I.I.E. has recently established overseas offices to assist United States colleges and universities that receive applications from foreign students concerning whom information, or means of evaluating information, is lacking. These offices will also provide information on higher education in the United States to foreign institutions and individuals. Offices are located in Lima, Peru (for South America), Nairobi, Kenya (for Africa) and Bangkok, Thailand (for Southeast Asia). The new service of the I.I.E. is extremely significant, and its experience will be invaluable in expanding educational advisory services and in improving the placement of foreign students in U.S. institutions.

2. Relevance of Study Programs

Increasing attention is being given to the relevance to the objectives of foreign students of the training and education offered by U.S. institutions. One frequently hears complaints that our educational requirements should be more flexible in meeting their needs. Another suggestion is that our curricula are linked so closely to the American economy and culture that readjustment to conditions in his home country is made difficult for the returning foreign student. Still another claim is that the pace of our educational process is too leisurely, that our smörgåsbord approach to education is not sufficiently compact, unified, and efficient for the purposes of students coming from the developing countries of Africa, Asia, and South America.

These matters have been considered by an International Study Group at a meeting of the Association of State Universities and Land-Grant Colleges in 1961. The position taken was that modification of educational offerings is urgent in order to prepare foreign students for constructive work upon their return home. Study programs now available to foreign students are rooted in traditional American patterns and reflect social, economic, and scientific needs in a highly industrialized economy with large-scale businesses, organized labor, a free market, and a democratic government that are "worlds removed" from the economic pattern in their home land. Knowledge and skills acquired here must somehow be adapted for application in a social and economic environment quite different from that of the United States. Apparently, this particular study group was suggesting a pattern of education involving a combined program of technical training and liberal arts education. The traditional pattern, the group said, "will have to transcend both the present limited aim of technical assistance as the government defines it, and also the smug departmental isolation that often dominates the university world."[11]

Another study group, the Committee on the University and World Affairs, also observed that our traditional educational program is rooted in American conditions, and asserted that university and college curricula must often be redesigned to meet the distinctive needs of foreign students and the countries from which they come. Foreign students may obtain the type of training they need and seek by absorbing the best we have, but revision is often required to meet their particular needs. The group pointed out that some risks are involved in developing a new educational pattern, such as those of limited faculty competence, lowering of academic standards, and separating foreign students from the mainstream of college life. It is implied, however, that these risks are worth taking if we are to face up to the challenge of providing the type of preparation foreign students need for meeting their future responsibilities.[12]

These criticisms should not be brushed aside lightly. Clearly, there is need for continuous re-examination of our educational process, achievements, and goals. The implications of restructuring courses of study primarily for foreign students (aside from special programs that may be worked out through contractual arrangements with a U.S. Federal agency) are somewhat disturbing. It is evident that foreign students come here for graduate study because of what we have to offer, and if the knowledge acquired in the United States in the 1960's seems somewhat inappropriate for the realities of their own societies, it does not necessarily follow that our educational pattern should be revamped. Furthermore, since the economy in many foreign countries, particularly the developing nations, is changing rapidly, it seems that the interests of these young graduate students can best be served by preparing them for the future and for life in a changing world rather than by placing the emphasis on their immediate requirements by means of curricula quite different from those provided for American students. The presence of large numbers of international students in our institutions is only one aspect of the whole complex of factors underlying and affecting our changing society. There are also criticisms from American students about courses, sequences, and distribution requirements that must be met in fulfilling degree programs. Planning should be and is being directed not only to the foreign student but to American students as well.

The problem of the foreign student, so far as graduate schools are concerned, can be met to a considerable extent by acceptance at admission time of those who show the greatest potentiality for study at the graduate level. Even if a student appears to be qualified, he may need additional preparation before undertaking advanced work, which, incidentally, will also provide him an opportunity to adjust to a new educational system and environment. Certainly his proficiency in written and spoken English should be such that he will be able to participate fully in courses and seminars since, without this command, he will fail to reap the full benefits of study in this country. Also, careful examination needs to be made to determine whether he is sufficiently grounded in the academic discipline in which he plans to specialize. To this end, greater use should be made of placement examinations to determine adequacy of preparation. If assurance on these factors can be obtained at the beginning of a student's period of study, he can hasten accomplishment of his objectives. It is no favor to a foreign student to permit him to plunge into subject matter for which he is not prepared.

From the standpoint of graduate education and increasing enrollment pressures, we must obtain the best-qualified students and attempt to place them where they will gain the greatest profit from their advanced study. Progress is being made, but a great deal remains to be done in achieving better placement and distribution of graduate students as well as the best utilization of our educational resources.

NOTES

1. John L. Thurston, "The Education Explosion: Foreign Student Enrollments in the U.S.," *Overseas, The Magazine of Educational Exchange* (Institute of International Education), March 1963.
2. Unless otherwise indicated, all of the statistical information on foreign students was obtained from the annual publication of the Institute of International Education, *Open Doors, 1964* (New York: The Institute, July 1964; 70 pp.). See also Kenneth Holland, "The Foreign Student in the United States," *American Universities and Colleges,* 8th ed., ed. Mary Irwin (Washington: American Council on Education, 1960), pp. 68–73. A "foreign student" is defined by the Institute of International Education in its annual census as a citizen of a country other than the United States who intends to return to his home country when he has completed his period of study in the United States.
3. I.I.E. breaks down this figure: 3,057 from the Republic of China and 2,353 as "China, Unspecified."
4. The remaining 10 percent are those who are enrolled as special students or who did not answer the I.I.E. questionnaire.
5. Thurston, "Foreign Student Enrollments," *Overseas,* March 1963, p. 4.
6. Holland, "The Foreign Student in the United States," *American Universities and Colleges,* 6th ed., ed. Mary Irwin (Washington: American Council on Education, 1952), p. 137.
7. *Open Doors, 1964,* pp. 18–21.
8. During the fiscal year 1963, the Department of State, under its educational and cultural exchange programs, made grants to 5,595 citizens of 130 countries and territories to come to the United States, of which 2,029 were for university study. Grants to go abroad were made to 2,325 U.S. citizens, of which 830 were for graduate study. (*Open Doors, 1963,* p. 13.)
9. A mimeographed report was issued by the American Council on Education, Nov. 23, 1960.
10. This problem is also considered by Thurston, "Foreign Student Enrollments," p. 4.
11. Report of International Study Group II, *Steps Needed to Improve or Develop Programs to Meet the Needs of Foreign Students and Trainees,* Centennial Convocation, Association of State Universities and Land-Grant Colleges, November 1961, p. 346.
12. *Report of the Committee on the University and World Affairs* (New York: Ford Foundation, 1960), pp. 29, 31.

New Trends in Graduate Study in the Social Sciences

JOHN PERRY MILLER

GRADUATE training and research in the social sciences have changed dramatically in the last three decades. The changes reflect several developments: the rise of new disciplines and subdisciplines; greater emphasis on scientific analysis as a complement to policy-oriented research and training; the use of powerful new research tools; the impact of such extra-university influences as the foundations, government (Federal and local), and the Social Science Research Council; the rise of autonomous or semiautonomous research institutes; a greater concern with the social systems of non-Western cultures; and the increasing demand for social scientists to staff research and operational positions in nonacademic institutions.

While some of the social science disciplines have been affected more than others, notable changes have taken place in all. The developments in the various disciplines have led to corresponding changes in the character of the training programs in the leading centers of graduate study. The major graduate schools have, of course, responded differently and with varying speeds. Although the leading graduate schools with each of the disciplines have important common characteristics, equally important differences reflect, in part, planned or accidental specialization and, in part, dif-

JOHN P. MILLER (Ph.D., Harvard) has been dean of the Graduate School of Yale University since 1961. Since 1939 he has been a member of Yale's Department of Economics. He has served on numerous state and national economic study commissions and has written extensively on economic subjects.

ferences in the way the tensions between the old and the new have been reconciled in various universities.

The social sciences had their origins in history and moral philosophy.[1] But one after another, each of the social sciences was differentiated from the parent disciplines and recognized as a separate field of study. The leaders in each new discipline have sought to define a distinctive field of study, to formulate its concepts with increasing precision, to articulate a body of theory, and to develop or borrow meaningful methods for analyzing the phenomena distinctive of the discipline and for testing its theories. As the new disciplines became more precisely differentiated and their concepts and tools more powerful, efforts were made to relate the disciplines to one another through programs of multidisciplinary or interdisciplinary research and training and through the development of new disciplines or subdisciplines, such as political sociology, economic history, and social psychology.

In this essay, I interpret the social sciences to include anthropology,[2] economics,[3] history,[4] political science,[5] psychology,[6] and sociology.[7] History is, of course, equally related to the humanities, and several fields in psychology are more closely related to the biological than to the social sciences. But the outside ties only emphasize the interrelatedness of the conventional fields of study. We live not in "two worlds" but in "many worlds" which interact with one another in a constantly changing pattern. Statistics and linguistics are not included in this discussion, although statistics is a subject of considerable relevance to the social sciences, and some aspects of contemporary linguistics are more fruitfully treated as a social science than as a part of the humanities.

The growth of the social sciences over the last three decades is suggested by a few salient statistics.[8] The average annual number of Ph.D. degrees awarded per year in the social sciences increased 470 percent from 462 in the years 1930–31 to 2,179 in 1960–61. Ph.D. degrees in anthropology increased 840 percent; in psychology, 740 percent; in political science and public administration, 520 percent; in sociology, 400 percent; in economics, 350 percent; and in history, 300 percent.

The reorientation of the disciplines and the growth of new subdisciplines may be illustrated by the experiences of economics or psychology. In economics, the field of macroeconomics has undergone a great change in the last three decades. In 1930, the field was generally conceived as the study of "money, banking, and business cycles." This field has been revolutionized by the convergence of two developments: first, the elaboration of a theory of income and employment, stimulated in part by the work of John Maynard Keynes, and, second, the systematic compilation of theoretically meaningful series of national income and product statistics. These innovations, each of which had a long history that came to fruition in the 1930's, were truly "creatively destructive." They had significant repercussions, not only in the field of money, banking, and cycles, but also in other fields, including fiscal policy, taxation, and international trade. The story of how individuals and institutions adapted to this revolution is a fascinating study in intellectual history. Adaptation was not easy; the impact upon individual careers was, in some cases, serious and even pathetic. These developments had a great effect not only upon economics and economists, but also substantively upon the content and process of public policy. They provided an important new body of information regularly available to the public and to policy makers in labor, industry, and agriculture, as well as in government. The inevitable consequence was to make economics and economists operative factors in the problems of the public and private economy, with the result that many more economists have become involved in the world of affairs.

An example of a new subdiscipline in economics is linear programing. Although its impetus came from the needs of the military establishment for criteria for rational planning, the technique is being applied extensively to problems of industrial economics. Other new subdisciplines in economics that have developed mainly since World War II encompass the application of game theory, input-output analysis, regional economic analysis, and the theory and policy of economic development. These various innovations, which have led to important new areas of research and training, are timely examples of the interplay between the needs and problems of the public and private economy on the one hand, and the development of new techniques of analysis and new subdisciplines on the other.

Although the very success of economics has tended to inhibit cooperation in many interdisciplinary programs, several of the new developments have been based on or led to closer cooperation with other disciplines. The increasing use of mathematics and statistics has led to fruitful collaboration by economists with scholars in these fields. It has also led to growing emphasis on mathematics and statistics in the training of students. The renewed interest in economic development, particularly in the underdeveloped countries, has led to cooperation of economists with anthropologists, historians, political scientists, psychologists, and sociologists. In the field of labor economics considerable cooperation has taken place with other social scientists and lawyers.

Developments in psychology also illustrate changes brought about in a discipline as a result of new research techniques and the insistent pressure of practical problems. Important new developments in neurophysiology, in particular the use with animals of the implanted electrode and the microelectrode, have made it possible to correlate neurophysiological phenomena with observed behavior and thus opened up new directions of research in physiological psychology in which psychologists cooperate with zoologists, physiologists, and neuroanatomists. Likewise, the discovery of new tranquilizers and related drugs has led to important research on the relation between the physiological effects of the drugs and observable normal or abnormal behavior. Two other changes within psychology exemplify the extension and expansion of older fields of training and research. The pressing needs for clinical psychologists to deal with problems of disturbed persons in the armed services during World War II induced a substantial expansion of research and training of clinical psychologists. The result has been the rise of new techniques and improvement of old ones for the study of personality and its treatment. The field of industrial psychology has experienced a similar expansion since World War II because of the need for developing improved techniques for the selection, training, and management of personnel at all levels, including top management. Finally, the earlier child psychology, which contented itself with recording ages at which certain behaviors appear, has been replaced by a child psychology infused with newer ideas from studies of the learning process, psychoanalysis, problem solving, concept formation, and other fields.

The proliferation of subdisciplines and the rise of interdisciplinary fields of training and research have raised serious problems for the universities. In order to develop strength in the newly emerging areas of knowledge, they have had to increase the size of their staffs and graduate student enrollment. But few, if any, universities have been able to maintain real strength in all of the newly developing areas in the kaleidoscopic "mosaic" of the social sciences.[9] Consequently, universities have had to specialize. Some have allowed their social science departments to expand strongly in one or two directions. Others have insisted upon more diversification. A common policy is diversification within each of the major disciplines combined with depth in a few of the subdisciplines. As each of the disciplines has developed a body of theory and of research methods, the tendency has been to emphasize the common core in the training programs and in the staffing of departments.

Guiding the direction of the social sciences within a university poses serious administrative problems. An optimum use of limited resources requires some central direction. Much may be accomplished by encouraging related departments to develop complementary or reinforcing strengths. For example, where the economists are strongly interested in economic development, economics, as well as the other disciplines, will gain strength if political science, sociology, psychology, and history are developed in ways that reinforce the interest in economic development. If the administration wishes to maximize the fruitfulness of its resources, it will not relinquish responsibility for choosing areas of strength to the departments. The administration has a special responsibility for nurturing developments that fall between departments and for coordinating the developments of related social science disciplines. Needless to say, this requires the use of the budgetary and appointment processes as tools to implement the university's broad strategy. And this assumes that the administration has some idea of the university's comparative advantages and some philosophy for the university's growth.

In breaking away from moral philosophy and history, the social sciences have placed increasing emphasis upon scientific method and analysis. The role of the scientific element, in contrast to the humanistic, philosophical, and normative elements, varies among the social science disciplines. Psychology and economics have perhaps gone furthest in developing the scientific component; history and political science, perhaps the least. But these are misleading generalizations. Political science, traditionally historical, descriptive, and prescriptive in its orientation, is moving to adopt the various research methods of psychology, sociology, and economics, including mathematical and quantitative techniques, survey methods, and game theory. Moreover, historians, whose methods have long contributed to the other social sciences, are increasingly adopting the concepts and methods of the newer social sciences to their own uses.

At all times, the stimulus of problem solving has played a large role in the social sciences. But in their early stages, especially in the case of economics, political science, and sociology, the formulation of the problem was often biased by inarticulate normative assumptions.[10] As the social sciences have developed, there has been a healthy differentiation between the analytical and the normative, or prescriptive, components, with increasing emphasis on the scientific, or analytical. This has improved our understanding of social processes and social behavior and thereby fostered the development of a truly scientific body of knowledge. But in the process something has been lost, namely, a continuing awareness of the philosophical assumptions of the social sciences and of the significance of the resulting body of knowledge. This loss is particularly apparent in the programs of graduate and undergraduate training which, with their increasing emphasis on technique, often fail to convey a sense of relevance.

The complaint of the loss of relevance is a recurring one. In part it is unjustified. The social sciences are being applied in more and more situations—in industry, education, medicine, government, and many other aspects of modern life. Increasingly, they are being found to be relevant to very practical and pressing problems. The element of truth in the complaint lies rather in two factors. First, with increasing specialization and sophistication, it becomes even more difficult for one person to master enough of the social science disciplines to enable him to feel at ease with any major problem.

Second, as suggested above, the social scientists have increasingly ignored the philosophical and normative foundations of social life. In consequence, the layman faces more and more "scientific" knowledge of social life with less and less guidance to its meaning and significance.

The mounting emphasis on the scientific component of the social sciences has been made possible by the use of new research tools and techniques. As indicated above, several of the social sciences have been affected by the increasing application of mathematics and modern statistical methods.[11] These play an ever-growing part in the training of economists, psychologists, and sociologists. In some departments of political science they are now a regular part of the training. The growth of econometrics, one of the most fashionable and rapidly developing fields in economics, is symptomatic. And mathematical model building is becoming more and more common in several of the other social sciences. Sample surveys have become increasingly significant in political science and sociology, and are being employed in several aspects of economics and social psychology. Game theory is being used by sociologists, political scientists, and economists. The psychologists and sociologists have developed new measurement techniques and new experimental techniques for a wide variety of problems. The computer has proved useful, not only for carrying out elaborate statistical computations which would otherwise be prohibitively expensive but also for simulating human behavior. Cooperation between various fields of learning is facilitated by the tendency of various social scientists to draw on these common research techniques.

The proliferation of tools and techniques of research has tended to shift the emphasis in graduate training from the substantive content of the social sciences toward a study of research methods. As indicated above, this shift explains the growing decline of some traditional training programs and the increased emphasis on research experience as part of the early graduate training experience. In this respect, as in others, graduate training in the social sciences is moving away from the patterns familiar in the humanities and taking on characteristics similar to those of the sciences. This trend has gone far in psychology and sociology; it is noticeable in economics, but is only beginning in history and political science. The anthro-

pologists have long insisted on field work as part of graduate training for many students.

Frequently, the graduate training provides for research training
as part of a group activity.[12] In the Department of Economics at the
University of Chicago the device used is the workshop, in which
persons engaged in similar lines of research work together under
the guidance of a senior professor. More frequently, in psychology
and sociology, the student receives an introduction to research
training as a member of a research team associated with some major
project. Often the project is sponsored by a research center or institute such as the Columbia Bureau of Applied Research, the Michigan Survey Research Center, or the Harvard Social Relations Laboratory. The organizational arrangements differ from one university
to another.

The presence of major social science research projects in the university or some related research institute is largely a post-World
War II phenomenon. The research center serves a useful function
in providing opportunities for graduate training and may offer the
individual faculty member research facilities not easily available
otherwise. Experience indicates, however, that unless the relation
between the related departments and the research facility are carefully planned, and unless the university is willing to assume substantial financial risks, problems may arise. Pressure to give departmental appointments to members of the research staff may create a
teaching faculty without a desirable balance of talents and interest.
And the dependence of the research facility on term contracts and
grants may divert faculty into research not in line with the faculty
members' genuine research interests and may be of little scientific
merit. These problems are not insurmountable; specifically, they
require careful attention by the administrative authorities.

The impact of extra-university institutions on the development
of the social sciences and consequently upon graduate training programs has been significant. Since its establishment in 1924, the Social Science Research Council has played a major role in stimulating and supporting innovations in graduate education and research.[13] Many of the newer developments in the social sciences
have been fostered by the council's research committees which,
today, include committees on agricultural economics, analysis of

economic census data, comparative politics, comparative development behavior, economic growth, economic stability, genetics and behavior, intellective processes research, national security policy research, personality development in youth, simulation of cognitive processes, and urbanization, to mention but a few. In its early years the council was primarily concerned with graduate training programs. More recently, it has done much to explore the problems of training in mathematics for social scientists. Its fellowship programs have sought to strengthen interdisciplinary and multidisciplinary training for both predoctoral and postdoctoral students.

The large foundations have likewise had a major effect on the social sciences through stimulating particular lines of research, underwriting self-study of graduate training programs, and financing graduate fellowships and experiments in graduate training.[14] By their selection of areas of research, universities, and individuals for support, they have had a substantial and, I believe, beneficial effect upon the character and direction of training and research in the social sciences. The major foundations, as well as the Social Science Research Council, have had a major impact on all of the social sciences although the support of history has been less substantial.

The influence of the Federal Government has long been great in the field of agricultural economics and rural sociology. Since World War II it has played an increasingly important though selective role in all of the social sciences.[15] All the social sciences have received some support under title iv of the NDEA. Psychology and some aspects of sociology have received substantial support from the research and training programs of the National Institutes of Health. The more mathematical and quantitative aspects of anthropology, economics, and sociology have been supported by the National Science Foundation. Federal support for political science is in an embryonic stage; and history has, to a large extent, been neglected. The direction of the Federal Government's support of the social sciences reflects in part the problem-solving orientation of Federal support to education and research. But it also reflects the principal concern of the various Federal programs with those aspects of the social sciences most closely related to mathematics and the sciences in contrast to the more politically sensitive aspects of the disciplines.[16]

The selective nature of foundation and Federal support of the social sciences presents the university with serious policy problems. The impact of Federal support on a department of economics illustrates the matter well. Some fields—for example, econometrics and economic development—are generously supported by the Federal Government and foundations, which provide funds for research and summer salaries for faculty and generous financial aid on a twelve-month basis for graduate students. But faculty and students interested in many other fields of economics depend almost entirely on university funds. So far as funds make a difference, this situation tends to divert students and faculty alike from doing what they prefer to do, to doing what an outside group prefers them to do. Moreover, the resulting inequities raise serious problems of morale.

The post-World War II period has seen increasing concern with the cultures of the non-Western (non-Graeco-Roman-European-North American) world. The war itself was a stimulus to this interest. Postwar revolutions in the non-Western world, the cold war, and concern for economic and social development have reinforced this concern. The response of the university world has been the establishment of various area programs. The area program is, of course, but a temporary response to a woeful lack of linguists and historians, a deficiency of library and supporting training resources, and in some cases a difficulty of access to the area under study. The long-run objective is to train sufficient persons in basic linguistic, historical, and cultural aspects of these areas to satisfy the need for personnel with knowledge of these areas for positions in universities and colleges and for the many positions in government, industry, and other agencies of the world of affairs. When this day arrives for any area, there will no longer be a reason for an area program. Area specialists will be infiltrated into the relevant disciplines. Meanwhile, the concern for these "other" areas of the world has broadened the horizons of the university and, particularly in such social sciences as economics and political science, has given a new stimulus and different dimension to comparative studies. It has also given considerable impetus to the study of anthropology. Finally, the concern with the non-Western areas has led to a greater awareness of the preconceptions of much of modern social science and has stimulated various joint, interdisciplinary, or multidisciplinary research and training projects. Although some universities offer the Ph.D. in area studies, this is not generally the case.

Along with the changes in the nature of the social sciences has gone a shift in the types of careers open to graduates of the training programs. No longer are social scientists predominantly concerned with careers in college and university teaching and research. Many opportunities have opened up in government, industry, and private research organizations which are eagerly sought by the very best students, in many cases for long-term careers. Research departments in industry staffed, wholly or in part, with social scientists are becoming increasingly numerous; their staffs include economists, psychologists, sociologists, and, to a more limited extent, anthropologists and political scientists. Private and semiprivate research organizations devoted to defense studies have attracted many social scientists to work in close cooperation with engineers, scientists, and military officers. International organizations and the foreign aid and related agencies of the Federal Government offer similar opportunities as do the more traditional agencies of government, whether Federal, state, or local. Regional development authorities, water conservation authorities, foreign investment agencies are further examples of agencies employing social scientists of various types.

The needs of these various agencies are having a significant impact on university training programs. Generally, social scientists seeking such careers are trained in regular graduate programs. But in some cases, special programs have been developed. For example, programs in clinical psychology have been developed in many universities for training practicing psychologists. Likewise, programs in public administration have been tailored to the needs of those intending to go on to government service, and programs in foreign and international economic development have been established to meet the particular needs of persons training for careers in international economic agencies or in foreign central banks and planning agencies. The creation of such special programs for "operators," or practitioners, raises serious problems for the university that would at the same time protect the integrity of its regular programs for training Ph.D. candidates for careers in research and teaching.

A related development of the last thirty years has been the appointment of social scientists to the staffs of various professional schools. The law schools have long made use of economists in connection with training in corporate law, tax law, labor law, and antitrust law. Political scientists, sociologists, and psychologists have also been added to many law faculties. Schools of business and industrial administration have been drawing upon social scientists. In fact, two recent reports on the training for business careers have emphasized the importance of training in the basic social science disciplines as the core of an ideal educational program.[17] Schools of city and regional planning have added economists, psychologists, and political scientists to their staffs. In a somewhat more limited way, other professional schools, such as nursing and theology, have been experimenting with the appointment of social scientists. This development represents a happy convergence of the interests of the social scientist in research and the professional school in training. It gives promise of enriching the social sciences as well as the professional training programs by providing the social scientists with closer association with the world of affairs and consequently with rich fields for research. Properly fostered, this trend should promote greater communication and cooperation within the university community, and serve thereby as a means for preserving the university concept.

Similarly, social scientists are being called upon as advisers and consultants to private and governmental agencies both here and abroad (a development that has fostered the image of the social scientist as the "professor who is never there"). Much social science research is still best pursued in the laboratory or in the campus library. But the world of affairs, the world of people and of social institutions, is and always will be the true laboratory of the social scientist. Inevitably, more and more research will be carried on away from the campus. Moreover, involvement in the affairs of the world in an advisory or an administrative role for a limited period of time is a useful part of the training of some of our social scientists. Although the resulting absenteeism presents problems to university administrators, in moderation off-campus service increases the social scientist's effectiveness in both teaching and research by providing him with new insights and easier access to his true laboratory. Carried beyond some undefinable limit, absenteeism may reduce his effectiveness both as teacher and researcher.

The social sciences are relatively new disciplines. Most of them have come of age only in the second quarter of the twentieth century. They are in great ferment because of the development of new and refined concepts, new research techniques, and the demands upon them from all sides to aid in the understanding of man and his institutions. These changes are making new demands on the universities and generating many new developments in graduate training. Having come out of the humanities, the social sciences still incorporate in their training programs many of the traditions of the humanities. But increasingly the social sciences are taking on the characteristics of the physical and natural sciences. The needs of the social sciences, however, are unique. Imagination and inventiveness will be required to bring harmony between the dynamics of these disciplines and the principles of the university within which they should flourish.

NOTES

1. Bernard Berelson (ed.), *The Behavioral Sciences Today* (New York: Basic Books, 1963); Daniel Lerner (ed.), *The Human Meaning of the Social Sciences* (New York: Meridian Books, 1959). Two of the best sources of information on developments in the social sciences over the last forty years are the *Annual Reports* of the Social Science Research Council and, for the last sixteen years, *Items,* the quarterly publication of the council. For the earlier history of the social sciences, see "Introduction, Part II: The Social Sciences as Disciplines," *Encyclopedia of the Social Sciences,* I, 231–349.
2. Alfred L. Kroeber (ed.), *Anthropology Today: An Encyclopedic Inventory* (Chicago: University of Chicago Press, 1953); *Some Uses of Anthropology: Theoretical and Applied* (Washington: Anthropological Society of Washington, 1956).
3. For developments in economics, see Howard R. Bowen, *Graduate Education in Economics, American Economic Review,* September 1953, Part 2; *Graduate Training in Economics: A Report on Panel Discussions at Yale* (New Haven, Conn.: Yale University, 1956).
4. For research and graduate training in history, see Dexter Perkins, John L. Snell, and others, *The Education of Historians in the United States* (New York: McGraw-Hill Book Co., 1962); *The Social Sciences in Historical Study,* Social Science Research Council *Bulletin* 64 (New York: The Council, 1954).
5. For research and graduate training in political science, see Harold D. Lasswell, *The Future of Political Science* (New York: Atherton Press, 1963); also Committee on Standards of Instruction of the American Political Science Association, "Political Science as a Discipline," *American Political Science Review,* June 1962, pp. 417–21; Robert Dahl, "The Behavioral Approach in Political Science: Epitaph for a Monument to a Successful Protest," *American Political Science Review,* December 1961, pp. 763–72; Dwight Waldo, *Political Science in the United States* (Paris: Unesco, 1956).
6. Ann Roe (ed.), *Graduate Education in Psychology: Report of a Conference*

184   *John Perry Miller*

Held at Miami Beach 1958 (Washington: American Psychological Association, 1959); also "Education for Research in Psychology: Report of a Seminar Held at Estes Park," *American Psychologist*, April 1959, pp. 167–79.

7. See Elbridge Sibley, *The Education of Sociologists in the United States* (New York: Russell Sage Foundation, 1963); also Robert K. Merton and others (eds.), *Sociology Today: Problems and Prospects* (New York: Basic Books, 1959); Hans L. Zetterberg, *Sociology in the United States of America* (Paris: Unesco, 1956).

8. These statistics are based on *Doctorate Production in United States Universities, 1920–1962* (Washington: National Academy of Sciences–National Research Council, 1963).

9. See Robert K. Merton, "The Mosaic of the Behavioral Sciences," in Berelson, *The Behavioral Sciences Today*, pp. 247–72.

10. For discussion of the ideological biases of economic theory, see O. H. Taylor, *Economics and Liberalism* (Cambridge, Mass.: Harvard University Press, 1955), especially chaps. 4 and 9. For discussion of the application of social sciences to problem solving, see Daniel Lerner and Harold D. Lasswell (eds.), *The Policy Sciences: Recent Developments in Scope and Method* (Stanford, Calif.: Stanford University Press, 1951).

11. James C. Charlesworth (ed.), *Mathematics and the Social Sciences: The Utility and Inutility of Mathematics in the Study of Economics, Political Science, and Sociology* (Philadelphia: American Academy of Political and Social Science, 1963); William G. Madow, "Activities of the Committee on Mathematical Training of Social Scientists, 1952–57, and Suggestions for the Future," Social Science Research Council *Items*, December 1957, pp. 44–47.

12. Paul F. Lazarsfeld and others, *Observations on Organized Social Research in the United States: A Report to the International Social Science Council* (Mimeographed; New York: 1961).

13. See Social Science Research Council, *Annual Reports*.

14. See the *Annual Reports* of the Carnegie Corporation of New York, the Ford Foundation, and the Rockefeller Foundation.

15. On the effects of the Federal Government on higher education in general and the social sciences in particular, see Harold Orlans, *The Effects of Federal Programs on Higher Education: A Study of 36 Universities and Colleges* (Washington: Brookings Institution, 1962), especially pp. 95–99; Homer D. Babbidge, Jr., and Robert M. Rosenzweig, *The Federal Interest in Higher Education* (New York: McGraw-Hill Book Co., 1962); "Twenty-six Campuses and the Federal Government," *Educational Record*, April 1963, pp. 95–136.

16. Harry Alpert, "The Social Sciences and the National Science Foundation, 1945–1955," *American Sociological Review*, December 1955, pp. 653–61.

17. Robert Aaron Gordon and James Edwin Howell, *Higher Education for Business* (New York: Columbia University Press, 1959); Frank C. Pierson and others, *The Education of American Businessmen* (New York: McGraw-Hill Book Co., 1959).

New Trends in Graduate Study in the Humanities

GUSTAVE O. ARLT

I
T IS both fitting and humiliating that a discussion of humanistic
studies in our day almost inevitably begins in a defensive, not to
say apologetic, tone: fitting, because the humanities today occupy a
most equivocal position in the academic galaxy; humiliating, because they once were the vital force that exercised spiritual and intellectual leadership which, somewhere in the last century, they either lost or abdicated. These are blunt, perhaps even harsh, words
but they inevitably constitute the background against which the
present status of humanistic studies must be assessed and from
which a more hopeful future may be projected. To sketch in the
broad outlines of this background it is essential to look briefly at
the history of higher education since the Middle Ages. For the
structure and much of the content of higher education in the Western world comes to us as a heritage of the cultural upheaval of the
Renaissance and the concomitant intellectual movement known as
Humanism.

The medieval pre-Renaissance centers of learning, chartered by
the Church and recognized as self-governing bodies by the secular
authorities, had, by the fifteenth century, developed a stabilized
curriculum common to all of them. The university consisted of four
faculties, or, as we would say today, of four separate schools or colleges. These, in order of importance, were the faculties of theology,

GUSTAVE O. ARLT (Ph.D., Chicago) is president of the Council of
Graduate Schools of the United States. Formerly he was graduate dean
and professor of German at the University of California at Los Angeles.
Dr. Arlt has been a leader in the effort to establish a National Humanities
Foundation.

185

philosophy, law, and medicine. Again, without laboring the comparison, we would say that the university consisted of three professional schools while the faculty of philosophy is analogous to our
college of liberal arts. Indeed our term is literally translated from
their designation *artes liberales*. These were seven in number:
grammar, logic, and rhetoric—the triple road to eloquence—and
music, arithmetic, geometry, and astronomy—the quadruple road to
knowledge. The faculty of philosophy was designed to provide students with a "liberal" education; the professional faculties trained
them for the three learned professions.

At this point the similarity between the medieval university and
its later counterpart abruptly ends. The former was dedicated to
the preservation and dissemination of knowledge. The creation of
new knowledge was not its business. Indeed, the creation of new
knowledge was a perilous exercise and he who engaged in it was in
danger of crossing the thin line between orthodoxy and heresy. As a
result, the medieval university was a static institution and its teaching was strictly traditional. The student learned what the teacher
had in turn learned from his teacher. There was nothing to add.
Therefore teacher and student alike could live and work with the
comforting thought that the limits of knowledge are finite, that
with sufficient diligence one could know everything that was worth
knowing. There were no problems, no differences of opinion, for all
controversial questions had long ago been answered by the axio-
matic dicta of Holy Writ and of the Church Fathers. It is no wonder
that the medieval university became sterile and that its most exalted intellectual exercise took the form of endless debates on hypo-
thetical topics of dogma.

The second half of the fifteenth century brought with it the
discovery—or perhaps only the rediscovery—of a great body of long-
forgotten literature, first Roman and Greek, later Hebrew. Obviously these writings were heretical and subversive and had no
place in the authoritarian medieval university. Nevertheless, small
groups of adventurous men, first in Italy, later in France and Germany, found a new world of learning thrown open to them in these
ancient works on mathematics, philosophy, and natural sciences,
and they began to study them, at first surreptitiously, then openly.
They banded themselves together and called themselves "Human-

ists" to indicate their preoccupation with all that is human in con-tradistinction to the Scholastics with their calcified book learning. They soon found the existing universities too confining for their interests—or perhaps too dangerous for their heresies—and estab-lished the first Humanistic university at Padua, soon to be followed by those at Prague, Heidelberg, and elsewhere.

The Humanistic university inherited the structure and organiza-tion of the medieval, church-established institutions and kept the four traditional faculties—theology, law, medicine, and philosophy. But it expanded the curriculum, particularly in the latter, to in-clude the new disciplines—the ancient languages and the Latin, Greek, and Hebrew classics, the history and philosophy, the poetry and drama, the religions and legal systems of these ancient peoples. Into the medical faculty it introduced Hippocratic medicine and into the legal faculty Roman law on a par with canon law. Profes-sors of law and medicine were Humanists as much as were their colleagues in philosophy. Thus Humanism and Humanistic studies eventually permeated the entire university and brought about significant changes not only in the content but in the philosophy of higher education. *In the postmedieval university, from the Renais-sance to the nineteenth century, Humanism was not a discipline, not a field of study, it was the heart and soul of the university, it was a way of life.*

While the Humanistic university retained much of the structure of its medieval predecessor, it broke sharply with authoritarian Scholasticism and its rigid system of *a priori* deductive logic. The Humanists had no desire to overthrow the authority of the Church; in fact their most distinguished leaders—Erasmus, Reuchlin, and Beatus Rhenanus—actively opposed the reformatory movements of Luther and Calvin. Nevertheless, it was inevitable that their intro-duction of the empirical method of arriving at the truth should come into violent conflict with the dialectical method of reasoning and instruction.

The bitter feud between the Humanists and Scholastics ended about 1510 with the complete defeat of the latter and with the firm establishment of empiricism as the primary means of extending the frontiers of knowledge. This is without a doubt the most significant contribution of Humanism, for it opened the way not only to free inquiry in the realm of human affairs but also to observation and experimentation in the realm of the natural sciences. The acceptance of empirical methods had another far-reaching result, the full effects of which were not to become apparent until much later. It broke the philosophical faculty into two distinct areas, natural philosophy and moral philosophy. The former concerned itself primarily with the physical world and eventually developed into the four basic natural sciences—chemistry, physics, biology, and geology, although these actual terms did not come into use until much later. The concerns of the moral philosopher, on the other hand, were the more abstract disciplines of the mind—philosophy in the restrictive sense, ethics, esthetics, history and its allied subjects.

In the ensuing three centuries the structure of the European university changed very little, if at all. A gradual sharpening of dividing lines between disciplines becomes evident and with it a slowly growing tendency toward specialization. There is also evidence that the natural philosophers tended to separate their creative activities from their teaching, if any. The great advances of science in the seventeenth and eighteenth centuries took place almost entirely outside the universities. Johann Kepler, René Descartes, and Isaac Newton were humanistically educated natural philosophers who pursued their scientific studies privately. Gottfried Leibnitz discovered integral calculus but lectured on moral philosophy. In the eighteenth century, Joseph Black, who proposed the theory of latent heat, and Henry Cavendish, the discoverer of the composition of water and nitric acid, were English gentlemen of leisure. Joseph Priestley, the discoverer of oxygen, was a clergyman, and Antoine Lavoisier, who invented the chemical nomenclature in use to this day, died on the guillotine as an aristocrat.

By the beginning of the nineteenth century the European universities—and the few then existing in America—might be described in this way: They were primarily training schools for the three learned professions—theology, law, medicine. Natural philosophy had achieved its division into the four basic sciences, and the old common name was fast disappearing. But the role of the sciences was a distinctly secondary one, and they were tolerated rather than fostered in the academic scene. Humanistic studies, by virtue of three centuries of tradition, survived and held the position of prestige in the university, but they were showing signs of splintering and fragmentation into particularistic and even competing disciplines. In the German universities particularly, and elsewhere under their influence, research and also teaching in the humanistic fields were becoming more and more highly specialized. Humanism (with a capital H) and the Renaissance ideal of the Whole Man were fast disappearing.

Engineering and other aspects of technology, industrial and applied arts, and even the fine arts had not yet made their appearance in the universities. Institutes for higher technical education and for the advancement of technology were developed outside the universities and were generally regarded as inferior to them. The first degrees ever awarded in engineering in any English-speaking country were conferred by Rensselaer Polytechnic Institute in Troy, New York, in 1835. The first chair in engineering in England was established in 1838 at King's College of the University of London, and Cambridge did not follow until 1878.

This, then, was the university in which the epigonists of Humanism flourished in the late eighteenth and in the early nineteenth century and in which humanistic scholarship produced works which, by any standard, must be described as monumental. To name only a few, there were the philosophical systems erected by David Hume, Immanuel Kant, Johann Fichte, Georg Hegel, Friedrich Schelling, not to forget Henry and William James and perhaps John Dewey. There were the fundamental historical writings of Edward Gibbon, George Bancroft, and Theodor Mommsen. Cultural anthropology is represented by Thomas Percy, Johann Herder, and Francis James Child. Finally there are such polyhistorians as Jacob and Wilhelm Grimm whose far-ranging erudition filled volumes on such diverse subjects as mythology, legal history, folklore, and linguistics. All these and many others that should be named are works on a grand scale, concerned with fundamental concepts of Western civilization and endowed with validity and permanence far beyond the decades or even the centuries that produced them. They represent a flowering of humanistic creativity on a scale that the twentieth century—so far—cannot rival. This is not to call the past fifty years barren or to minimize the quality of what they have produced—the new philosophical concepts of Bertrand

Russell, Karnap, and Reichenbach; the great definitive editions of Chaucer, Luther, and Goethe; the folklore studies of Antti Aarne, Wesselski, and Archer Taylor. The existence of these works and of the men who wrote them gives the assurance that the spirit of humanistic scholarship lives and flourishes in spite of external and internal adversities.

The first major impetus for the development of science and technology in American universities came from the original Morrill Act of 1862 which provided for Federal aid to agriculture and the mechanic arts in the land-grant colleges. But even with this and subsequent more substantial support, the acceptance of science and technology in these institutions was a slow and discouraging process. It took half a century for the sciences to establish a firm beachhead in the erstwhile humanistic university and another twenty-five years for them to consolidate their position. But even while the sciences were still struggling for recognition within the academic hierarchy, their impact upon humanistic studies made itself felt. With astonishment and admiration the humanist observed the effectiveness of the research techniques of the sciences and the satisfaction that comes with measurable and demonstrable results. He can hardly be criticized for trying to adopt and adapt the analytical, empirical techniques that served the natural scientists so well and with such reliable results. And he could scarcely have foreseen the ruinous effect of these techniques on humanistic scholarship unless he had perceived with great clarity that the scientist deals with facts and the humanist with values and judgments.

It would be difficult, perhaps impossible, to prove that the rapid development and growing prestige of the natural sciences played a major role in the final great blow to the humanities: the secession of the social sciences from the humanistic orbit. On the other hand, it would be equally difficult to believe that this was not the case. Remembering that the social sciences are the offspring of moral philosophy, we might reasonably expect that their disciplines would collectively be called "social philosophy." It almost seems as though the term "social sciences" is intended to imply their consanguinity with the natural sciences and to abnegate their affinity with the humanities. ("Deny thy father and refuse thy name . . . and I'll no longer be a Capulet.") At any rate, the social sciences, originally economics, political science, and sociology, use the techniques of the sciences with a good deal of success.

The secession of the social sciences left a confused, not to say chaotic, situation in the residuary area of disciplines that we now imprecisely designate as the "humanities." "The fact is," writes Charles Blitzer,[1] "that there is no convenient and simple way to define this word, although it is possible to elicit fairly substantial agreement on a list of the disciplines that are included within the humanities." Even the last part of this statement is open to question. Carmichael[2] quotes a dictionary definition without source, defining the humanities as "The branches of learning concerned with human thought and relations, as distinguished from the sciences." This definition not only begs the question but is equally applicable to the social sciences. The long current edition of *Webster's New Collegiate Dictionary* defined the humanities briefly and impudently, as "the branches of polite learning, esp. the ancient classics and belles-lettres."

The American Council of Learned Societies, in its announcement of fellowship programs in the humanities, states, "The fields of specialization included in them are: philosophy (including the philosophy of law and science) ; aesthetics; philology, languages, literature, and linguistics; archaeology; art history and musicology; history (including the history of science, law, and religions) ; cultural anthropology; and folklore." This is a good useful listing for practical purposes, and none of the disciplines named would be likely to disclaim membership since it betokens fellowship support. But it does not reveal the fact that there are gray areas about which there is no complete agreement. There are many historians, for example, who prefer to think of themselves as social scientists, and, indeed, in many universities that divide their liberal arts colleges into the convenient four divisions, history is carried in the division of social sciences. Thirty-odd years ago, when the University of Chicago first instituted the divisional system, the members of the history department were permitted to choose their allegiance, with the result that half of them became social scientists and half humanists. And even today this university lists history in both the Division of the Humanities and the Division of the Social Sciences.

Similarly, the social scientists sometimes lay claim to philosophy and, with respect at least to some of its areas, with justification. Ethics, for example, is an area of philosophy, but since it treats of man's relation with his fellow-man, it may properly be a social science. On the other hand, anthropology, sister-german of sociology, should certainly be classed as a social science. But when it concerns itself—as it currently does—with archeology, with the religions, mythologies, and folklore of primitive peoples, with their languages and even with abstract linguistics, it comes dangerously close to returning to the humanistic field.

No one, so far, has questioned the humanistic character of studies in language and literature, although the inevitable linking of the two words has never been quite clear. Language as a medium of communication—not as a subject of research—is simply a tool which one must learn to use. Language as a subject of research—historical, structural, or semasiological—comes very close to being an exact science. Literature is the precipitate of the human spirit, the distillate of man's faith and doubt, hope and fear, joy and grief, in short, all that is human and humane. Historically, nevertheless, the two basically incompatible yoke fellows have been linked together with no great profit to either. Any graduate department of Romance—or Germanic—languages and literature is composed of two kinds of people who have little in common and nothing to communicate to each other. Yet they are solidly married with no prospect of divorce.

In the latter part of the nineteenth century the linguists began to learn the use of the techniques of science for their discipline. They found that by the collection and collation of innumerable examples they could create a body of factual knowledge from which hypotheses, theories, and conclusions could be drawn that were susceptible of scientific proof. Jacob Grimm, as a forerunner of the new science, discovered Grimm's law of phonetics which is as sound as any law of physics. In 1875 a Danish philologist, Karl Verner, added a second law of phonetics explaining the apparent exceptions to Grimm's law. In 1890 a German, Eduard Sievers, on the basis of an Anglo-Saxon manuscript fragment, postulated the existence of an Old Saxon original from which the former was translated. Five years later his analytical technique was vindicated when the original was actually found in the Vatican Library.

Today the scientific method of language study has been brought to a state of high development in our graduate schools. In several of them computer techniques are being used with great success. The project of the "American Dialect Atlas," for example, is progressing rapidly. Just as in the natural sciences, applied research and development generally follow basic research, so linguistic research is now being pushed into the area of machine translation and linguists are working with mathematicians in the computer centers of universities.

The National Defense Education Act singled out the study and teaching of languages for particular consideration and favor. Under the various sections of title VI, it provided language institutes for the improvement of secondary school teachers; language and area centers for the study of "neglected" languages; graduate fellowships for the study of certain "critical" languages; and, finally, a language research program to promote pure and applied research in the complex procedures by which languages are taught and learned.

There is no question that title VI has had a tremendous impact on the study of modern foreign languages from the secondary schools through the graduate schools. Foreign language enrollments in the public secondary schools in 1960 increased by 44.5 percent over 1958. The percentage of public high schools offering at least one foreign language increased from 44 percent in 1955 to 61.8 percent in 1961. The number of applications from teachers to attend language institutes each year far exceeds the number of openings. For 1962–63, 19,204 applications were received for 4,418 available places in institutes.

The number of language and area centers for the study of neglected languages increased from 19 in 1959 to 55 in 1963. In the same year 1,006 graduate students in 59 universities were awarded fellowships for the study of 55 different languages. Of the total 8,733 graduate students enrolled in courses in neglected languages throughout the country in 1962, more than 5,500 had begun their studies as undergraduates. Moreover, more than 75 public high schools are now offering Mandarin and between 500 and 600 offer

Russian. This vastly increased activity in the foreign languages on the secondary and undergraduate levels is creating an unprecedented demand for qualified teachers which, in turn, is reflected in the graduate schools.

The humane scholar who has long regarded the American neglect of foreign languages—not to say aversion to them—as a symptom of provincialism and a rejection of cultural values cannot help but feel satisfaction in this sudden renascence of language studies. But his pleasure is clouded by the uneasy question, is this really a revival of the humanistic spirit or is it a pragmatic movement in the name of that overworked motive, national defense? There can be no doubt that these two words are the key to the Federal coffers from which the funds in support of these studies flow and that no other key could have unlocked them. Any lingering hope that the Congress had suddenly developed humanistic leanings must be dispelled by the Educational Facilities Act of 1963 which provides Federal money for buildings and equipment for engineering, mathematics, physical sciences, and modern foreign languages. This categorization makes it quite clear that the foreign languages have been admitted to the charmed circle of disciplines essential to national security, with all the rights and privileges thereto appertaining.

It is too early, of course, to judge what impact the new status of the foreign languages will have on the study of literature. One may speculate that out of the large numbers of students who are already enrolling in language courses, a fair percentage will eventually be drawn into the study of literature, and the net result for the shrinking humanities would be advantageous. On the other hand, one might easily foresee the ultimate divorce of language from literature, first on practical grounds, later rationalized into philosophic reasons, just as political science divorced itself from history, business administration from economics, or, more recently, speech from English. This would presumably result in a further erosion of the complex of disciplines now defined as humanistic. One is reminded of the fact that mathematics (arithmetic and geometry) was originally a part of the old humanistic quadrivium, then, along with astronomy, became a sort of associate member of the division of physical sciences, and eventually reached a category of its own defying conventional classification.

It is not unlikely that language science will finally separate itself from the broader complex that was once called "language arts." Thus philology and linguistics, with their subdivisions of morphology, semantics, historical and comparative grammar, and so forth, which effectively employ both empirical and theoretic methods of research, would receive logical recognition of their particular character. Whether they can then still lay claim to membership in the humanistic disciplines or whether they will lead an autonomous and lone existence like mathematics, is a question that will be answered fifty years from now.

Among the newer encouraging developments in the humane fields is the strong trend toward interdisciplinary study and the growing acceptance of interdisciplinary degrees. Some twenty-five or thirty years ago the first feeble attempts were made to secure recognition for programs leading to degrees in comparative literature. These attempts generally were impeded by the rigidity of departmental lines and departmental requirements. Departments of English, French, German, or Italian professed willingness to entertain dissertations in comparative literature but each insisted upon its pound of flesh in the form of the full requirements of its Ph.D. program. The few hardy individuals who survived this ordeal found themselves at the end with a degree for which there was no ready market.

During World War II a sudden need developed for persons with at least a nodding acquaintance with the regions in which the Armed Forces were engaged. This need was met by the establishment of so-called area studies, in which the language, geography, history, economics, and even a little literature of a country or a region were intensively studied. Area study programs, all on the undergraduate level, mushroomed on large and small campuses, largely subsidized by Federal funds. Their graduates proved the worth of these programs—and showed up their weaknesses—in many countries of Europe, Asia, and Africa.

It is interesting to note that a wartime exigency achieved what years of peaceful discussion in faculty meetings had not done. It proved that sacrosanct departmental lines could be crossed without destroying the integrity of the disciplines and that reasonable breadth and reasonable depth were not necessarily incompatible.

After the war many of the area programs became fixtures, adjusted to a less frenetic pace. Cautious experiments were made to expand them to the graduate—master's degree—level. By the mid-1950's a number of them had grown into "study centers" or "institutes." Some now have programs leading to the Ph.D. degree, and a few are even sought by postdoctoral scholars. Today there is scarcely an area in the world that is not represented by graduate programs in several universities. Moreover, their graduates find a ready market for their degrees. Specialists in African studies, for example, are in such short supply and long demand that it is hard to keep track of them as they move from one high bidder to another. Doctoral degree holders in American studies are in greater demand at the moment than doctors in conventional American literature.

One of the commendable by-products of the weakening of departmental lines has been the great burgeoning of folklore studies. Twenty-five years ago there was no professor of folklore in the United States, no university in which a degree in folklore could be earned. There were, to be sure, a few notable scholars who had achieved international reputations by their folklore publications. But they were professors of English or of German and they gave their courses almost surreptitiously to avoid the wrath of departmental budget-makers. The struggle, frustrations, and final victory of these lone scholars and their few loyal allies to achieve recognition for a humane discipline that had been regarded in Europe for more than a century not only as respectable but distinguished, will make interesting reading some day when the history of humane studies in the United States is written.

After World War II, in the wake of the area studies, a few of the leading universities timidly initiated interdepartmental programs leading to the master's degree in folklore. These generally involved at most the departments of English, various foreign languages, anthropology, and perhaps archeology. It was not until the late 1950's that the first folklore institutes were established. There are still not many today but a few have already achieved high distinction. Best of all, they now cut across the lines of a dozen or more departments, typically including, besides those previously mentioned, art, history, linguistics, music, philosophy, psychology, and theater arts.

Merely as a bizarre footnote, it is worth noting that in 1960 the

Congress specifically designated folklore, along with classics and ancient history, as disciplines not eligible for support from Federal funds.

In the field of history—a humane study, not a social science—the trend toward interdisciplinary collaboration is also apparent. Of course, the history of culture, law, medicine, religion, and science has long been regarded as falling within the purview of history proper. (Curiously, the history of education and philosophy, not to mention art, literature, and music, has generally been delegated to the subject disciplines.) However, again probably as a result of rigid departmentalization, historians, with few notable exceptions, have generally confined themselves to the study and writing of military and political history. This is hard to understand, since history, of all academic disciplines, is—or rather should be—the most universal. History is not a subject discipline, although unfortunately teachers often try to make it such. History is a technique, a method of study of all things past. If Emerson is right, that "There is properly no History; only Biography," or Carlyle, "History is the essence of innumerable biographies," then indeed nothing is outside the historian's domain.

In recent years, in some of the major universities, doctoral dissertations on the history of law, science, and technology have appeared with some frequency. At one university, a dissertation of monumental size on "The History of Industrial Design" was jointly sponsored by a committee of professors of archeology, art, engineering, and history. At least two universities have made joint appointments in their schools of medicine and history departments to facilitate research in medical history. Joint appointments between law and history or law and political science are becoming quite common. This gradual loosening of the structure of strict departmentalization—a process which has been going on in the physical and biological sciences for some years—will be increasingly advantageous for the humanities. It will restore their character of universality without which humanistic research must degenerate into arid, particularistic pedantry.

This brief overview of the state and prospects of some of the humane fields would hardly give a clear picture without some mention of the fine arts and their relation to the humanities. The previously cited announcement by the American Council of Learned Societies includes art history and musicology in the fields of specialization labeled as humanistic, but it does not include the creative aspects of the arts—musical composition, painting, sculpture—nor does it specifically mention theatrical history or theory. The inclusion of art, music, theater arts, and dance in the university structure is a peculiarly American development and a fairly recent one at that. Europe has traditionally segregated the fine arts in state-supported academies of music and of arts. The American counterparts of these in the nineteenth century were without exception privately supported and were, therefore, subject to the vagaries of economic cycles and the whims of donors. As more and more of these academies closed their doors, the task of educating teachers of music and of art for the public schools fell to the universities. Out of this relatively modest operation, usually confined to the school or college of education, departments of art, music, and theater arts burgeoned in practically all public and, more recently, also in private universities.

As long as these departments restricted themselves to the undergraduate level and to the education of teachers, their relation to the total university was comfortable and happy. But when they inevitably expanded to the graduate level, uneasy questions about their academic respectability could not be avoided. Over the past twenty-five years, practically every major university in America went through a long period of soul-searching trying to justify doctoral degrees in composition or in painting, or the appointment of a distinguished composer or painter who himself had no graduate degree. The adjustment has not been easy to achieve and required good will and understanding on both sides, but it has now, generally, been achieved. The fine arts departments have, for the most part, agreed that the Ph.D. degree should be reserved for the areas that involve substantial research—history of art, music, and theater, musicology, dramaturgy, esthetics. On the other hand, advanced work in creativity or performance leads to the Doctor of Musical Arts or the Master of Fine Arts, the latter being, like the doctorate, a three-year program.

In this year 1965 there are at least a dozen highly distinguished schools or colleges of fine arts in our universities and several dozen more that are good or better. They have more than adequately replaced the defunct conservatories and art schools in the preparation of teachers and performers of the arts. They train, side by side, creative practitioners and scholars of theory. Perhaps most importantly, they have given new life to the American theater when it was not moribund but actually dead and buried. It lives and breathes today not in the commercial hothouse on Broadway but on a hundred university campuses.

There can be no doubt that the development of distinguished work in the fine arts has greatly strengthened the humanities. It has not only added new areas of study but has also added new and stimulating colleagues. It provides opportunity for the humanistic scholar to discuss his theories with the creative artist who translates the theories into visual or auditory experiences. For the product of the artist's creativity is the material for the humane scholar's research. In fact, it seems almost absurd to try to draw a sharp line between the humanist and the artist. The one deals a little more with the intellect, the other a little more with the emotions. But the intellectual and emotional elements are present in the work of both. They both differ from the scientist whose ultimate objective is fact, whereas the humanist's and artist's objective is value and judgment. Thus in a very real sense, the fine arts should be, and therefore are, included in this examination of the humanistic disciplines.

Although a review of the humanities in the American university in 1965 shows many encouraging signs of progress, of new approaches and techniques, and of healthy interdisciplinary cooperation, it cannot truly be said that all is well with the humanities. There is a pervasive spirit of uncertainty and insecurity, almost a sense of futility. There is an uneasy feeling, especially among younger scholars, that contemporary materialistic society neither needs nor wants the contribution that the humanist makes. Above all, the humanist feels himself overshadowed by the natural scientist and even by the social scientist who has learned to copy the other's techniques. As a result he feels himself reduced to second-class citizenship, if not in the academic community, then in the community at large. He sees honors and material rewards showered on his colleague in the sciences while he explains to the P.T.A. why it is important to write a commentary on Proust.

Much has been written and said in the last few years about the growing imbalance in the universities resulting from the vast Federal subsidies poured into the natural sciences as contrasted with the pittances expended on the humanities. It is indeed true that such imbalance exists and it is likewise true that it has a destructive effect on the humanities. Any scientist worth his salt can get a complete Federal subsidy for his research, including a staff of research assistants. The humanist has no comparable source of funds. Any science student who is qualified for admission to graduate school is assured of a fellowship, traineeship, or research assistantship. The best that a student in the humanities can hope for is a teaching assistantship, for which he renders at least ten hours per week service. It is little wonder that it takes him twice as long to attain his degree.

Early in 1963, the American Council of Learned Societies, the Council of Graduate Schools in the United States, and the United Chapters of Phi Beta Kappa jointly sponsored the establishment of a Commission on the Humanities, "to consider the state of the humanities in America and to report its findings and recommendations to the sponsoring organizations." This commission, composed of twenty distinguished persons in the fields of education, science, industry, and business filed its report and recommendations in May 1964, supported by individual statements from twenty-four learned societies.[3] The commission recommended the establishment by the President and Congress of the United States of a National Humanities Foundation, to develop and promote a broadly conceived policy of support for the humanities, the arts, and those aspects of social science that have humanistic content and employ humanistic methods. The recommendations include specific details regarding fellowships, scholarships, training and travel grants, summer and full-year institutes for teachers, support for libraries, and so forth.

There is no doubt that substantial subsidies would be beneficial to the humanities. They would attract more and better students. They would stimulate the quantity and perhaps even quality of the research productivity of scholars. They might restore the humanist to a place of esteem in the community and they might even restore his self-esteem. But let no one delude himself that the lack of money is the root of all evil in the humanities or that money alone can cure all ills. The process of erosion of the humanities began long before educational and research subsidies were available to anyone. It began when the humanist fell prey to the blandishments of dialectic materialism. It began when the humanist forgot that his responsibility is to interpret the past to the present and the present to itself, to make the whole of contemporary civilization accessible, *in fact to help give civilization its purpose and direction.*

When the humanist recognizes, faces, and lives up to that responsibility—and a fearful responsibility it is—then and only then will the humanities regain the spiritual and intellectual leadership which they once held.

NOTES

1. "Commission on the Humanities" [Cosponsored by the American Council of Learned Societies, the Council of Graduate Schools, and the United Chapters of Phi Beta Kappa], Staff Paper #1 (Washington: May 1963).
2. Oliver Carmichael, *Graduate Education: A Critique and a Program* (New York: Harper & Bros., 1961), p. 74.
3. *Report of the Commission on the Humanities* (New York: American Council of Learned Societies, 1964).

New Trends in Graduate Study in the Biological Sciences

W. GORDON WHALEY

B EFORE describing the graduate student aspiring to become
a biologist as he is today, let me prepare the background by
drawing a contrasting picture of his professional ancestor from my
own graduate student days. The gap represented is about a quarter
of a century.

Most of my own professors brought to biological science a basic
preparation ranging from the classics to physics and intense personal interests as far apart as music and theology. They shared a common concern for the world to which Linnaeus had given structure
and Darwin had given a sense of continuous change. The majority
of them were observers, cataloguers, and categorizers, and their purpose was to absorb and then to transmit to their students the vast
body of accumulating knowledge of organisms which, if properly
ordered, would let them, after some years, reveal some new relationships or some new organisms or some new stage in a life cycle.
Their most important tool, an apochromatic light microscope, was
a superior instrument to one which can be purchased today (despite
the fact that many new advances in microscopy have been made),
and they learned to use it with great effectiveness. They were aware
of the developments in the physical sciences of their day, aware too

W. GORDON WHALEY (Ph.D., Columbia) has served as dean of the
Graduate School of the University of Texas since 1957. He has been a
member of the Texas Department of Botany since 1946. Under his direction the *Graduate Journal* has become an influential scholarly magazine.
He has had important committee assignments for the Association of Graduate Schools, the Council of Graduate Schools, and the American Council
on Education.

that the pace of development in this kindred field was quickening. The great advances in physical science that have made analyses of the processes of life possible, however, were still in the future. Darwin, on one side, and some distinguished literary agnostics not withstanding on the other, these men worshipped the Lord with the certainty of their forebears of the late nineteenth century, thanked Him for a magnificently varied world, and fully expected that when they came to understand the character of its orderliness, the basic problems of life would be solved.

Their complacence was, however, beginning to be disturbed by the emergence of a minority group, a group increasingly interested in the now rapidly developing physical sciences. This minority had strong interests in the functioning of organisms, in analytical methods, in quantitative relationships, in experiments frankly patterned after those in the physical sciences. They looked upon organisms or populations or communities of organisms as models that could be analyzed, taken apart, and perhaps put together differently.

Ironically perhaps, the traditional habit of dividing life into tight categories had led to a division of biologists into two groups designated, in an oversimplification, vitalists and mechanists. Even then, however, there was a vague general awareness that the facts of life were not that simple, despite the hope of the vitalists that understanding order among organisms would supply the answers and the conviction of the mechanists that analysis of the parts or processes would do so. If biological science has learned a single paramount fact in the past quarter of a century, it is that life is indeed more complex than it once seemed.

Before I leave my old professors let me give them due credit for some matters of great concern that my graduate students ignore or are too impatient to contend with. First, they were literate. They spoke English and understood it. They wrote papers that employed appropriate scientific terminology, but did not require the reader to know highly professional jargon. Second, even if they were mechanists, they looked upon organisms as unified unfolding wholes of some sort—a view vastly different from the attitude that either an assembly of parts or knowing enough about the DNA molecule (see below) will provide ultimate answers to almost everything. If they could return, these older biologists would be pleased that many of the questions which intrigued them have been answered. Yet in a population of biologists ten times as large as their own, they would have to search far to find one capable of using language that would explain these matters clearly. Let me add only that these professors were clean-shaven descendants of fully bearded ancestors. If the new biologist is bearded, one can almost be sure it is because he feels impelled to conform to the current concept of nonconformity rather than follow his own convictions, independent of his ancestors.

A new day has come in biology. Those who were once in the majority have become a minority—defensive, puzzled, and not infrequently resentful. A few of them, of course, are slowly picking up new approaches and techniques. Basically they are still dedicated to the amassing and ordering of knowledge of the whole organic world as the aim of graduate education as contrasted to the analysis of the functional processes of organisms.

Those once in the minority have now become the dominant group in biology, thanks in part to advances in the physical sciences, to some hard self-training on the part of a few of them, and, in no small measure, to some only partially intended effects of the project method of support generally used by agencies of the Federal Government and imitated nearly everywhere else. This group, often termed the "problem-solvers," with interests in such discrete studies as one stage of intermediary metabolism or the action of one particular gene, comprises the individuals who can most easily command both the attention of the better students and the support of the granting agencies.

In the 1960's most biological science groups, no matter how they are formally subdivided, into botany, microbiology, and zoology, or into taxonomy, genetics, physiology, etc., are in fact split by a formidable schism between those once in the majority, now the underdogs—the observers—and the now dominant and dominating problem-solvers. Like pediatrics and surgery, the two groups attract vastly disparate types of personalities, and the result is something between an uneasy truce and a bitter civil war. Although part of the situation is inevitable because of the many different areas included in the biological sciences, it is most unfortunate; some settlement of what we offer the graduate student in the biological sciences must be made. We can no longer insist that he accumulate all the knowledge of the observers and master the advanced techniques of the problem-solvers.

Although the scope of knowledge in almost every field of science is reaching beyond the limits of human absorbability, there are several means of preserving this knowledge and keeping it accessible. The biologist would do well to investigate them.

Much of what the observers attempt to teach first hand could be learned second hand if inspired students knew how to use libraries. Despite their quite proper emphasis on direct observations, these biologists have partly lost sight of the fact that the learner is now confronted with so much new information from the experimental areas of the newer fields that he simply does not have the time, if indeed the patience, to concentrate his attention on the spate of observations made by several generations of workers. The student cannot learn everything; he must be taught how to pick and choose carefully. Medical diagnosis has already advanced into information storage-computer analysis techniques, as have several branches of the physical sciences that relate to biology. Biological science would do well to stop trying to pass along impossibly large bodies of information. The information itself must be handled in a different manner and presented in new ways to the student. It is high time for the older biologists to stop defending their handling of biological knowledge in the nineteenth-century pattern. It is also high time for the problem-solvers to cease disdaining the work of the observers. The problems they solve are largely drawn from the work of the observers; this work is still critically essential. But to say that it is critically essential is not to say that it is any longer the best basis for education in biological science, and that is how one still-large but fast-dwindling group of biologists would have it. They seem to believe in the mutability of organisms but not in the mutability of biology itself.

Let me approach issues in graduate education in biological science through a description of the problem-solver, who has become the dominant man on the scene. Unlike my professor in the 1930's who often sought to comprehend the whole field of knowledge, the problem-solver has entered biology because he is aware of many discrete problems or ones that may be made discrete. He can single them out and apply himself to them. He is far more the technologist than his predecessor, and he has at his command an expanding number of techniques from the physical sciences and even engineering, combined with a high respect for, if not direct knowledge of, the application of instrumentation to biology, particularly electronic instrumentation. He is an impatient young man who spends his first years matching his techniques against problems in the hope that he can select the problem which, if solved and solved speedily, will bring him prestige and security at an early age.

His state of hurry is related in part to a greatly heightened competition. Ten laboratories work on the same problem and the prize goes to the first to cross the line. Although his ancestor could be satisfied with a lifetime output of ten papers of which three were major contributions, he is expected to produce a hundred papers—but he will be lucky if as many as two are considered major. While this search for problems of a very specific kind and the competition in publication are frequently regarded as bad, they are often good because they can lead to deep delving and creativity. These, in turn, can lead to highly significant work. Furthermore, secondary work in science may have great data value. One man's attempts may miss or only come close but nevertheless inspire another. All this is part of the accelerated pace. The new style biologist is basically interested in methodology, in the making and testing of models, in the design and execution of critical experiments, and in proof to the extent his tools and thinking seem able to provide it at any given time.

What sort of graduate education in biological science will produce the best biologist for the later part of the twentieth century? Let me begin with what seem to be the essential characteristics of this biologist: intense interest in a problem or problems in biological science and a willingness to learn experimental approaches to this problem or problems; thorough training in the principles and experimental techniques of physical science; motivation; imagination; creativity; and total dedication. If these are the characteristics we are looking for in a potential graduate student, how do we evaluate them?

I shall treat these characteristics in an inverse order of our ability to recognize and plan for dealing with them.

Motivation: We know next to nothing about how to evaluate it. It may be conspicuous, it may be spurious, and it is often hidden within an individual to be brought to flower by some problem, by some teacher or investigator, by love, or by some unpredictable circumstance. Being unpredictable, it cannot always be aroused or even counted on to exist in a dormant state. We had better reject the student who has as yet given no sign that a spark has been ignited within him. Yet, we rarely do so. There are too many assistantships open. Thus, we dilute biological science with more of those for whom it is a living than for whom it is a life. With such students only a modest degree of motivation can be hoped for, whereas what is demanded for great achievement is nothing less than intense motivation.

Imagination: It is really the key to graduate work in biology as it is to all of man's other intellectual efforts. But graduate programs, and specifically the particular problems toward which students are oriented for dissertation work, frequently give a higher value to conformity than to imagination. There are perceptive exceptions, of course, but I shall support my case with a single example. Until recently I held in my files a warm note from a distinguished biologist colleague in an Eastern institution. Being then a very junior faculty member of that institution, I had sought his assistance in evaluating a student's honors paper. His note told me bluntly that I had better grade the paper low, for the student had ignored the work of X and Y and Z, and had presumed to put forth an imaginative hypothesis of his own, not in line with the accepted work in the field. Less than two decades later, this transgressing and neglectful student had contributed several brilliant hypotheses and had been honored by a share of the Nobel prize.

Creativity: The great biologists I know are not plodders or followers. They are intuitively interested in the new, in the expression of ideas, in the seeing of new relationships. To be sure, in biological science, as in the other sciences, experiment is an essential part of the process and it has its just rewards. It is an underpinning but no substitute for the ideas themselves that may come with the lonely walk or the cold gray dawn. How do we evaluate or measure creativity? We do not know, and the psychologist is at a loss to tell us. He prefers, in fact, to deal with what is common to all well-adjusted men.

Total dedication: I can tell you even less about it, except that it comes from the inner self and is essential to great work. Total dedication obviously begins with motivation, but the degree of dedication necessary to great achievement is something extending beyond simple motivation. I think that the graduate schools do more to inhibit than to foster its development with their systems of security and a sense of well-being produced by carefully measured semester hours of credit and properly-approved-by-committee dissertations that are not too adventurous, and thus lessen the dedication as well as inhibit the imagination by denigrating the challenge. The graduate schools tend to make of their students what T. S. Eliot described as unadventurous, modern man—"Deferential, glad to be of use,/- Politic, cautious, and meticulous;/ Full of high sentence, but a bit obtuse." Of course, a sustaining interest in biological science is the keystone of any distinguished career in biological science. It may be shaped by some undergraduate training or it may be brought from elsewhere. It needs no discussion, because if it is absent, the student does not wish to pursue biological science.

Advanced training in the physical sciences: Here we can do effective planning; but from the biologists' point of view, there are difficulties. The physical sciences have become by and large the dominating influence on the academic scene in the later half of this century because of their bearing on national defense and international problems and the large amounts of money poured into them. The physical sciences have succeeded other studies in disciplining man's mind, but their position of prominence is more related to a very old spirit of adventure and conflict with established ideas. Remember Galileo's fate and listen to the words of John Tyndall:

> A hint of Hamlet's, however, teaches us how the troubles of common life may be ended; and it is perfectly possible for you and me to purchase intellectual peace at the price of intellectual death. The world is not without refuges of this description; nor is it wanting in persons who seek their shelter, and try to persuade others to do the same. The

unstable and the weak have yielded and will yield to this persuasion, and they to whom repose is sweeter than the truth. But I would exhort you to refuse the offered shelter, and to scorn the base repose—to accept, if the choice be forced upon you, commotion before stagnation, the breezy leap of the torrent before the foetid stillness of the swamp. In the course of this Address I have touched upon debatable questions, and led you over what will be deemed dangerous ground—and this partly with the view of telling you that, as regards these questions, science claims unrestricted right of search.

It is not the accepted and easy that challenges man to progress. It is the unorthodox, provided it is founded upon wisdom and defended objectively. Because the physical sciences early presented man with a challenge of high adventure, their strong position is easily supported today. I confess that I have never understood why the biologist, with more exciting and more personally related bases for experiments, insisted until fairly recently upon teaching most of his students by the dull road of recited fact rather than the personal experience of experiment based directly upon ideas. But he has, and at the expense of losing too many of the best minds to the physical sciences. When we add the advertisements in the Sunday *New York Times* for physicists, chemists, and engineers, we make still more good physical scientists out of students who might become good biologists. Then, when we add the attractiveness of medicine, which holds the personal challenge of momentary and perhaps even fairly long-lasting triumph over death itself, we find the candidates for graduate education in biological science just where a national committee found them a few years ago—fifth on a list in which the distance between the stages in the pecking order is great.

Some persons will respond that we have turned out biologists of note in the last few years. My reply is that we have not turned out nearly enough of the right sort, and where we have done so we have achieved the result more because of the determination of a few biologists than because of planning in graduate education. We have, in a limited measure, succeeded in spite of ourselves. If biological science is indeed the most vital of the sciences because man's fate is in a large measure dependent on it, I respectfully suggest that we alter our ways.

Part of the alteration can be in graduate training in biological science. It should begin with rigid selection of the best students, along with purposeful barring of the weakest. It will be objected by many that the reduction of students will render useless many faculty members. Some of these faculty members will find new means of usefulness, and any university administrator knows he has to fence off a few people. The new biology is well on its way to replacing the old; its direction and its ultimate fusion with much of what is now called physical science is inevitable. Those who cannot adjust will fall by the wayside. What universities could do to retrain their established faculty members in many fields has never been explored. In time, rigid selection of graduate students will heighten the challenge and will attract more as well as better ones.

We can insist that much of the basic graduate education in biological science be strongly physical science-oriented and thus concerned with basic principles and experimental models. The current understanding of energy relations in cells and organisms would not have been possible without such a basis. The picture of the cell obtained by electron microscopy is an excellent example of instrumentation and technique adaptation. By combining several physical science approaches, we can now often relate function to form even at the molecular level. The current understanding of respiration as a function related to the molecular structure of the mitochondria is an example. When we have gone further in these directions, we shall have more proficient, more perceptive experimentalists in an age in which the cry for more capable experimentalists in biology is high—from agriculture which has become increasingly a biological science, to medicine where the essential biological science often hinges directly upon use of highly sophisticated instruments, and to the undefined demands of the space-age projections.

Three or four years in graduate school necessarily require specialized effort, and much of what our modern biologist needs, he must receive long before this period. It has been demonstrated to my satisfaction several times in recent years that one can make a better Ph.D. biologist out of an undergraduate physical science major than out of an undergraduate biological science major. Sometimes he is, I admit, merely better trained than educated and he may have neither sensitivity to, nor concern for, more than a narrow part of man's world. It is a pity not to produce biologists who are also men of great human awareness. The scientists' tendency to concentration and specialization is usually cited as the basis of his callousness to values, but something like equal responsibility lies in the humanist's failure to inspire.

The term "general education" too often connotes some easy way out. Yet general education, offered in a highly selective manner and designed to show the many different aspects of the will and the mask of man is what the would-be biological scientist needs at the undergraduate level. Only rarely can he get it, for only rarely does the academic hierarchy leave to undergraduate teaching the most accomplished and sensitive teachers. Rarely can he get it, because the collegiate system puts a premium on conformity and security that is little different from what the educationist has built into the elementary and secondary schools. Where in the system does the student get, or should he get, this general education? What do we actually do with the college years? We impart a sense of security, educate a few students well, and train some who may not be further educable. For the most part, we swing far toward specialization with intense relationship to the personalities in and the powers of the departments involved.

We should not avoid attention to biological science at the undergraduate level for it is the student with an interest in life and its processes that we wish to entice into a career of high adventure in biological science. But as a general comment on college curriculum planning, it seems to me that, if a student has superior reading ability, we sometimes succeed in spite of ourselves.

I do not know how much the schools have to do with development of superior reading ability and an intense desire to read and understand. Surely far less than a home environment with books and reading persons, less than discussions of writing and its meaning among family and friends, and less than early exposure to the exciting, moving passages from which things apart from the everyday world are gleaned intuitively, even though a child's maturity may not be great enough for understanding. Near the top of the list of fundamentals in the education of a human being is this matter of perceptive, sensitive reading. Left to the school system and the

P.T.A., it ends up where one would logically suppose—at the mean reading level of the general population.

Close to sensitive reading is the capacity for critical thinking. The trait relates to daily living. It is the *sine qua non* for the scientist. We know very little about how to nourish it (and I have carefully not said how to teach it). It seems to have roots put down early in life, and it grows through a succession of associations with strong examples: parents, teachers, or others.

It is obvious that the elementary and secondary schools must teach large numbers of children what they need to know to lead orderly, satisfying lives; but I want them, or their parents, or someone, to send my would-be biologist to college with an advanced ability to read sensitively and to think critically. Perhaps we may have to violate one of the spurious precepts of democracy and sort out this fellow from his classmates early in his education.

What do I want to put into the graduate program in the biological sciences in the late twentieth century? A strongly trained biological science major, crammed with facts and enormously enthusiastic about dealing with living things? Heavens, no. I ask for a sensitive, widely read, communicative, liberally educated man with a high spirit of adventure, an interest in critical experiment and reasoned argument, and a solid foundation in physical science, yet with concern for the biological questions that physical science can answer. I would have this would-be biologist, who has learned to read and think critically, and who has some idea of the importance of writing, neglect the labels of botanist, microbiologist, zoologist, insofar as possible.

Biological science is now concerned with the ordering of knowledge at a vastly different level than in an earlier day. In working with gene-controlled reactions at the level of molecular processes, the biologist has no concern for the once seemingly important boundaries between academic disciplines. His interest must be in some aspect of the organic world important to man, and he will do best to select his experimental organisms and procedures in terms of the problems of his day rather than the way a university department is organized for budgetary or other reasons.

Why, when we have been doing with far less, does it seem to me now that the situation calls for more? Not least important is the tremendous advance in the physical sciences. They may well open the universe to man and, whether they do or not, they have already greatly altered his environment. He can persist and continue to evolve only with far greater understanding of himself, his limits, and his alterability than he now possesses. He may well ultimately have to take a hand in the direction of his own evolution, and he is by no means knowledgeable enough to do so.

Modern genetics has lent validity and a mechanism to Darwin's great scheme of evolutionary change and interrelationships among organisms, and at the same time it has posed the possibility of directed, if not controlled, evolution. As we have come ever closer to the chemical structure of the gene, we have approached the possibility of constructing the flow diagram of life itself. There is yet much to be accomplished, but there are limitless possibilities for the use of such knowledge once it is complete enough and if man is wise enough to use it. Our knowledge of DNA as the genetic material and our recently gained understanding of its structure and patterns of replication now seem to give us possible means for modifying genetic controls. Man-made "life" and its management are indeed frightening in the light of man's limited wisdom and responsibility. These are no longer considerations for science fiction alone for they have already brought into focus awesome questions of ethics and morals.

The communications code by which genetic material commands the activities of the cell has now been broken and it can to some extent be modified. More knowledge of it might permit correcting many metabolic errors and strengthening much faulty metabolism. There is much direct evidence that DNA activities and RNA activities control protein development, particularly enzyme protein development and hold the key to the sort and form of organism developed. But how? Here also presumably is the barrier to the surgeon's attempts to prolong life by organ transplants. But exactly what is it and how do we overcome it? The immunity and susceptibility relationships of man, mouse, and oats also fall within a broad problem here, and there is yet much to be learned. Further ability to synthesize hormones or substitutes for hormones or hormone antagonists would give the physician many new ways of dealing with human ills. Merely more comprehensive knowledge of metabolism itself and its genetic basis would make much possible.

While we are this close to DNA, RNA, and the proteins, let me raise the whole subject of the viruses, long known but only recently subject to fairly direct investigation. Where do they really fit in the scheme of things? How do they relate to the genes? Perhaps, afield from the viruses, but still in this weft, is the question of the genetic factors outside the nucleus, in the cytoplasm. Are they unique to some organisms or general?

We are somewhere near an understanding of photosynthesis and various facets of the energy transfer and utilization problem. Formidable undertakings remain but so does the possibility of newly developed means of capturing and converting energy. In relation to the energy capture-transfer-utilization complex, there loom large issues in relation to permeability, the excitability of cells, and motility, which can, in part, already be interpreted in terms of protein contractibility.

Radiation is known to be a factor in genetic mutation, but the other effects of radiation on cells are little understood, a factor of direct importance for man's hopes in conquering space.

Such problems as the differentiation of species that the biologist once thought largely morphological have now become susceptible of approach by physical science techniques and of definition in terms of molecular differences. But the whole world of plants and animals remains to be explored in such relationships. The question of the development of life forms from ordered molecular structures and the varied functioning of these life forms in light of these molecular structures has just barely been opened by the development of applicable techniques. Perhaps the greatest challenge to the biologist is that he knows certain facts about the physics and chemistry of the nervous system, but he has little knowledge of how the system works. He does not know how man thinks, any more than deans know how to make graduate students or themselves think. Here is a challenge of a high order.

One could, of course, give hundreds of examples of the opportunities facing the new biologist. They would differ depending on the writer's particular interests and his hopes. There now seems no discernible limit either to the complexities of the organic world or to the future of biological science.

I have written this essay around the contrast between the biologist of an earlier day and the biologist of today. This contrast exists, in fact, because of progress. The search is still one having to do with order and change, but now largely at the level of molecules and atoms. When we understand more about this order and change, many things will become possible; but the great diverse organic world will still exist and man will still be faced with problems concerning his place in it.

New Trends in Graduate Study in the Physical Sciences

BRYCE CRAWFORD

THE SUBJECT of this essay brings forth a very quick reaction from most superficial observers, even members of university faculties. The impression is that of enormous expansion in this area, of limitless support for research projects, of numerous and easily obtained fellowships, and, in general, of very strong support from society, especially from the Federal Government. The impact of such concentrated support is alleged to have overexpanded the physical sciences and to have tended toward distortion within our universities. Several forms of distortion are seen: an imbalance between support for the physical sciences and for other disciplines; an orientation in graduate programs with too much emphasis on research and too little effective teaching by the faculty; and an orientation of the research work itself toward applied problems rather than problems in basic science.

It is my thesis in this essay that such a view is exaggerated, and arises from a misunderstanding of the basic causes of the changes made in graduate studies in the physical sciences (including engineering) in the period since World War I. There has been a change in the relationships between the physical sciences and the engineering disciplines, so that the "EMP area"—engineering, mathematics, physical science—needs to be considered as an entity. But there has not occurred a disproportionate increase of graduate work in this area as compared to other areas. It is not true that every graduate

BRYCE CRAWFORD, JR. (Ph.D., Stanford), dean of the Graduate School, University of Minnesota, since 1960, is a distinguished physical chemist. He has played an important role in the activities of the Association of Graduate Schools and in the Council of Graduate Schools.

216

student working in the EMP area is fully supported. It is not true that any faculty member with a research project which is even barely acceptable will find ready money to support that project. I find no substantiating evidence for the idea that students engaged in team research projects have no opportunity to develop their own independent scholarly abilities. Nor do I find evidence of vast numbers of degrees awarded for research which is of an applied nature or directed strictly to the solution of practical problems.

Although there is statistical support for several of these statements, I will cite only one set of numbers, to be found in Table 11, in Dr. Cartter's essay in this volume. These data on the production of doctoral degrees in the various fields certainly show a tremendous increase in the *number* of degrees given in the EMP area—and in other areas of scholarship. But a careful look at these figures also shows no gross distortion over the past three decades; the *percentage* of degrees awarded in the EMP area, in particular, has risen by only one percentage point. (I am referring to the actual results of experience, not to the projections for the next decade. Those projections, in my opinion, greatly overestimate the probable increase in percentage of production in the EMP area; similarly in my opinion, they underestimate the effect of the very exciting developments in the biological sciences.)

I believe that, if we wish to understand recent trends in the EMP areas so that we may grasp the opportunities and avoid the dangers which these trends bring, we shall gain little from studying enrollment trends, or degrees achieved, or availability of Federal support funds. Instead, we must look into the nature of the disciplines themselves and into the changes which these fields have undergone with regard to their intrinsic character. And I believe we put it backwards when we assume that changes are occurring in EMP graduate studies because of society's increasing interest in these fields. It is, rather, the developments which have occurred in the EMP disciplines that have caused society to become more interested in them. Indeed, I suspect that, with regard to any field of scholarship, it is a poor approximation to describe the development of the scholarly field as dependent on social interest in it. Scholarship is seminal, and advances in a scholarly field are causes rather than effects of social progress.

If we look to the basic developments in the disciplines themselves, seeking to understand changes in graduate work in the EMP area, the root of the present trends and recent changes can be stated quite precisely: *in the years since World War I, the physical sciences have become successful.* They have progressed from the description of natural processes, through the understanding of them, into the control of them. The conceptual models, which at first merely reproduced the qualitative behavior of nature, have been successively refined to the point where they described the essential characteristics, and most recently to the point where the models approximate the real phenomena rather accurately; one may say that the theories of physical science have made contact with reality. I do not wish to repeat the errors of nineteenth-century physicists and claim that everything is understood, of course; but in many areas, including many relevant directly to the practical world, it is possible to proceed with accuracy from first principles of science to a successful prediction. Up to and into the twentieth century, practical advances were the result of intuition, empiricism, and trial and error; it was the "handbook engineer," proceeding empirically and guarding his uncertainties by judicious "safety factors," who directly influenced human affairs. The scientist was essentially a scholar, observing and interpreting phenomena, providing some enlightenment and stimulation but few accurate and reliable quantitative predictions. The steam engine was not developed as a result of advances in thermodynamics; rather the converse was true, and thermodynamics developed as a branch of physics partly in order that the steam engine might be more fully understood. By contrast, the atomic reactor was conceived and predicted and developed as a direct result of the theory of relativity; and the maser and laser were conceived and developed by the direct application of quantum mechanics.

"Nam et ipsa scientia potestas est," wrote Francis Bacon, "knowledge itself is power"; but the justification and demonstration in the physical science area has come largely in the last few decades.

The effects in the EMP area are not difficult to understand. With regard to the physical sciences themselves, there has been no discontinuous change in the nature of graduate study. As the range of physical science developed, as the sciences became more successful, there have, of course, been increased numbers of graduate students in these fields. The sciences themselves are more exciting and attractive for being successful; and with the demonstrated success there has been a steadily increasing opportunity for industrial employment of scientists with graduate degrees. There has, however, been a discontinuity and a dramatic change in the nature, as well as the volume, of graduate study in the engineering fields. When empiricism was the only root to practical solutions of problems, the practical engineer profited more from getting out of school and into the field early, to begin his practical experience, rather than spending years in studying advanced scientific topics that still would not provide reliable answers. The situation has now changed, and we have, as the data cited show, a dramatic increase in the number of graduate students in the engineering fields, pursuing advanced studies because they—and their future employers—realize the practical applicability of such study. And the programs of graduate work in the engineering fields contain less and less empiricism, and increasing amounts of advanced basic science. It is indeed difficult these days to distinguish a graduate program in electrical engineering from one in physics, to distinguish one in chemical engineering from one in physical chemistry.

These changes in the EMP disciplines do, of course, make some demands on our graduate schools, requiring basically an understanding of the nature of the changes and the provision of that flexibility which every graduate school should demonstrate regarding all active fields of scholarship. In the physical sciences themselves we must recognize some redefinition of fields as the disciplines progress, and provide at appropriate times of development for study in such fields as "chemical physics" or in "control sciences," seeking, as we always should, to "keep the happy mean between too much stiffness in refusing and too much easiness in admitting variations in things once advisedly established."

In the engineering fields we must adjust to and wisely accommodate far more than merely slight modifications or redefinitions of fields; we must understand the discontinuity, and provide what is needed. That has involved and will continue to involve, for one thing, an enormous quantitative increase in the number of graduate students in the engineering fields; this implies appropriate increases in the size of the faculties. But far more drastic have been the changes in the nature and substance of graduate work in these fields, changes in the nature of the courses which must be offered for graduate students, and especially changes in the nature of the research studies that are appropriate. And these changes have placed a real demand on the graduate teachers in the engineering fields; they have always needed to be "practical men" and this need continues, but now, in order that they may indeed be practical men, they must have a competent and scholarly understanding of basic, pure theory. Both the engineering professions and the engineering faculties in universities have been meeting this challenge; universities must understandingly help them to continue to meet it. There have been and will continue to be new degrees offered, and more frequently new degree programs will be offered under old degree names.

There are several challenges implied for our graduate schools. Quite obvious is the challenge to our faculties in the EMP area that they must keep up with and preferably keep ahead of the field, and must both expand and revise their graduate programs. University administrations also need to understand the basic nature of these changes, to encourage proper development of these fields of graduate study, and to provide the appropriate flexibility of forms and procedures. And, perhaps most important of all, the scholars in all parts of the university must understand the nature of the changes in the physical sciences. They must understand that, if their EMP colleagues are involved with graduate students whose ultimate goal is in the world of affairs, this does not imply any contamination of scholarship or the reduction of the EMP departments to mere trade schools. Scholarly work at its best is relevant to the real world and not confined to the ivory tower. The most scholarly of all societies takes its name from its motto: let scholarship be the steersman of life.

It is true, as always, that success also has its perils. Society has indeed a tremendous interest in the EMP area and feels the need of many more men with graduate training in these fields. This is, to be sure, part of a feeling of need for many more highly trained men in all fields of scholarship; but the chief thrust is in the EMP area, as the Gilliland report[1] makes plain, and the numbers of estimated manpower needs are large indeed.

Such interest of society along a particular direction always carries the danger of distortion of universities. This phenomenon is, however, not a new one, nor is it unique to the EMP area. There have always been those who would use universities for their own purposes, careless of distortion or violence done to the universities themselves—nor have the purposes always been evil. The record of the universities, though it carries some blots and smudges, shows remarkable strength and integrity in resisting such forces of distortion. And I believe that the American academic scene today shows the same integrity. I would reach the same conclusion with regard to the character of the research done by graduate students in universities in the EMP area, believing that in truth it has not been distorted toward unscholarly or applied goals by the pressures of society.

It seems to me readily possible to identify two basic strengths of our universities in resisting any distortion arising from the success of the physical sciences, and once again these two bulwarks of academic integrity are not peculiar to our times. The first is that the universities are by no means powerless; they are masters of their own destiny. If increasingly the universities are dependent on the Federal Government, the government and society in general is far more dependent on the universities. The universities do have an obligation to meet the real needs of society; they also have an obligation to maintain their integrity, and the insistence by the university on meeting society's needs in such a way as to defend their integrity will find understanding and acceptance and support.

Indeed, this measure of understanding of the nature of universities, by society and by leaders in public affairs, supplies the second bulwark. Informed men do realize that a distorted university cannot serve the ends either of scholarship or of society; they do realize that the best education for a future scientist cannot be restricted to studies in the sciences alone. And this understanding of and concern for proper relations between the universities and society is evidenced in such reports as the Seaborg report[2] and the Kistiakowsky report.[3]

I therefore conclude by repeating my central theme: the universities of this country show little evidence of distortion in favor of the EMP disciplines as a result of social pressure. It is well, I am sure, for us to maintain our concern about such possible distortion; for the danger is present, and the continuing concern over this danger is doubtless one of the reasons why it has not seriously materialized. But while we maintain the balance of our institutions undistorted, we must keep faith with the obligation to pursue scholarship vigorously in all fields and to offer graduate education which keeps pace with scholarly development. In the EMP area we find that graduate education is in a ferment of change and growth, whose many different currents we can understand if we grasp the basic fact: that in the EMP area the theoretical and the practical have become unified, and that this field is now in a period of exciting creative activity. Our graduate offerings should follow these new directions and keep pace with the scientific advances—even if some of the feared distortion should come about. Let us suppose even that a few of our universities should approach the imbalance of California Institute of Technology or the Massachusetts Institute of Technology. Are these institutions unworthy members of the academic community?

NOTES

1. President's Science Advisory Committee, *Meeting Manpower Needs in Science and Technology* (Washington: Government Printing Office, 1962).
2. President's Science Advisory Committee, *Scientific Progress, the Universities, and the Federal Government* (Washington: Government Printing Office, 1960).
3. Committee on Science and Public Policy, National Academy of Sciences, *Federal Support of Basic Research in Institutions of Higher Learning* (Washington: National Academy of Sciences—National Research Council, 1964).

The Decades Ahead: Trends and Problems

ALLAN M. CARTTER

PREVIOUS essays have dealt with graduate education yester-
day and today; what can we say about the graduate education
of tomorrow? In what ways are the character and scope of graduate
education likely to change in future decades? What are likely to be
the most pressing problems? What lessons can we learn from the
past?

Anyone closely concerned with higher education today can safely
make one prediction for the future: the changes will be vast. The
past few decades have seen a marked alteration in the nature of the
university on the American scene. Only thirty years have passed
since Abraham Flexner rather bitterly noted that "American universities look like bedlam," describing them to an international au-
dience in terms reminiscent of Thorstein Veblen's description of
higher learning in America:

> All of them possess colleges, which are secondary schools, inferior in
> solidity to the secondary schools of England and the Continent. Many
> of them possess teacher training departments, in which an absurdly
> artificial technique is communicated to an inferior student body—this
> being one of several reasons for the poor quality of American high
> school and elementary school; even more common are business de-

ALLAN M. CARTTER, formerly graduate dean at Duke University,
is now vice-president of the American Council on Education. His chief
assignment at the Council is director of the Commission on Plans and Objectives for Higher Education. A native of New Jersey, Dr. Cartter attended
Colgate (A.B., 1946) and Yale (Ph.D., 1952). He began teaching economics
at Duke in 1957, and in 1959, at the age of thirty-seven, was appointed professor and dean of the Graduate School. Dr. Cartter has written several
books and articles on economic subjects.

partments, schools of journalism, schools of practical arts, and even a department of hotel management. Not satisfied with the miscellaneous aggregation thus brought together to reside in the university, correspondence and home study courses are organized, which endeavour to give by mail the equivalent of resident study. Most of this, of course, is not education; it is not even "service," the catch-word by which it is usually designated.[1]

The representative university of the 1930's was an essentially insular establishment, not deeply involved in the affairs of government or industry, and only sluggishly responsive to the evolving needs of contemporary society. The unparalleled demands made by World War II in the areas of science and technology heralded a new phase in the life of the university. No longer isolated from mundane society, called upon to staff greatly expanded industrial and governmental activities in a variety of areas, and encouraged to probe systematically the frontiers of both knowledge and practice in a host of fields, the contemporary university is far different from its predecessor of a generation ago. The difference is most marked in the graduate education and research functions of the university.

Graduate education, once considered an expensive luxury by many university administrations and boards of control, is today the heart of the institutions that have achieved full university status. The prestige of these institutions in academic circles, their ability to attract outstanding students at both the undergraduate and graduate levels, their support through grants from private foundations and government agencies, come primarily from the strength of their graduate schools. This trend is not without its problems, and is viewed as a not unmixed blessing by many, but graduate education is truly the signature of the university today.

ENROLLMENT PROJECTIONS

In recent years graduate education has been one of the most rapidly expanding sectors of higher education. Doctorates awarded have doubled in nearly every decade since the turn of the century, and graduate enrollment increased nearly 80 percent during the 1950's while the number of baccalaureates at the end of the decade only barely regained its 1950–51 level.

Projections of the future are always hazardous, and one cannot but be mindful of Sir Thomas Browne's warning:

> Amuse not thyself about the Riddles of future things. Study Prophecies when they are become Histories and past hovering in their causes. Eye well things past and present, and let conjectural sagacity suffise for things to come.

Nevertheless, some tentative projections may provide a measure of the likely magnitude of change in the decade or two ahead.

Undergraduate enrollment is important both because the source of graduate students is the undergraduate student body of a previous year, and because it is a rough indicator of the demand for doctorates for the teaching profession. Projections ahead to 1980 are moderately safe in the sense that the college-age population—barring plague, pestilence, or war—is predictable; its members are already born and approaching elementary school. A major revolution has occurred in the last decade, however, in college attendance patterns, and how many of the future 18–21-year-olds will enter college is a more dubious guess. Beyond 1980 one must make assumptions about future birthrates, assumptions which are likely to compound the errors. Table 9 hazards such assumptions in an attempt to assess the relative magnitude of changes ahead.

In case the reader is tempted to choose projection I as the most likely, it should be recalled that almost every enrollment projection made in past years has turned out to be much too conservative. When the U.S. Office of Education began gazing into its crystal ball in 1959, it projected enrollment patterns for ten years ahead. Its projection of the ratio of college students to the college-age population for 1965 was surpassed by 1961! The current estimates of the Office, reflected in projection II in Table 9, are probably a good median guess of the future pattern.

Table 9 clearly indicates that higher education is not faced with a one-time tidal wave or bulge in enrollment, but with a continuing expansion of about 1.5 million students in each five-year period (except for the slight breathing space in 1980–85). The supply of potential graduate students, and the demand for doctorates as college faculty, can, therefore, be expected to rise continuously over the foreseeable future.

Table 10 goes further out on a limb, attempting to predict the impact of expanding undergraduate enrollment on the graduate-student population. Concentrating just on the next seventeen years, one can make moderately good guesses on the size of the pool from which graduate students are drawn. Column 1 projects baccalaureates and first professional degrees ahead to 1980, assuming that

TABLE 9: *Undergraduate College Enrollments,*
Actual and Projected, 1930–2000*

(in thousands)

YEAR	POPULATION AGED 18–21	COLLEGE ENROLLMENT			
		Actual Enrollment	Projection I	Projection II	Projection III
1930.....	9,027	1,101....	....	....	....
1939.....	10,015	1,365....	....	....	....
1950.....	8,948	2,297....	....	....	....
1960.....	9,546	3,296....	....	....	....
1965.....	12,282	.....	5,021	4,675	4,973
1970.....	14,278	.....	6,556	6,182	6,688
1975.....	16,107	.....	7,773	7,655	8,366
1980.....	16,790	.....	8,103	8,843	9,495
1985.....	16,957	.....	8,183	9,367	10,296
1990.....	18,880	.....	9,111	10,429	12,176
1995.....	21,570	.....	10,410	11,915	14,648
2000.....	23,730	.....	11,452	13,108	16,648

* Figures in non-italic type are actual or, in the case of population figures for 1965–80, projections based on persons already born. Beyond 1980 population estimates are based on Census series B and data supplied by the Census Bureau. Enrollment projection I is a conservative estimate, assuming that the college attendance ratios rise to .48 by 1975 and then level off. Projection II is based on U.S. Office of Education estimates through 1975, the attendance ratio leveling off at .55 in 1985. III assumes an attendance ratio rising at a constantly declining rate, reaching .71 by the end of the century. For more detailed analysis, see A. M. Cartter and R. Farrell, "Higher Education in the Last Third of the Century," *Educational Record*, Spring 1965.

these degrees continue to total about 13 percent of the entering fall enrollment five years before (a fairly reliable measure in the past). The pool will not quite triple between 1960 and 1980.

Figures on total graduate enrollment are quite untrustworthy, since they include a high and varying proportion of part-time students, and often include non-degree students, auditors, and the usual share of unknown names that turn up on early fall class rolls, and they often exclude those completing dissertations once they have completed their minimum residence requirements. The best available figures are those gathered by the Office of Education since

1959 on entering full-time students. In Table 10 the figures on entering full-time graduate students prior to 1959 are enlightened guesses by the author, based on fragments of information; figures after 1962 are estimates based on the assumption that the percentage of bachelors going on to full-time graduate study will stabilize at 20 percent.

TABLE 10: *Entering Graduate Students and Doctorates: Actual and Projected, 1950–80**

(in thousands)

Year	Bachelor's and First Professional Degrees	Entering Full-Time Graduate Students	Column 2 as Percentage of Column 1	Doctorate Degrees Awarded
	1	2	3	4
1950............	384	38	10.0	6.4
1953............	305	36	13.5	8.3
1955............	287	41	14.3	8.8
1959............	385	59	15.3	9.4
1960............	395	69	17.4	9.8
1961............	402	73	18.1	10.6
1962............	420	80	19.1	11.4
1965............	523	105	20.0	15.0
1970............	740	148	20.0	23.1
1975............	919	184	20.0	31.1
1980............	1,094	219	20.0	36.8

* Baccalaureate degrees are estimates based on projection II enrollments in Table 9. Projected doctoral degrees are about 20 percent above U.S. Office of Education estimates but nearly 40 percent below estimates by the National Science Foundation. See *Projections of Educational Statistics to 1973–74*, U.S. Office of Education Circular 754 (Washington: Government Printing Office, 1964) and *Comparisons of Earned Degrees Awarded 1901–1962—with Projections to 2000* (Washington: National Science Foundation, 1964).

Doctorates awarded in past years have averaged between a fifth and a quarter of entering graduate students five years before, and in column 4 of Table 10 it is assumed that this percentage will be approximately 20 percent in 1980. Combining what appear to be a number of relatively conservative assumptions gives a nearly fourfold increase in doctorates awarded from 1960 to 1980.

A number of conclusions are suggested by Table 10. The first is that the pool from which graduate students are drawn has been relatively stable over the last few years, and only 10 percent larger in 1962 than in 1950, so the recent expansion of graduate enrollment has involved going deeper into the pool of qualified persons. The marked growth in national fellowship programs (Woodrow Wilson, NSF, NDEA, etc.) may well have meant awards to less well qualified students, a charge often made by critics of these programs. More important, however, no matter how accurate the actual projections for the next decade or two, the direction and magnitude of change are clearly indicated; the supply of potential graduate students should more than triple during the 1960's and 1970's, and perhaps the increase will be even more marked as undergraduate honors programs expand and student motivations and aspirations

TABLE 11: *Doctorates by Area of Study: Annual Average for Periods between 1938 and 1962, and Projections to 1968–72*

SUBJECT AREA	1938–47		1948–52		1953–57		1958–62		1968–72	
	No.	%	No.	%	No.	%	No.	%	No.	%
Engineering.....	49	1.9	417	7.0	583	6.7	863	8.6	2,000	9.0
Physical science.	719	28.3	1,577	26.5	1,977	22.7	2,251	22.5	6,000	27.0
Biological science.......	639	25.2	1,403	23.6	2,300	26.5	2,433	24.3	5,000	22.5
Social science...	387	15.3	872	14.7	1,212	13.9	1,450	14.5	3,200	14.4
Education......	293	11.5	876	14.7	1,488	17.1	1,697	16.9	3,600	16.2
Humanities.....	452	17.8	806	13.5	1,130	13.0	1,326	13.2	2,400	10.9
Total......	2,538	100.0	5,952	100.0	8,691	100.0	10,020	100.0	22,200	100.0

Source: Data for 1938–62 are from Allan M. Cartter (ed.), *American Universities and Colleges,* 9th ed. (Washington: American Council on Education, 1964), p. 54. Figures for 1968–72 projection are the author's.

continue to improve. The graduate deans, who for decades were pictured as recruiting agents beating the bushes for scarce talents, will soon be sharing the woes of present undergraduate admissions officers in trying to bolster the dikes to keep out waves of students for whom they have insufficient facilities. This pressure will have serious consequences for admissions policy and screening procedures, which will be noted below.

The over-all projections conceal important trends in the various fields of study. Table 11 summarizes these trends for the last twenty-five years by six broad classifications of disciplines, and hazards a guess for the 1968–72 half-decade. The projections for science are based on estimates made by the National Science Foundation and the President's Science Advisory Committee; projections in other areas are the author's. Table 11 is not intended to represent an "optimum" or even a "satisfactory" distribution, but rather a likely distribution ten years hence, given present trends and prospective support programs.

The most rapidly expanding areas are likely to be in the sciences, led by mathematics, engineering, and a number of the fields that cross traditional disciplinary boundary lines (genetics, biophysics, and the like). In the nonscience areas, education (predominantly Ed.D., rather than Ph.D.) is the most rapidly expanding field. Most other fields are growing absolutely but account for smaller proportions of the larger graduate enrollments.

This expansion in graduate education will raise (or further complicate) many problems concerning admissions, fellowship needs, faculty requirements, and imbalance in support of educational programs, not to mention the physical problems of providing university facilities, equipment, and housing for a graduate-student population three or four times larger two decades hence. In the moments when one's prophetic zeal weakens and the size of the task appears impossibly great, a sobering reminder is that graduate enrollments in the United States have approximately doubled in each decade since 1900 with very little encouragement from government or private foundations. With the active support of both government and foundations today, and the increasing recognition that highly specialized manpower is a critically scarce national resource, it seems likely that the envisioned expansion will in fact be accomplished.*

If the author seems optimistic about the continued increase in numbers, he is considerably less optimistic about the implications of this expansion for the quality of graduate education. It is quite clear that the number of "graduate centers of excellence"—to use the fashionable parlance of the day—will be enlarged over the coming decade or two, but it also seems highly likely that the percentage of doctorates awarded by the recognized high-quality graduate schools will continue to decline. Although there is no general agreement about what constitutes "optimum" size of a graduate program (and the optimum size obviously differs for various disci-

* A recent National Science Foundation study, *Comparisons of Earned Degrees Awarded 1901-62—with Projections to 2000* (Washington: The Foundation, 1964), projects the following totals for doctorates (excluding medicine): 21,000 in 1970, 56,000 in 1980, 87,000 in 1990, and 123,000 in A.D. 2000 (computed from Table 36, p. 54).

plines), few would doubt that there are real disadvantages of scale in qualitative terms as a program expands beyond some moderate size. The general expansion of graduate enrollments will enhance the quality of graduate programs at some institutions that are presently too small to utilize fully their faculty, library, and plant facilities, but it will tend to lessen the effectiveness of programs at many more, already sizable universities. Somewhere between Mark Hopkins' log and a department with 1,000 graduate students and senior professors serving concurrently on dissertation committees of forty students—somewhere there lies a happier median. Holding to this median position, once found, has been a difficult—if not impossible—choice for some private and many public universities. The choice is more difficult in an age when external funds are available primarily for "new and expanding" programs, rather than for the improvement and strengthening of existing ones.

ADMISSIONS PROBLEMS

The swelling of graduate enrollments has begun to create an admissions problem of major proportion. The number of applications received by each graduate school is rapidly rising, partly because of increased numbers of potential students, but also because of multiple applications. The fellowship selection process is becoming more burdensome to departments, and most institutions will no longer give "admission without award" to more than a small fraction of the moderately well-qualified applicants because of faculty and space limitations. As noted by one director of graduate studies in a department with adequate fellowship funds: "We are in the anomalous position of saying that if we can't pay them to come, we won't admit them." Just as many younger students (or more important, their parents) feel that it is their "right" to gain admission to a public undergraduate college if they have met the minimum qualifications of high school graduation, an increasing number of bachelors are claiming this "right" of entrance to graduate school. Most public institutions are considerably more selective in graduate admissions than in undergraduate, but as advanced study becomes the accepted pattern, this problem will become more acute.

No general data are available to document the admissions problem, although deans and admissions committees are familiar enough with their own experience. There is a general impression that a decade ago most applicants for graduate study completed two or three applications to schools they would like to attend. Currently the typical student appears to be submitting four or five applications in the quest for admission and fellowship support. In all likelihood the average will rise to seven or eight a decade hence. If these impressionistic figures are approximately correct, this probably means a total national volume of about 100,000 completed applications in 1950, approximately 300,000 today, and an expectation of 1,000,000 or more by 1970. Since the number of doctorate-awarding institutions will probably not even double in the period from 1950 to 1970, this projection suggests that most graduate schools will have a five- to tenfold increase in volume of applications, and perhaps much greater if the number of master's candidates increases more rapidly than doctoral students.

The Council of Graduate Schools or the Association of Graduate Schools may wish to study this problem seriously in the near future. Recommendations have been made in the past for a possible centralized admissions service, and serious consideration of such a proposal may be timely. Under such a central program a student could fill in one complete set of applications, and indicate the schools to which he would like to apply. Copies could quickly be reproduced (for example, by Xerox or, conceivably, through some microfilm or microcard process) and forwarded to the indicated institutions. A standard charge of perhaps $20 could be levied on the applicant, with an additional $10 charge for each institution over three to which the dossier would be sent. This central file could also be used by all the national fellowship programs, and thus considerably reduce the volume of requests for transcripts, letters of recommendations, Graduate Record Examination scores, and so on. Conceivably, the system might proceed to the point, somewhat akin to the centralized procedures used by the medical schools in distributing interns, where the student would list his order of preference, and the central office would match these with institutional responses. Although this procedure may appear at first to be rather dehumanizing, it might make more sense than some of the chaotic selection results that now occur. It could also simplify the present fellowship award process, which takes weeks or months of offers, declinations, and alternate offers, and which produces in even the most prestigious institutions in the country fellowship declination rates of nearly 50 percent.

A centralized admissions procedure (without centralized awards decisions) could be begun by a small number of institutions on a voluntary participation basis, provided only that some of the more prestigious institutions take the lead. When one remembers that the projected one million applications of 1970 will mean three million or more letters of recommendation written by perhaps not more than one hundred thousand faculty members, this burden alone may make the effort worth serious consideration.

The present experiment with standard centralized language examinations being conducted by the Educational Testing Service in cooperation with about twenty graduate schools is a somewhat analogous attempt to bring order and meaning out of a similarly confusing situation.

FACULTY DEMAND AND SUPPLY

As the economists long ago learned—although still occasionally forget—the problems of any one institution may be solved by money, but the problems of all institutions may be insoluble simultaneously, even with adequate finances. This has long been clear in recruiting outstanding graduate students: attractive awards may entice students to Melrose U, but merely have the effect of redistributing a given number of students. Similarly in the case of faculty, higher salaries in the long run may make an academic career more attractive than some alternative career, but in the short run one institution can rapidly progress only by drawing faculty away from other similar positions. So too in the case of rapidly expanding graduate programs, the supply of future doctorates can be expanded by diverting more of the present stream of doctorates back into teaching; therefore, specialized skills in short supply may have to become temporarily scarcer before they can become more abundant.

Table 11 indicated a projected increase in the number of doctorates awarded annually in engineering from 863 for the 1958–62 period to about 2,000 for the 1968–72 period. Just the increase in the operations of one Federal agency, NASA, could probably absorb this total output. To increase the number of doctorates, however, requires diverting a larger number of new Ph.D.'s for the next few years into teaching or, alternatively, pulling a larger number of engineers with doctorates out of current nonteaching positions. The extent of this diversion is difficult to estimate accurately, but some rough calculations will indicate the magnitude of the problem.

In most academic disciplines it takes, on the average, about one graduate faculty member (full-time equivalent) to turn out one new doctorate a year. Thus a department which awards, say, five doctorates a year ordinarily requires about five full-time faculty members—perhaps ten faculty spending half their time on graduate instruction. Even if undergraduate engineering enrollments remained stationary for the next decade, which seems most unlikely, 1,200–1,500 doctorates in engineering would have to be added to graduate faculties. At the present time about 300 engineering doctorates enter teaching each year, but nearly 200 are needed merely to meet attrition owing to current retirement, deaths, and net losses to nonacademic positions. Thus, to accomplish the projected doctorate rate, a significantly larger fraction of those now completing their studies will have to be retained by the universities.

A similar problem exists in several other critical fields, and the rapid rise in faculty salaries over the last five years is largely accounted for by the increasing competition from industry and government for such highly skilled personnel. This is a familiar enough problem in wartime, and can easily be met for periods up to five or ten years by what might be called "manpower cannibalism," that is, temporarily swelling present government and industry ranks by reducing current use of these resources in education. But just as a business firm cannot survive long by living out of its capital, similarly a nation cannot easily provide for an increasing supply of engineering doctorates *and* reach the moon in two or three years—although it may be able to achieve both over a longer period of time.

Awareness of the impact of expanding Federal programs on the demand for scarce personnel in science and technology is evidenced in the current work of the Office of Science and Technology and the President's Science Advisory Committee. Serious consideration is being given to improved means of estimating present and future manpower needs and to the inauguration of a manpower budgeting process parallel to traditional fiscal budgeting procedures. In many areas of government concern, financial constraints are less imposing than limitations in the supply of highly skilled personnel, and the overlooking of this facet of the resource problem may endanger the major functions of the universities by drawing away their teaching and research faculty.

The problem is more complicated than it might at first appear, for more than three quarters of the scientists and engineers employed from government funds are not in government service per se, but working in industry or universities. Thus a million dollars spent on one type of hardware (for example, a rocket booster—may involve the employment by a government contractor of twenty or thirty scientists, whereas an equivalent amount spent on another type of hardware (say, Jeep carburetors) may involve only workers on an established production line. Neither the Congress nor the executive branch can make rational decisions on Federal budgets without much better information than now exists.

The expansion of graduate education over the next decade or two will bring about a wider dispersion of graduate facilities. This is a desirable move from many viewpoints, but it is likely to create a greater demand for outstanding graduate faculty than would a comparable expansion of present institutions. In older institutions graduate enrollments can be expanded by adding junior staff as instructors. In new graduate programs an equivalent number of graduate students requires the addition of many experienced senior professors who can direct student programs and supervise dissertations. Institutions such as Duke in the 1930's, U.C.L.A. in the 1940's, and Michigan State during the last decade illustrate the peak demand for new faculty of experience and stature in graduate education as a young institution moves to full university status. The added demand for senior faculty over and above what would have been needed to expand existing large graduate schools is a temporary phenomenon, and in the long run such dispersion of graduate facilities is both needed and desirable. The extra burden is nonetheless real, and must be met if the quality of graduate education is not to suffer.

On the brighter side of the faculty supply picture is the fact that the percentage of college teachers holding the doctorate has increased over the last decade, rising from a little over 40 percent to 51 percent in 1953–62.* This situation has evidently occurred as the result of a much lower attrition rate owing to deaths and retirements, a more rapid increase in the number of persons earning the doctorate, and the greater attraction of college and university teaching in bidding people away from industry and government, than was projected in the well-publicized earlier studies by the National Education Association, the Fund for the Advancement of Education, and the U.S. Office of Education.[2] Berelson's estimates in 1960 have turned out to be more accurate than those of his more pessimistic critics, and his conclusion that there is a problem but not a crisis in the supply of college faculty appears justified.[3]

IMBALANCE IN GRADUATE EDUCATION

"Imbalance" has become a popular term in recent years, although it may refer to a multitude of sins. Imbalance may be felt to exist between the relative emphasis placed on graduate and undergraduate education in an institution. It may refer to the relative value society places on pragmatic, utilitarian disciplines (characteristic of what Veblen called the "barbarian university") as against truly scientific and scholarly pursuits. It frequently refers to the decline of traditional humanistic studies coincident with the emergence of the natural sciences. Most commonly, in reference to the situation of the modern university in America, it is used to describe what many feel to be an undesirable pattern of external financial support in recent decades.

Some few voices will argue that there is absolutely too much support for research studies in some disciplines and that such support actually harms the university through the diversion of its own resources into matching grants and into covering unreimbursed indirect costs. More commonly it is argued that new outside support programs are needed to redress the imbalance in fields less directly

* This improvement will be indicated in the forthcoming publication of the results of the major Study of College Faculty undertaken by the U.S. Office of Education. Other studies under way at the American Council on Education indicate that the percentage of faculty with the doctorate has increased steadily for all categories of colleges and universities—public and private, large and small, university and college of liberal arts, etc.

concerned with the immediate research and national security needs of the Federal Government.

Approximately 95 percent of all Federal funds going to colleges and universities in support of educational and research activities are for "science," for example, the physical and life sciences (including medicine) and engineering. For the institutions fully reporting in the recent Carnegie study of "Twenty-six Campuses and the Federal Government,"[4] Federal funds for research were equal to approximately 25 percent of their total educational and general expenditures (the University of California at San Diego, California Institute of Technology, Stanford, M.I.T., and Princeton indicated more than 40 percent, exclusive of the governmentally sponsored national research laboratories). For the same group of institutions, however, only about 40 percent of Federal funds were for research in the arts and sciences, the remaining 60 percent being divided almost evenly between their medical and engineering schools.

Closer to the heart of graduate education is the distribution of funds to support predoctoral students. It is not surprising that information in the Federal Government is poor on the extent of Federal support of graduate students, since few graduate deans have complete information on federally financed fellowships, traineeships, and research assistantships even for their own institutions. Perhaps the most ambitious attempt to categorize such student support is found in the 1963 report of the House Committee on Education and Labor.[5] For the fiscal year 1962 it is estimated that 182,911 students received support from Federal monies totaling $256,562,000. Of this number approximately 40,400 were full-time predoctoral students, distributed as shown in Table 12.

Approximately 70 percent of the students were supported either on research grants and contracts or through traineeships administered by departments—awards which do not regularly come under the control or scrutiny of the graduate school office. Only about 8,000 of these students received outright fellowship awards administered through the graduate office and/or a national fellowship program. Of the approximately 40,000 students supported, roughly 4 percent were in institutions not directly connected with a college or university (separate teaching hospitals, research institutes, etc.), 27 percent were in professional fields normally outside the province of the graduate school of arts and sciences (medicine, nursing, public

TABLE 12: *Federal Support of Full-Time Predoctoral Students, 1962*

Support Source	No. of Students	Amount (000's)
Atomic Energy Commission....................	261	$ 1,325
Department of the Interior....................	17	200
National Aeronautics and Space Administration..	100	1,866
National Institutes of Health..................		
Fellowships...............................	995	3,753
Traineeships..............................	6,900	24,150
National Science Foundation..................	2,749	10,871
U. S. Office of Education		
Teachers of deaf..........................	151	453
Mental retardation.........................	168	933
NDEA title iv fellowships...................	4,041	21,371
Foreign language fellowships.................	1,006	3,918
Office of Vocational Rehabilitation		
Fellowships...............................	20	68
Traineeships..............................	1,921	3,896
Public Health Service		
Fellowships...............................	31	133
Training grants...........................	170	601
Traineeships..............................	2,534	7,925
Research assistants on research contracts and grants (estimate)...............................	19,350	48,375
	40,414	$129,838

Source: *The Federal Government and Education* [report by Edith Green, chairman of the Special Subcommittee on Education], Committee on Education and Labor, House of Representatives, 88th Cong., 1st Sess., June 1963, p. 33. Two adjustments have been made in the figures as originally published. Late information supplied by the National Institutes of Health on traineeships has been substituted, and the value of research assistantships on research grants and contracts has been estimated at an average of $2,500.

health, social work, etc.), 56 percent were in the mathematics, sciences, and engineering area, and 13 percent were in the humanities and social sciences. Of the latter nonscience category, about one third were in humanities, chiefly the NDEA title iv and title vi (language and area studies) fellowship programs.*

* One reader has raised the question of how some forty thousand predoctoral students supported on Federal funds can be reconciled with only about eleven thousand doctorates awarded in 1962. As the above paragraph indicates, probably less than 30,000 of the students were in fields in which the Ph.D. is the highest degree. In addition, the average student enrolled in graduate school in 1962 who completes the doctorate successfully will probably be in the class of 1965, when total doctorates awarded (excluding medicine) will be about 15,000. Thus the ratio is closer to 2:1 than the apparent 4:1. Full-time work toward the doctorate normally requires at least four years, so the 15,000 expected degrees implies at least 60,000 students now in the "pipeline" who will be successful in obtaining the degree, plus perhaps another 75,000–100,000 who will not complete degree requirements. Predoctoral support of graduate students should be compared with this larger universe of full-time students in doctoral programs. It would appear that about 20 percent of such students now receive some Federal support, the proportion approaching 50 percent in the physical and biological sciences.

Thus, although only about 1,600 of the 40,000 predoctoral students receiving Federal support were in the humanities, this is a much larger share of the total than is to be found in the support of faculty research in the humanities. There is some concern in Congress over the issue of imbalance, particularly in the House, and one senses a growing understanding of the needs and responsibilities in the broad field of scholarship. Even within the major science grant agencies—NSF and NIH—there is now a movement to make broad "general research support" or "institutional" grants to supplement the large amounts now spent on specific project support. The Higher Education Facilities Act authorizes approximately $150 million in general support funds for centers of quality graduate education. In addition, a number of members of Congress have proposed the creation of a counterpart to the National Science Foundation for the nonscience fields, and the recently appointed Commission on the Humanities will give further momentum to measures to alter the present and past balance of Federal support in higher education.

Although the coming decade will undoubtedly see some shift in this balance of support, it is likely—and probably desirable—that there will continue to be a marked asymmetry in Federal programs. The social sciences and humanities do not lend themselves to the same kind (much less, the same magnitude) of aid which the sciences have received. The critical needs of government and private industry in scientific research and technology are unlikely to be matched in classics, philosophy, or anthropology. And while the humanist may echo Blake's prayer on occasion:

> May God us keep
> From single vision and Newton's sleep,

his needs are not fully competitive with those of his colleagues in science and engineering. As President Goheen of Princeton stated the case recently:

> Personally I do not judge wide-ranging Federal support, comparable to the Government's investment in the sciences and engineering, to be a desirable solution for the substantial needs of America's colleges and universities in the fields of the humanities or in many of the socio-scientific fields . . . a Federal investment in the humanities and social sciences of any scope comparable to that in the sciences seems to me

not only hard to justify but potentially dangerous. For one thing, potential research results in these nonquantitative fields of learning are
harder to identify and measure concretely; thus they make a poor
basis for contractual relationships. Second, and more fundamentally, I
believe that Federal interference and other sorts of adverse political
pressures are much more likely to follow entrance of the Government
into these fields.[6]

The burden of balance rests in large part upon the institution
itself, for it is within the province of the administration of a university to make decisions that will help to compensate for the imbalance of external support. Attempts to legislate balance within universities by diminishing Federal support will be no more successful
than attempts to legislate "purity" by banishing Henry Miller and
D. H. Lawrence from the public library. Perhaps it would be fair to
conclude, however, that the opportunistic university administration
which has a Pavlovian sensitivity to the scent of Federal funds may
be less led astray (or only randomly) if funds are more available
across a broad spectrum of fields.*

EVALUATION AND ACCREDITATION

In the decades ahead there is likely to be growing pressure for improved evaluation, and perhaps for formal accreditation, of graduate programs. In an informal sense universities are in fact continuously being evaluated—by students seeking admission, by faculty deciding on academic positions, by foundations in program support,
by state legislatures, by review panels and visiting teams of major
Federal agencies, and so on. The quest for excellence presupposes

* This argument is more applicable to the private institution, which has
greater freedom in reallocating private funds at its disposal, than it may be to
many public institutions. It is also not an argument in support of some voices
in government who maintain that Congress has no responsibility for aiding
the balanced growth of higher education. (On this point see the very excellent
case William G. Bowen has made in *The Federal Government and Princeton
University: A Report on the Effects of Princeton's Involvements with the Federal
Government on the Operations of the University* [Privately printed; Princeton
University, 1962].) The anguished cries of some Princeton alumni in recent
months over the disclosure that approximately 45 percent of Princeton's annual
income comes from Federal grants and contracts will, one may presume,
strengthen the university's future fund raising for nonscience programs. In New
Haven the shoe has been rather on the other foot, and recent fund raising has
helped to redress the imbalance in favor of the "underprivileged" sciences.

the means of measurement, although for too long we have tended to judge by purely quantitative standards—enrollments, number of Nobel prize winners, Ph.D.'s granted, amount of government and foundation grants received, and the like. The Association of Graduate Schools for years has wrestled with this problem, and despite occasional interest on the part of their presidents in the American Association of Universities, formal evaluation or accreditation proposals have never seriously been entertained. A special committee of the A.A.U. recommended in 1960 that "a recognized list of institutions offering acceptable education at the graduate level" be compiled, but the report was filed without action.[7]

Growing pressures from the regional accrediting associations and a number of professional associations, particularly the National Council for the Accreditation of Teacher Education (N.C.A.T.E.) and the American Society for Engineering Education (A.S.E.E.), were called to the attention of the newly organized Council of Graduate Schools by the National Commission on Acrediting in 1962. The C.G.S. in December of that year issued a policy statement: "That it is the conviction of the Council that no group should undertake to evaluate or accredit institutions with respect to their programs of graduate education unless it is responsible primarily to an organization of the institutions themselves." A special committee of the council was created to review current practices and to study "the characteristics of graduate education of high quality."

Both graduate associations (C.G.S. and A.G.S.) can be expected to maintain their firm stand that *if* there is to be anything akin to accreditation in the field of graduate education, it should not be done by an outside group which is not ultimately responsible to the graduate schools or their parent universities. The opposition of some college and university presidents and many graduate deans to N.C.A.T.E. in accrediting teacher preparation programs has arisen because it was felt that N.C.A.T.E. did not adequately represent the institutions themselves and the subject disciplines under review.

At present the six major regional accrediting associations in the United States do accredit institutions with graduate schools, and in the case of at least two of these associations (Southern Association of Colleges and Schools and Northwest Association of Secondary and Higher Schools) guidelines are laid down for the review of graduate education. None of the associations, however, accredits graduate schools as such, in the way that the American Bar Association, the A.M.A. Council on Medical Education and Hospitals, and the Engineers' Council for Professional Development accredit schools in their respective professional fields.

Perhaps accreditation has seemed less necessary in graduate education in the arts and sciences partly because the public welfare is not as critically dependent upon the qualifications of scholarly practitioners as it is upon physicians and lawyers, and partly because Gresham's law has not prevailed in the field of scholarship. The academic man is continuously under review by his peers, and the low-quality or "diploma mill" doctorate has been notably unsuccessful. The high cost of graduate education has also helped to deter marginal institutions from inaugurating doctoral programs.

Historically, accreditation of undergraduate colleges has performed a useful service in bringing the institution of dubious quality up to some mutually agreed upon minimum standard. Even with accreditation, however, there is perhaps greater variation in the quality of baccalaureates awarded by approximately 1,200 accredited four-year institutions than there is in the quality of doctorates awarded by the approximately 200 universities awarding this highest degree.* The existence of major state universities has tended to act as a check upon state legislatures in approving funds for graduate programs in weaker public institutions, thus providing a kind of informal review and evaluation medium for state-supported institutions, and the cost factor has deterred the less well endowed private institution from dubious ventures.

* This is a personal judgment, although a casual sampling of the views of a number of colleagues tends to support it. Oliver Carmichael, however, in his recent *Graduate Education: A Critique and a Program* (New York, Harper & Row, 1961), concluded the reverse and my respect for his judgment has made me add a qualifying "perhaps." Although there are no "facts" on which a firm conclusion can be based, I would cite one piece of evidence, for which I am indebted to Harold Orlans' stimulating paper "Federal Programs and the Quality of Higher Education" (given at the University of Illinois Graduate College on March 21, 1963). One-quarter of the four-year colleges in the United States did not have a single graduate who went on to obtain the doctorate in the 1936–56 period; one-half did not have a graduate who obtained a doctorate in the natural sciences. I doubt if there is a single graduate school which cannot boast of at least a few graduates who have received scholarly honors in their later careers.

Accreditation in a formal sense is unlikely to be established in graduate education in the foreseeable future. The regional accrediting associations, however, are likely to pay increasing attention to graduate programs in assessing the over-all strength of universities. To be truly effective, accreditation would have to be quite explicit and restrictive in standards; and the more restrictive it was, the greater would be the opposition by the better institutions, which would view this as unwarranted limitation on their freedom. An excellent institution with outstanding faculty and good students need not obey any rules to be a highly successful educational enterprise; Harvard fellows are perhaps the most outstanding example.

There may be good reasons, however, for periodic *evaluation* of graduate programs. The fact that it is being done already—haphazardly by individual faculty and students, and in piecemeal, if more systematic, fashion by foundations and review panels of government agencies—may be sufficient reason to try to improve existing means of evaluation. As Riesman pointed out in his essay on higher education:

> Thus, data are publicly available for only a limited number of institutions, and even then they are often out of date. Moreover, the question of what is "quality" remains elusive: it refers to a complex of variables and . . . no single scale suffices. . . . While autos carry their advertising, so to speak, on their body shells, which speak as loudly as print or TV commercials, colleges can change inside their shells with hardly anyone's noticing. And the result can be tragic, not only for misled students, but for imaginative faculty and administrators who may not live long enough to be rewarded by the appearance of good students attracted by those changes.[8]

Periodic attempts have been made to evaluate the quality of graduate programs, although the climate of opinion has not always been favorable. Hughes's studies in 1925 and 1934 attempting to rank A.A.U. institutions in various fields of study were the subject of considerable debate in their day.[9] Keniston's study published in 1959 was accepted as an interesting, but not necessarily conclusive, subjective ranking of institutions.[10] Keniston queried department chairmen in twenty-five "leading" institutions, asking them to rate graduate departments according to their prestige. Some critics doubted that department chairmen were necessarily the best judges, and questioned the basis of inclusion or exclusion, but apart from many reactions that one's own institution did not come out in the "right" place on the scale, the study was taken as a rough measure of relative quality. Berelson added to the Keniston ratings and extended the categories to include forty-nine universities in three major groups.[11]

The climate for evaluation studies has perceptibly changed in recent years. Perhaps this in part owes to the fact that the A.A.U. is no longer a group including *all* the better universities; many non-A.A.U. members have larger graduate enrollments than some members, and quite a few of the newer universities would compare favorably in quality with the member group. Perhaps a stronger reason for the changing climate is that the trend in Federal aid to education (and to a lesser extent, in aid from private foundations) is to seek out and support the promising "second-rank" universities. It is becoming a matter of public policy to expand the number of "centers of excellence," to provide a broader geographic distribution of graduate schools of high quality. It may, therefore, be a mark of favor to be ranked thirty-fifth rather than tenth, since the trend in Federal support is toward altering the imbalance in its research and general support to a small number of long-recognized universities.

Future evaluation studies could be made much more meaningful than they have sometimes been in the past, by sampling the views of a broader spectrum of the educational community and by seeking to measure factors in addition to the research prestige of graduate faculty. How do the views of department chairmen compare with those of the most distinguished research scholars in various fields? with those of the most knowledgeable young scholars? How marked are the time lags in the opinions which outsiders hold of a rapidly changing institution? Do the views of Midwestern or Southern scholars on the caliber of education in Northeastern or Far Western universities approximate what scholars in those regions think of themselves? How do the assessments of individuals within a university differ from those who view it from the outside? How do the views of persons in liberal arts colleges differ from those of their counterparts in the large universities? How does one's own educational background affect the view one holds of his alma mater? Does an institution with a prestigious faculty necessarily offer the best graduate education? How close is the correlation between size and reputation? between both size and reputation and outside research support?*

Traditionally, educators have done less questioning about themselves and the processes of which they are an integral part than they have about the world outside the university. A few among the historians have analyzed the evolution of our educational structure over the last century or more, but only in the last few years have the social scientists occasionally turned their analytic skills to their own institutional environment. There has been almost a professional code that encouraged free inquiry and public discussion of issues and institutions outside academia, whereas self-analysis and informative debate within have been minimal. In an age when it is increasingly recognized that the quality of our educational system may be a critically determining factor in the future well-being of the nation, and when a rapidly rising proportion of financial support is coming from public monies, the claim of society on higher education for improved information and guidance becomes greater.

The graduate schools may be able to avoid the adoption of formal accreditation procedures as long as the Ph.D. degree does not suffer serious devaluation as the number of granting institutions rises over the coming decades. They will do so, however, only if there are commonly recognized standards and informal processes of sanctions imposed on the self-satisfied inferior institution. Public exposure is probably the best safeguard, and institutional vanity the best guarantee of corrective measures. Few would doubt that on balance the publication of faculty salary ratings by the Association of American University Professors has had a favorable effect on both the level and structure of faculty salaries. Perhaps occasional evaluation studies of graduate education would have a similarly beneficial effect on universities.

This essay has touched on some of the more prominent general problems that the continued rapid expansion of graduate education will generate.

* Six months after this was written, perhaps encouraged by his own logic, the writer undertook a study for the American Council on Education which included a questionnaire to some 5,400 scholars for the evaluating of graduate programs in approximately 100 major universities. This study will be published in 1965.

Financial needs, both for student aid and for physical facilities, have been overlooked, not because they do not pose major problems, but because they are part of a larger problem affecting all colleges and universities and have been frequently treated elsewhere.[12]

The major problems in the decades ahead will be complicated by the entrance of many new institutions into graduate education. The first fifteen universities in quality as classified by Berelson,[13] awarded 76 percent of all doctorates in 1925, 59 percent in 1934, 49 percent in 1950, and only 41 percent by 1960. If, between 1950 and 1980, these first fifteen institutions only double in the number of doctorates awarded (and they had increased only 15 percent from 1950 to 1960), they will account for less than 20 percent of all doctorates by the end of this period. The ten private universities among these fifteen awarded 32 percent of the total in 1950, 24 percent in 1960, and will probably award less than 10 percent of all doctorates by 1980. In earlier periods, when a handful of prestige institutions dominated the scene not only in quality but also in numbers, it was a simpler matter for them to set standards which the smaller and younger institutions could emulate. As the center of gravity shifts to the non-A.A.U. institutions, and from private to public universities, standards of high quality may be more difficult to maintain merely by emulation and self-interest. A large responsibility devolves on the Council of Graduate Schools to help its member schools meet the problems of the coming decades in a manner which will maintain the quality of graduate programs. The older and more restricted membership of the Association of Graduate Schools may find its continuing role as the guardian of standards in graduate education.

NOTES

1. Veblen, "American Universities as Institutions of Learning," Walter M. Kotschnig and Elined Prys (eds.), *The University in a Changing World* (London: Oxford University Press, 1932).
2. See the biennial reports of the National Education Association, *Teacher Supply and Demand in Universities, Colleges, and Junior Colleges* (Washington: The Association); *Teachers for Tomorrow* (New York: Fund for the Advancement of Education, 1955); and occasional papers by the Higher Education Personnel Section of the U.S. Office of Education.
3. Bernard Berelson, *Graduate Education in the United States* (New York: McGraw-Hill Book Co., 1960), pp. 69–80.

4. See *Educational Record*, April 1963, pp. 95–136. Twenty-six institutions participated, but some did not report comparable figures. The twenty-six institutions, ranging from Harvard and California to Lawrence College and Arkansas State Teachers College, accounted for 28 percent of Federal funds for research in educational institutions in 1959–60.
5. *The Federal Government and Education* [report by Edith Green, chairman of Special Subcommittee on Education], Committee on Education and Labor, House of Representatives, 88th Cong., 1st Sess., June 1963.
6. Robert F. Goheen, "Federal Financing and Princeton University," *Educational Record*, April 1963, p. 176.
7. Report of the Special Committee to Study Growing Pressures in Graduate Work, Sept. 15, 1960.
8. David Riesman, *Constraint and Variety in American Education* (Garden City, N.Y.: Doubleday & Co., 1958), pp. 3–5.
9. See R. M. Hughes, *A Study of the Graduate Schools of America* (Oxford, Ohio: Miami University, 1925), and *Report of the Committee on Graduate Instruction* (Washington: American Council on Education, 1934).
10. Hayward Keniston, *Graduate Study and Research in the Arts and Sciences at the University of Pennsylvania* (Philadelphia: University of Pennsylvania Press, 1959).
11. Berelson, *Graduate Education*, especially pp. 124–28.
12. Seymour Harris, *Higher Education: Resources and Finance* (New York: McGraw-Hill Book Co., 1962); John D. Long and J. B. Black, Jr., *Needed Expansion of Facilities for Higher Education, 1958–70* (Washington: American Council on Education, 1958); Dexter M. Keezer (ed.), *Financing Higher Education, 1960–70* (New York: McGraw-Hill Book Co., 1959); Selma J. Mushkin (ed.), *Economics of Higher Education* (Washington: Government Printing Office, 1962), especially Part III; and John D. Millett, *Financing Higher Education in the United States* (New York: Columbia University Press, 1952).
13. Berelson, *Graduate Education*, p. 97.